CALCUTTA
1940–1970

CALCUTTA 1940–1970

In the photographs of Jayant Patel

CONCEPT Lila Patel

TEXT Soumitra Das FOREWORD Gopalkrishna Gandhi

NIYOGI BOOKS

Published by
NIYOGI BOOKS
Block D, Building No. 77,
Okhla Industrial Area, Phase-I,
New Delhi-110 020, INDIA
Tel: 91-11-26816301, 26818960
Email: niyogibooks@gmail.com
Website: www.niyogibooksindia.com

Editor: Jayalakshmi Sengupta
Design: Misha Oberoi

ISBN: 978-93-86906-02-1
Publication: 2017

In this book the old spelling of Kolkata, as Calcutta, has been retained for the sake of consistency.

Printed at: Niyogi Offset Pvt. Ltd., New Delhi, India

In memory of my husband, late Jayant Patel, whose abiding love for Calcutta and unfailing passion for photography encouraged me to put together this book.

With all my love

LILA PATEL

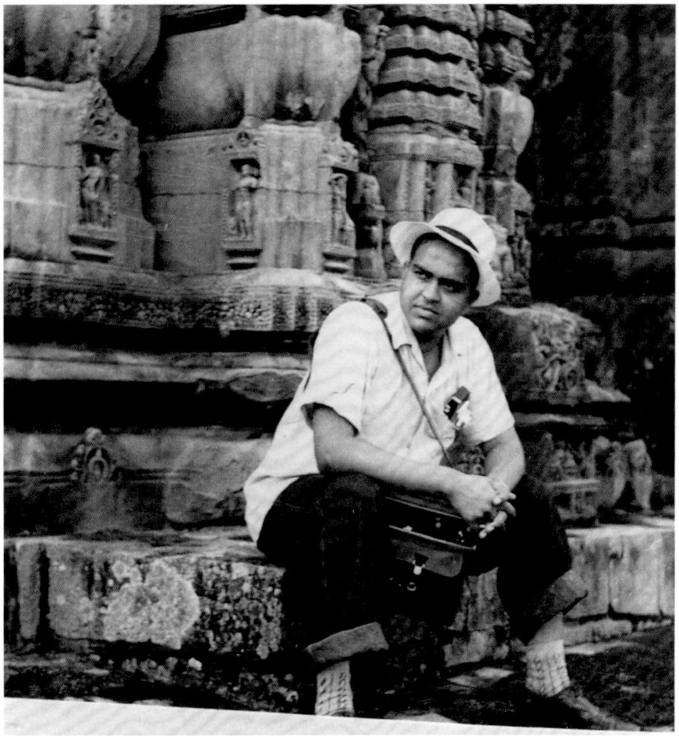

Jayant Patel was an artist.

The camera was his brush, the scene ahead of him, his canvas.

The paint?

It was his mind's ink, made to play with the white of the ambient light.

'No camera, no picture' is of course the plain fact. But it is when the camera is wielded by the artist's mind that we get photographs that are art. The rest are photographs, interesting and important, no doubt, but still not quite 'art'. And when the art of photography has as its subject the making of history, that art also becomes visual historiography.

Every moment in time is material for history of one kind or another. While some periods may see things of uncommon significance happen dramatically, others may pass without a fuss and yet become game changing.

The photographs offered in this volume give us a photo-artist's view of Calcutta in the 1940s and 1950s—a period when momentous history was being made in and around it. World War II saw dizzying action in theatres close to the city's east. There were moments when Japan seemed very close to the seaboard near the city, its airfield and its very heart. And then, the Bengal Famine of 1943, bared the ribs of hunger in Bengal as never before, with the city feeling its fangs. In 1946 came riots, manslaughter of unprecedented scale, presaging the strife that escorted Pakistan out of undivided India.

Having been the imperial capital of the British Raj from the end of the 18th century until 1912, Calcutta had its pride, its honour—home to the Brahmo Samaj, to Keshub Chandra Sen, the Tagores, to Sri Ramakrishna and Swami Vivekananda, Calcutta had its self-esteem—nursery to the poetic flashes of Michael Madhusudan Dutt and Toru Dutt, the brilliant truancies of Derozio and his 'circle' and the patriotic fervours of Aurobindo Ghose, C.R. Das and the Bose brothers, Calcutta had a sense of its place in the civilisational history of India. Its buildings spoke of different ages, discrete communities. They reflected phases, mores, and fashions. And so did the spaces that were not occupied by buildings, empty patches before buildings, roads, maidans, bridges, the land under bridges. These comprised a built heritage, a physical heritage that made Calcutta more than a city—a universe.

But going through the trauma of Partition, with hundreds of thousands leaving for the new East Pakistan, and hundreds of thousands coming into the new West Bengal, *that* Calcutta became, for a while, what it had never been—a city in transition, in flux, in an existential melt. That state, the state of being made, unmade, of being in some kind of 'shift' was new to Calcutta. Others could go through vestibules of change, Calcutta had been and become what it was, centuries ago. That sense of stability, that strong invulnerability, came under stress in the 1940s.

That silent stress was captured by the great photographer of the Bengal Famine, Sunil Janah, and the incomparable sculptor, Somnath Hore. Their work, in different mediums and yet complementary, chronicled Bengal's and Calcutta's travails with the daring and the compassion that only artists bring. Satyajit Ray's *Ashani Sanket* drew from Janah and Hore.

Jayant Patel's work belongs to their great ouvre.

A photograph does not comment in words. Captions to photographs are afterthoughts. Photographs comment wordlessly but comment they do. They speak non-verbally, non-vocally. Jayant Patel's black-and-white pictures speak, they describe but they do so non-judgmentally, non-prescriptively. They show buildings in strained repose, roads in tension. They show them ageing with struggle but without complaint, with dignity but without false prestige. Peeling plaster and sagging balconies in Calcutta's buildings have the kind of inevitability to them one associates with superannuation, not imminent demise. Be it Queen Victoria or one of her equestrian Viceroys, the statuary of the Raj, in India's once-imperial capital, bespeaks the grace of resignation. Jayant Patel captures the humour and the pathos behind those statues, which seems to have been abandoned by the departing empire to their fates.

The 'mugshots', as we now call full-face pictures of American GIs, stationed in Calcutta during the war, are a study in human psychology. Each one of them is a 'character', their faces holding great stories. The most striking of these is that of the nurse. Such determination lies in those eyes, and such calm! If Jayant Patel has shown himself a master of the long-shot he has shown himself to be an artist of the human face.

Government House, or Raj Bhavan, the Governor's residence now, and once the palace of the Governor General of India, is a favourite of Jayant Patel's lens. That building is the nerve centre of change. Flux is written all over the

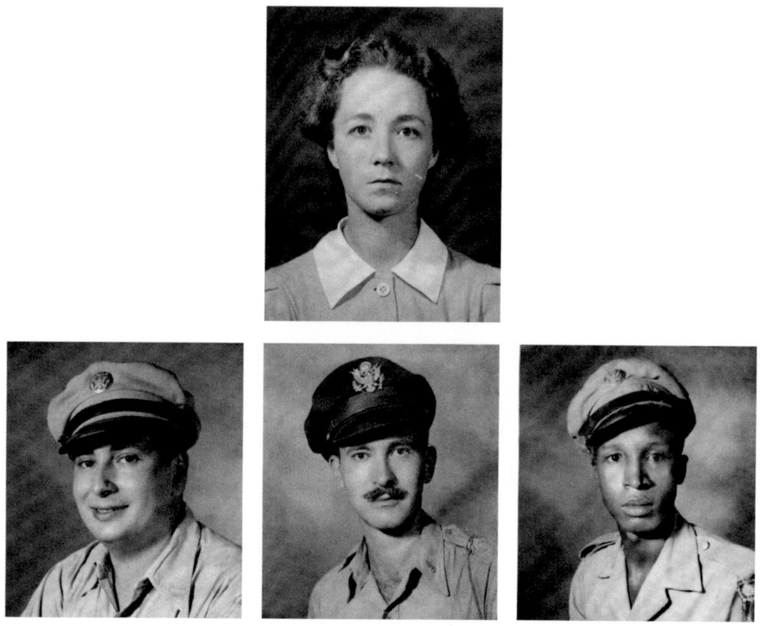

GI nurse and GIs based in Calcutta during Second World War. (c.1941)

photographs of Mahatma Gandhi in conversation with the wartime governor, Casey, in one of that building's gracious sitting rooms. The representative of the King-Emperor seems self-conscious even as the Mahatma sits at ease. I had known that photograph for years, without knowing which cameraman had captured that truly memorable moment. It is good to know the art-picture's authorship (p. 190).

The founder of Pakistan, is captured by the camera looking very tense, very preoccupied (p.192). A Premier of Bengal and future Prime Minister of Pakistan, H.S. Suhrawardy is seen at a swearing-in ceremony looking quizzically at one of his colleagues taking the oath of office (p. 193). He seems to ask with some self-assailing humour: How long is all this going to last?

If I were to choose one picture out of these as my 'favourite', I would choose the one in which Nehru and Patel are standing in a close knot, looking at a document. Nehru is the very picture of trusting optimism, Patel of cautious pragmatism. Nehru seems like he has accepted what he is reading, Patel is giving it a close look. While Nehru trusts, Patel seeks evidence. While Nehru believes, Patel wants proof (p. 195).

The photographs of Chakravarti Rajagopalachari, the first Governor of West Bengal and the first Prime Minister of India, Jawaharlal Nehru, in that house, are veritable nuggets of history (p. 197–201). CR is happy, Nehru radiant as they pose for photographs. Nehru is bright, beaming and ebullient. He has been wafted by history to the crest of a future India. That is the message these pictures convey. The PM and the Governor have seen their shared struggle reach its destination, if at a huge and guilt-laden cost. Are their smiles too broad, their joys too naive for those plangent times? They are, in a sense.

The picture of the urn in Raj Bhavan holding the slain Mahatma's ashes is a poem if ever a photograph can be one.

Lila Patel has placed us in her debt by nurturing her husband's art and then bringing it out of its rest to public viewing. It is my trust that this book will inspire the aspiring photographer to see technology as an art that records and documents human condition and thereby helps us better understand ourselves and our times.

—GOPALKRISHNA GANDHI

Preface

My Personal journey with my late husband, Jayant, and his camera began in the summer of 1955 when I arrived in Calcutta as his young bride. Calcutta was a bustling dynamic city, with a distinct culture and lingering echoes of the British Raj, yet quite different from New Delhi, my home town.

As Jayant was introducing his favourite city to me, he shared in depth his memorable photographs of Pre-Independence and Post-Independence Calcutta .Through his images I saw in him an artist, a writer, and a poet, who through his creative genius had captured the essence of images with a wide spectrum of subject matters, from photographing dignitaries to historical moments, to a lightning bolt during a monsoon thunderstorm. This was the magic of Jayant's keen eye and artistry expressed through a camera lens.

I would like to share the story behind some of the photographs.

It was the summer of 1969, a very hot and sultry day in April. Everyone in Calcutta was looking forward to a Nor'wester that usually brought rain and cooled the place down. We were dressed to go to a party, and I found that the sky had turned dark and there was a strong wind blowing. The trees were swaying, and there was thunder and lightning. Jayant realised that the thunderstorm would lead to heavy rains within no time! He decided to get his camera out to take some photographs. His eyes were alight with the thought of capturing the lightning. He took a few photographs and then placed his camera near the window, fixed the aperture, opened the shutter and left it there. We went to the party and returned after a few hours. Jayant closed his camera and took out the film for the next day. A few days later he came home and told me he had a surprise for me. I could see the excitement in his eyes as he pulled out the photograph from his briefcase. It was this lovely photograph of the stormy night, with lightning illuminating the swaying trees, Victoria Memorial, St Paul's Cathedral, and Nehru Children's Museum (p. 177).

Another interesting event WAS when he had gone to take photographs of Muhammad Ali Jinnah at the Muslim League meeting held at the Calcutta Maidan. He narrated this story to me much later, on a beautiful evening when we were resting on the steps of Victoria Memorial, after our walk. He was reminiscing the good old days when as a youngster he went to cover important events with his camera. On 16th August, 1946 Jayant had gone to the Calcutta Maidan to take photographs of Jinnah. The joy of being in the right place at the right time, was very important for him. The place was full of people shouting slogans, anxiously awaiting the arrival of Mohammed Ali Jinnah. Jayant found himself being pushed around and was afraid of losing his camera. Holding onto his camera for dear life, he tried to make his way through the crowd to reach a place from where he could capture the historic moment. For over an hour he tried to get near the dais but with no luck. Unexpectedly, the space before him opened up, and suddenly he found that he had a commanding view of the dais. There was a lot of excitement as Jinnah arrived. Once Jinnah started talking, there was complete silence and that is when Jayant's camera went to work (p. 192).

Jayant was the youngest of seven siblings born in Mombasa, Kenya on 28 November 1927. His father had the first, full-fledged photography studio with developing and printing facility in Mombasa, where his wife and sons helped him in the processing of films after school. Jayant's interest in photography goes back to his early childhood when he was gifted with his first Kodak box camera at the tender age of five by his father. His interest increased as he took photographs of his family members, school friends, and the sports and picnics he attended.

By early 1940, the political atmosphere was dramatically changing in India. The Patel family decided to move to Calcutta on 8 February 1942, to help the two older sons, who had opened doors of Bombay Photo Stores on Park Street in 1940 and needed help. Jayant was sent to study in Ahmedabad. Before long the schools were closed due to political instability. As a young 15-year-old teenager, in the midst of the Independence movement, with schools closed, Jayant decided to participate in the freedom marches in Gujarat. He went everywhere with his camera hanging around his neck. After two or three months his eldest brother, Jasbhai, happened to visit Bombay on a business trip and found Jayant participating in the freedom movement. He decided to take him back to Calcutta. With schools closed he was made to help in the business. Initially Jayant rebelled but ultimately decided to join Bombay Photo Stores. He enjoyed travelling with his father in the double-decker bus around the city, standing in the upper deck and taking photographs. Some photographs were turned into picture postcards and sold in the shop.

The Patels had the privilege of being the official photographer for the Government House and the American and British military. Jayant was sent to cover these assignments. This gave him the opportunity to be at the right time in the right place when history was being made, during the 40's, 50's and 60's. In his camera lens he captured a lot of historic moments; dignitaries and important personalities like Mahatma Gandhi with Governor Casey and with Chiang Kai-shek; Jinnah on the dais in the Maidan, prior to the Hindu-Muslim riots that took place on 16 August 1946. Time stands still when you look at these images and they take you back to that era…

Over the years, those beautiful statues in the Maidan and around the city have disappeared. They have been replaced by new statues. Today, we are left with just faded memories of those glorious days. Jayant always said, 'A camera never lies—with age, buildings deteriorate, people age, but a photograph brings back to life what has been captured in its lens.' He took photography more as a hobby and captured the passion of day-to day-life—people on the street, a vendor selling coconuts, a snake charmer, anything that caught his eye. An artist's way of expression is through his brush and colour palette, a sculptor has his clay, while a photographer sees his vision through his camera lens. His love for photography was etched in his psyche from then on and to the very end of his days when he was sequencing his treasure trove of images with events, which now I am working towards sharing with a larger audience.

Besides being an avid photographer, Jayant was a businessman who owned at the prime of his career three studios with a large processing lab known as Bombay Photo Stores, normally referred to as BPS, famous for studio portraits. As I reminisce about the 50 plus years of my life with Jayant, I feel so enriched with all that he shared with me about his love of photography and life. As a proud wife, I wish to share my memories of Jayant as a passionate photographer and a sensitive artist, whose keen eye and camera work have left behind images frozen in time, ever so alive, fresh, and new.

—LILA PATEL

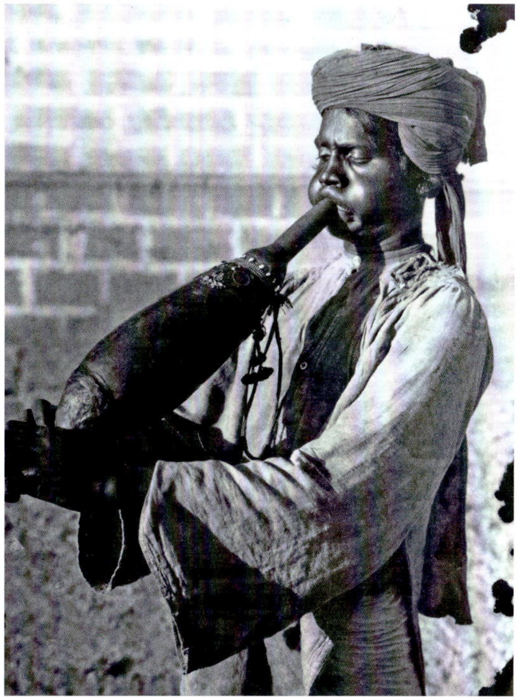

A snake charmer. (c.1951)

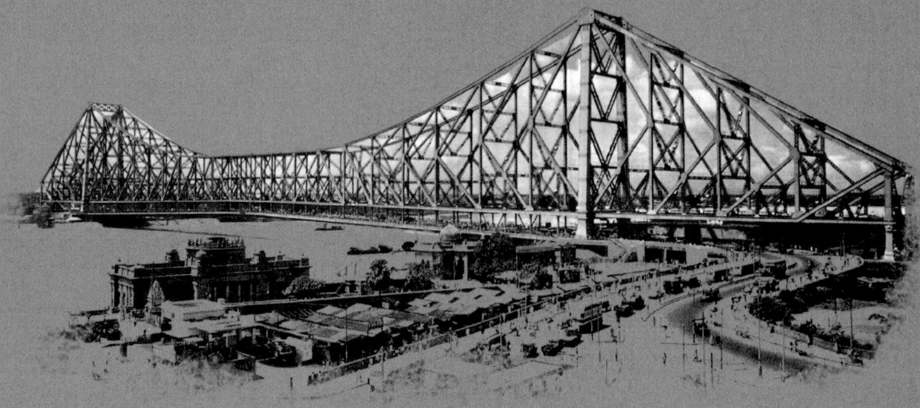

Calcutta, once serenaded as the 'City of Palaces', now a metropolis unhinged, was the creation of the British, who ruled the country from Writers' Buildings till 1911. Long after the capital shifted there, Delhi was little better than a village. Calcutta continued to flourish as a great mercantile city and was the cultural capital of the country. It reached its apogee in the 1930s and 1940s, when it was a truly global city attracting businessmen, fortune hunters, entrepreneurs, writers, scientists, performers and entertainers from all over the world. Calcutta held this prime position till well into the 1960s, Partition and the ensuing refugee problem notwithstanding. An unfortunate downslide began in the mid-1970s.

This Calcutta in its glory days was captured in the superb frames of Jayant Patel, who had also recorded some of the momentous proceedings at Government House, which was renamed Raj Bhavan after Independence in that highly eventful era. Born in 1927, Patel had inherited the renowned Bombay Photo Stores in Park Street and was himself a passionate photographer. This book examines his oeuvre of black-and-white photographs in which his focus is Calcutta and the events the city witnessed from the 1940s up to the early 1970s when the rot had just started setting in.

When Job Charnock dropped anchor on the banks of the Hooghly on 24 August 1690, Sutanuti already had a thriving cotton market and the Seths and Basaks dominated it. Belonging to the weaver community, they had turned it into a trading post. But it was little more than that. Kalighat was a popular pilgrimage centre, and it attracted devotees from far and wide. They used the pathway through the dense forests, which later became Chitpur, the arterial road of the city. But the cotton traders lacked the vision, the military advantages, and the gumption that the British possessed to lay the foundation of a pullulating metropolis in this malaria-infested bog.

At a time when Akbar ruled India, the East India Company was signed into existence by Queen Elizabeth I, in 1600. Over the 17th and 18th centuries the Company's powers and influence increased exponentially. It had already established trade and military posts along India's eastern and western coasts. The Company constructed Fort William on the western side of the great fresh water tank called Laldighi. Writers' Buildings was constructed in 1776. On the northern side of Laldighi, it resembled barracks, to accommodate the writers or secretaries—the cogs and wheels of the administration.

After Siraj-ud-Daulah sacked and plundered Calcutta and Fort William, which was then situated on the spot where the General Post Office came up later, and his ultimate defeat at the hands of the British at the Battle of Plassey thereafter, the Company rebuilt the city around the three villages of Sutanuti, Kalikata, and Gobindapur with Laldighi at its centre. What is now known as B.B.D. Bag was then Tank Square and Dalhousie Square later. Stately, occasionally ponderous, buildings came up around this great waterbody.

The fort was shifted to Gobindapur, and Lord Clive, who was the hero of the hour, cleared the jungles to create the Maidan, the lungs of the city. London was the prototype of this city, meant for the habitation of the white people. The 'natives', who lived in Gobindapur, were shunted to the northern outlands.

The British used the language of architecture to drive home their might to the 'natives' while, at the same time, bleeding them white to pay for the uber-luxurious lifestyles of the nabobs, as the thieving servants of the East India Company were known. The Company had been granted the Diwani of Bengal, and with the fall of Tipu Sultan in the south, by 1818 this corporate body became the virtual ruler of two-thirds of the entire sub-continent. However tainted the sources of funding may have been, there was no denying that Calcutta was a city of unmatched splendour. As ships sailing on the Hooghly approached, the city with its imposing rows of fine buildings, their *chunam*-polished facades, gleaming in the sun like marble, heaved into sight. And newcomers were awestruck.

By late 19th century and early and mid-20th century, the period when Jayant Patel was most active, Calcutta had turned into a fleshpot with glittering shops lining Old Court House Street, Esplanade, and Chowringhee. The streets boasted tailors and outfitters like the famed Ranken & Co., jewellers of royalty like Hamilton & Co and Cooke & Kelvey, hatters, glovers, drapers, gun makers, establishments that specialised in china and crockery ware, (including Osler & Co of crystal fountains fame), glassware, hosiery, cabinet makers, opticians, saddlers and harness makers, watchmakers, stationers, provisioners, and wine merchants of such pedigree that they would have made Oxford Street proud. Contemporary directories crawl with the names of such shops and establishments.

Way ahead of their counterparts in other regions, Bengalis, cutting across class, had developed a taste for Western-style food and drinks, and these along with a remarkable range of commodities found a ready market in the city. This in turn contributed to the flourishing of the advertising agencies and the creation of the most memorable and eye-catching campaigns in the print media and hoardings that were visible all over the city.

There were fine-dining places, such as the popular Peliti's, opposite Government House, which found mention in the writings of Rabindranath Tagore and Rudyard Kipling, besides the splendiferous Firpo's. Floor shows sizzled. Dancing cheek to cheek, one could while away the night in hotels like Spence's (a bank now and newspaper office), Great Eastern Hotel, and indeed the Grand, which true to its name became a byword for the good life. But these were the reserve of those with very, very deep pockets. Higher up on the pecking order were the exclusive whites-only clubs like Saturday, Bengal, and Calcutta, created by a breakaway group of Indians.

For a shopping experience that could only be replicated abroad, or simply to relax, one could drop by at the sprawling department stores like Whiteaway Laidlaw (today's Metropolitan Building) with its stained glass atrium and rows of stained glass windows at the corner of S.N. Banerjee Road and Chowringhee, and the upscale Army Navy Stores, further down the same thoroughfare.

The glitzy movie theatres were known as the home of the Hollywood stars. Even on a sultry Calcutta afternoon one could walk into Metro cinema, now being converted into a multiplex, and get chilled to the bones at a time when air-conditioning was a rarity. This hall with its plush carpets and red velvet seats exercised considerable influence even on the lives of ordinary Bengalis, who would think twice before walking past its portals bearing the 'waterfall' style engaged columns. Its architecture introduced art deco and classics like

Hindustan Building, which resembles an ocean liner, and numerous other Calcutta contemporaries.

Of the twin theatres New Empire and Lighthouse, the former doubled as a stage for theatrical and musical performances by international stars. Jamshedji Framji Madan, the Parsi theatre and cinema magnate, after whom a street in central Calcutta is named, was the first one in India to launch a bioscope show in a tent on the Maidan. He opened Elphinstone Picture Palace in Hogg Street, opposite the Calcutta Municipal Corporation building, in 1907. Later renamed Minerva, and till its last days in 2013 known as Chaplin, it was the first of his chain of cinemas, and the first permanent movie theatre in this city. It was a small theatre like Tiger on Chowringhee, where good Hollywood films were screened.

What made central Calcutta and the fashionable boulevard, Park Street, even more attractive and cosmopolitan was the presence of colourful bevies of Jewish, Armenian, and Anglo-Indian girls, who were permanent fixtures in offices long before Bengali women broke out of the bounds of their homes. Its largely westernised milieu contributed to the sophisticated urbanity of central Calcutta, and set it apart from other Indian cities.

Then came the dark days of World War II, and although the local populace had to bear the brunt of inflation and rising prices, many traders and speculators became rich overnight. Calcutta became the home of the Allied Forces, and soldiers poured into the city. The landmark Hindustan Building on Central Avenue was occupied by the GIs, who operated from there. It contained a post office, a radio station, officers' mess and living quarters and signal offices. It became risky for civilians, particularly women, to venture out after dark because of the presence of these rowdy and lusty men. The city of Calcutta, except for designated areas—the central Taltollah and Park Street precincts; Karaya/Park Circus and Kanarni Estate—was out of bounds for the uniformed men.

Photographer Clyde Wadell's original caption for Karnani Estates close to the Theatre Road crossing read thus: 'Karnani Estates, mammoth apartment hotel for US Army officers. Known to the many thousands of transient and locally based officers as a social center, it has been provided with one of the most elaborately decorated bars of any officers' club in the CBI theater.' The large hotels like the Grand, Spence's, Great Eastern, and Firpo's, and restaurants like Ferrazinni's (on Lindsay Street close to the Chowringhee crossing) were reserved for 'Officers Only'.

The fear of bombing by the Japanese cast a pall of gloom and fear over the city, and thousands of people began to flee like rats from a sinking ship. Yet the soldiers and privileged people had fun, and both the classy and sleazy joints swung to the music of the pianos and jazz bands. The crowds danced as if to save their lives, probably to stave off their terror and desperation. Red Road was turned into an air strip of the air force, and Victoria Memorial Hall was painted black to camouflage it during anticipated Japanese bombing.

The zeitgeist was captured perfectly in Jashoda Dulal Mandal's popular songs. I had heard this amazing song in childhood, when I first encountered the word 'Nazi'. It was a smart, snappy, and caustic number, and its title was: 'Hello World Today 1939.' The 78 rpm was produced by HMV, number N 27488. It was all about the international alliances and conflicts that culminated in World War II. Here is a line from that delightful ditty:

Hitler ese humki dilo/biswatake korbo chharkhar/Mussolini bollo Hitudada ami tomar pashe achhi.
(Hitler threatened that he would devastate the world.
Mussolini said Brother Hitler I am beside you)

The other cheeky Bengali rhyme about the British in a blue funk during the Japanese blitz has survived till today. It began with the seven notes of the musical scale in Indian classical music, and continued with the Japanese bombing and how the British were scared out of their wits by the cobra inside the incendiary device.

It was in such tumultuous times that Jayant Patel went around the city armed with his camera. He was a prolific photographer, but the pictures he took of the city were in the main of the central areas, the buffed and manicured white enclave—Dalhousie Square, Clive Street, today's Netaji Subhas Road, Chowringhee, and what later came to be known as Brabourne Road. There are some shots of Kalighat and the famous Parshwanath Jain temple in Badridas Temple Street in north Calcutta, Burrabazar and Jadubabur Bazar in Bhowanipur, but the focus is on the neighbourhoods that were powdered to perfection. The warts were rarely visible. Not in the ones we have in hand. For many others may have been lost over the years, and when the establishment was shut down. He did take photographs of the horrors of communal riots but they are gone forever.

Now let us go back to the beginning, and the paterfamilias. Chhotabhai Dwarkadas Patel (1885–1975) was from Boriavi, close to Anand in Gujarat. Chhotabhai went to the JJ School of Arts in Bombay and was a self-taught photographer. He moved to Mombasa in Kenya in 1915 and set up a photo lab named C.D. Patel & Sons. After establishing his business, he took his family to Mombasa in 1920. His entire family was there to provide support. Chhotabhai's school-going sons used to help him out, and so did their mother. So the children were involved with photography from an early age.

I made a trip to Chandannagar to meet Amiya Chakrobortty, a lithe and erect 86, who had worked in all three Bombay Photo Stores—in Park Street and the branches in the Grand Hotel arcade, next to the jewellery store named M. Walter, and in Gariahat. Trained at Fort William, he had been appointed to work in the darkroom.

Chakrobortty had some interesting stories to relate about C.D. Patel in Mombasa. His photographic store was close to the port and sailors came to buy picture postcards from him. The postcards were printed in Switzerland and they sold like 'hot cake.' Senior Patel was allowed to open shop in the 'white' area by a dignitary who had been impressed by his efficiency and punctuality.

Chhotabhai moved back to India, after his eldest son, Jasbhai, who had gone to study in London, set up Bombay Photo Stores in Calcutta on 15 February 1940 at 33–34 Park Mansion in Park Street. The family followed them and arrived in Calcutta in 1941. Jayant was the youngest of seven siblings—four brothers and three sisters—and was born on 28 November 1927.

When he was still very young he had received a Kodak box camera as a gift from his father. In Calcutta, Jayant grew up in turbulent times. Gandhi's Quit India movement had started and schools were closed. Jayant joined the Gandhian movement, much to the trepidation of his London-returned elder brother, Jasbhai, who was a royalist. He persuaded Jayant to join the family business. The family needed hands and he started working at the age of 15. In Calcutta, Jayant's hobby turned both into his passion and profession as he took up photography seriously.

Jayant Patel, who has left behind a vast archive of mostly black-and-white photographs of the whole country and particularly of Calcutta, used to accompany his father everywhere. Six feet tall, he would go to the upper deck of double-decker buses to take photographs of the city. I have recently gathered from Facebook that in 1944, there used to be a Shyambazar to Ballygunge double-decker service on route No 2.

Jayant, like most truly professional photographers, was inseparable from his camera. He carried it everywhere he went. It was his first love. Jayant had a Zeiss, a Kodak folding camera, a Pentax, a Linhof, and a Canon with a wide-angle lens. He would often turn photographs of popular destinations of Calcutta into picture postcards for sale at Bombay Photo Stores. No wonder they proliferate the Internet, although Jayant has never received any credit for these.

In 1941, Bombay Photo Stores was commissioned by Government House to take photographs of all its official events. And Jayant Patel was the one to be sent for these shoots. During World War II from 1940 to 1942, Bombay Photo Stores was also appointed the official photographer of the American and British military. Two American soldiers stood outside the establishment. All photographs of the military were processed at the studio. Each photograph was checked to make sure that the enemies did not have access to information of any important places they could target.

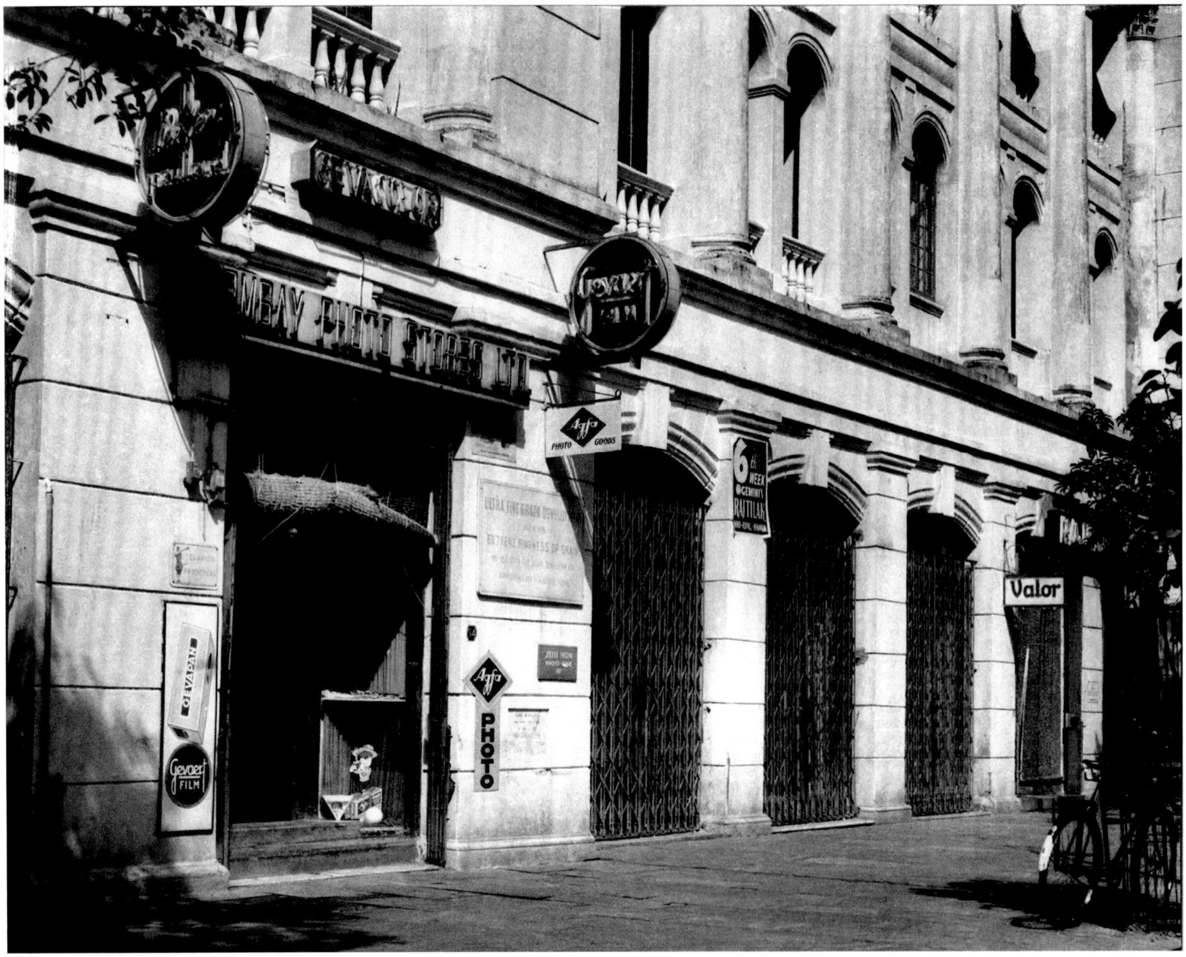

Bombay Photo Stores at 33–34 Park Mansion in Park Street

Government House, as Raj Bhavan was known in pre-Independence days, was built in 1803 and was the official residence of the Viceroy of India. The old Government House belonged to Mahomed Reza Khan, the Nawab of Chitpore, an official of the Murshidabad court. It was one of the buildings to be demolished to construct the new Government House or Raj Bhavan we are familiar with today. The then Governor-General of India, Lord Wellesley, had taken the initiative to construct it. When the capital moved to Delhi in 1911, it became the official residence of the Lieutenant Governor of Bengal. Since Independence in 1947, it has served as the official residence of the Governor of West Bengal. Gandhian though he was, Jayant Patel was forced to wear Western dress when he went for these shoots.

These assignments gave Jayant and his camera the privilege of witnessing some historic moments in the life of the nation at a moment when the situation was fluid and volatile. By 1947, Jayant's two elder brothers had moved out of Calcutta to pursue their own professions. Hence, Jayant, his brother Kanu, and their father took charge of the Calcutta studio.

The shop with an attached studio could not escape notice as it had a bold front. Adjacent to the famous restaurant, Skyroom, which has also closed down, Bombay Photo Stores was a landmark of Park Street.

Its first branch opened in the Grand Hotel arcade in 1942, and it was run by senior Patel. Between 1952 and 1953, Jayant received training in colour photography processing. and he went to Kodak in London, Agfa in Germany, and then the Gevaert factory in Belgium, where he worked on colour films processing for ten days, as Bombay Photo Stores processed Kodak films in Calcutta.

In 1953, Bombay Photo Stores started its first full-fledged colour processing laboratory in Free School Street, behind the Fire Brigade. The laboratory initially belonged to Kodak. That same year, Royal Calcutta Turf Club (RCTC) imported a special camera from London to conduct 'photo finishes' at the races in 1953, a first in India. This was done under the guidance of Jayant, who had a thing for horseflesh.

Jayant got married to Lila, a 19-year-old Delhite, in 1955, and about that time Bombay Photo Stores won the distinction of being awarded the Paillard Bolex Dealer of Year certificate for the third time in succession for record sale of Paillard Bolex Equipment in 1954. The Patel couple was given a free air ticket to visit the Paillard factory in Switzerland. In 1955, after the trip to Switzerland, Patel revisited all three colour laboratories he was trained at, for a few days, to update his knowledge of colour processing technique.

A second branch of Bombay Photo Stores opened with a studio in Gariahat in 1960. Kanu had, meanwhile, started his own business of making documentary films by 1955, and decided to leave Bombay Photo Stores by 1965. The Gariahat branch closed later in 1973 and Jayant's father died soon afterwards in 1975. In the late 1970s, the Chowringhee studio in the Grand Hotel arcade closed as well, as Jayant found it difficult to single-handedly take care of three shops and a large laboratory in four different places.

Jayant's pet name was 'Jayanti' among his close-knit circle of friends, most of whom were executives of commercial firms in the 1960s, when Calcutta was a more hospitable and cosmopolitan place. I met a couple of Patel's friends, all in their early 80s, in their flats and homes. They all spoke of Patel's good humour and bonhomie and his love of golfing and partying.

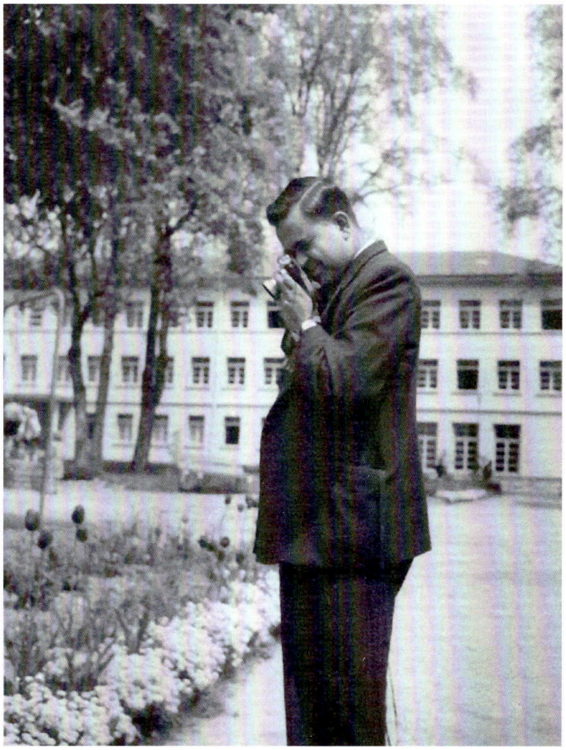

Jayant Patel

Gobind Bhagat came to Calcutta in 1963 and made friends with Patel two years later. He was seven years younger than Jayant. Bhagat recalled an incident as evidence of their camaraderie. 'He was one of the most kind and straightforward men one would have met. No conniving. When Jayanti was overlooked for captaincy of the RCGC (Royal Calcutta Golf Club) committee, three of us who were friends of his decided to resign,' Bhagat said in his terrace garden in Mandeville Gardens.

This group of friends—13 couples—who were basically outsiders and had come to work in Calcutta, formed a support group named Calcutta We Love in the 1980s. They had all made their careers in Calcutta, and now their sons were living abroad. 'There was a dossier on everyone,' said Bhagat. He rattled off the names of some of the members—Jagdish Sapru of ITC, Keshav Mathur of Birla, Vijay Kichlu and Harish Parekh, former chairman of J. Thomas & Company, Dr Rajen Watts, a well-known physician, and R.N. Deogun of Tata Tea.

Keshav Mathur lives in a duplex in Ballygunge Park, close to where Jayant Patel lived. He got to know Jayant when the Patels lived in Edward Court on Chowringhee, long before the monstrous hotel came up on the lawn in front of it. 'Jayanti loved the good things of life—racing and golf and was on the social circuit. He was very popular at RCGC. Everybody knew him. He was an easy person to get along with. I cannot say he was the greatest golfer but he enjoyed the game. He took a lot of interest in the welfare of the people he was friendly with. He was ably supported by his wife Lila.'

Haik Sookias of Alipore, one of the few Armenians still living in this city, was different from Jayant Patel's other friends. He lives in a comfortable house of his own and runs iron and steel foundries in Howrah and Falta.

Sookias said his elder brother, Malcolm, was a good friend of Jayant's, their friendship going back to their bachelor days. Malcolm was the best man at Jayant's wedding. Sookias added jokingly: 'I don't know if Gujaratis have best men, but ostensibly he was best man.' Haik Sookias played rugby for Armenian Club and the team would go to Bombay Photo Stores to get themselves photographed.

Jayant's brother, Kanu, once wrote to him about the struggle that preceded their success: 'Besides the social pleasures, remember those struggling days when we were building up Bombay Photo Stores from nothing—the hard work and dedication bring the dividends now—our contribution of making Bombay Photo Stores with two branches and a large laboratory—those were the most satisfying and happy days. Remember the photographic coverage of BOAC Comet air crash, and also of the Hindu-Muslim riots in '46, the visits of two Governors to our shop, and almost 1,000 rolls a day for processing during the Puja season. The stills we did of the Indo-American Film Venture—the rush of customers at the counter in the evenings, when even 8-9 attendants were not enough! Well, all these showed the prestige of Bombay Photo Stores.'

In its heyday, Bombay Photo Stores enjoyed the kind of standing that the century-old D. Ratan did at its Bidhan Sarani (earlier Cornwallis Street) establishment in north Calcutta. All prospective brides in the matrimonial market wanted to get their photographs taken there. Lila Patel reminisces: 'People used to come to have their daughters' photographs taken to be sent for the family to see prior to her engagement. I used to get a lot of calls from parents asking me if we had another location where they could go for their daughter's photograph, long after the shop was closed. I think the Marwaris, even the Bengalis felt that it was prestigious to send the girl's photo with the Bombay Photo Stores stamp at the back.'

Clyde Wadell, the photographer who has left behind a fascinating album of Calcutta, had come in contact with the Patels at one point of time. Lila Patel recalls the encounter: 'By the way, Bombay Photo Stores had started a counter in one of the GIs' residential places where Jayant used to sit and collect rolls for processing. That's where Clyde Wadell sold him his album of photographs of Calcutta for Rs 100, as he was short of funds.'

Jayant had health problems and his two children Ajay and Anjani, studying in the US, were not interested in running the business. So, Bombay Photo Stores folded up on 28 February 2004, five years before his death. Most of the photographs taken in the studio along with the equipment were lost. All that remains is a huge collection of photographs of Calcutta in its glory days, besides an equally prodigious number of images of picturesque destinations all over the country before the population explosion happened. The cut-off year is 1970. Calcutta was then caught in a web of events that sealed its fate. In actuality, Jayant had a larger collection of photographs of the city and other places too. A lot of 860 images was brought back home for the exhibition in 2004. But once the business closed, the remaining photographs were not brought back.

Jayant had travelled extensively all over the country from his youth with his camera as his companion. He has left behind a huge archive of those photographs along with the negatives, and since people rarely moved out of their home towns then, these images, dating back to the 1940s and up to the 1960s, give us a basic idea of what the country used to look like long before housing became a problem in cities, and when it was possible to move around without treading on each other's corns and without cars, trucks, and three-wheelers and slow-moving vehicles blocking every single road, pavement, and alley. The strangest thing about Jayant's photographs is that you can hardly find any human presence in these must-see tourist spots. One is reminded of Eugene Atget and his Paris photographs. We see Puri, Darjeeling and a paradisiacal Kashmir.

Lila Patel says her husband was a very good father, and he would take his two children to the Maidan daily and allowed them to play and cycle around. On Sundays, he would take the two to the zoo. Jayant's son Ajay, who was born in 1958 and is professor/chairperson of Wake Forest University in the US, recalled his father's boundless enthusiasm for photography in an email:

'My memories of Dad taking photographs go back to when I was less than four. My earliest memories of Dad with his camera are when he would take me to Victoria Memorial early in the morning. The sun would have just risen, the sky had a red hue to it, there was a fog in the air, people exercising, running or playing in the Maidan, and Dad would be taking pictures of everything around him—the Victoria Memorial with the rising sun reflecting off the white marble, people exercising, or playing in the Maidan, or the street.

'I also remember him taking pictures in front of Bombay Photo Stores during Christmas season when we would have a Santa Claus in front of the shop. People would stop by to take photographs of themselves in front of the studio. Each year, I always wondered what would show up in front of the studio. And Park Street, all lit up, was a wonderful place to be. Dad really wanted to make people happy during that time of year.

'Dad had an amazing eye and his ability to convert what he saw into a work of art was beyond anything I understood or could replicate. He just saw things I didn't. And, his ability to use his camera to create a work of art, without having had any formal study of physics and the impact of light on the negative, was amazing. He had figured out how to change the shutter speed, and the camera aperture to capture what he wanted. But, he never saw what he was doing as unique. It was just something he loved doing.'

Jayant Patel took straightforward shots. In his capacity as official photographer of Government House, there was no scope for experimentation with angles or filters or other modes of manipulating the image. His images had to tell their story in a simple, undemanding manner. They were essentially posed, carefully choreographed photographs, for documentation was the primary purpose of these images. There was no question of recording embarrassing situations, for everything was official. They had to be shot as formally and objectively as possible without the intrusion of his personality. It was unlikely that the photographer ever had to face a moral dilemma for people in distress were not his subject. The value of these photographs lies not so much in their artistry as in their role as witnesses to the chain of unfolding events that determined the fate and future of India. Which is why this is a priceless archive that enshrines the narrative of the establishment of the world's most populous democracy.

In this, Patel comes close to the work of Homai Vyarawalla, India's first woman photojournalist. Both presented authorised versions of India's history. And it is unvarnished truth. But carefully avoiding the pratfalls and disfigurements. Vyarawalla spelled out her personal philosophy of photojournalism in a handwritten note in 2006: 'Character assassination and ridiculing people in high position is no part of a photojournalist's work...At yet another time I was surprised to find one of my prints taken at Palam airport during Mr Ho-Chi-Minh's visit, showing Mr Nehru viciously holding his beard and the guest scowling at him in surprise and indignation. Such a freak photograph if circulated would naturally cause embarrassment for both the governments. I never circulated it. It was only 50 years later that I put it up for exhibition.' She could have been writing on behalf of Patel.

Although Patel photographed Gandhi and Nehru extensively, there is nothing quite as dramatic as Henri Cartier-Bresson's nocturnal shot of Nehru announcing Gandhi's assassination. Even when Jayant Patel ventured out of Government House with his camera, his stance remained almost the same. He did not wait for the 'decisive moment.' He did not wait for surprises with which to hold the attention of his viewers. His photographs were all carefully composed, even the outdoor shots. Although he did occasionally try out many shots where the focus was on chiaroscuro, what really drove him was the urge to record whatever he saw. He was mainly in the observational mode, and his role was that of the 'fly on the wall' using his camera to candidly document whatever he saw.

I had seen Patel's photographs of Calcutta when they were exhibited at the Victoria Memorial Hall in a show titled 'Majestic Calcutta' put together by then curator and secretary, Chittaranjan Panda, and inaugurated by the then West Bengal Governor, Gopalkrishna Gandhi. I never met him as I was commissioned to do this project long after his death. So I thought it would be a good idea to interview at least one living photographer of Patel's time. That way one could contextualise Patel's photographs. After all, he was not working in a vacuum.

I thought of the Delhi-based Madan Mahatta, known for his photographs of the modernist buildings designed by leading architects such as Kuldip Singh, Joseph Allen Stein, Raj Rewal, Kanvinde & Rai, Charles Correa, and Habib Rahman. They came up in the capital city, galvanised by the creative activity to give shape to and epitomise the secular spirit of a new nation. These brutal concrete structures without any hint of ornamentation were in stark contrast with the stolid Victorian buildings that Patel shot in Calcutta.

Mahatta was born in 15 May 1932, which makes him a little younger than Patel. He was very ill when I called him in 2014, and although he could barely be heard, he was eager to speak. He said he was born Mehta but changed his surname to Mahatta on a Frenchman's suggestion to make it easier for his mostly British clients. Mahatta began shooting sports events in his school in Srinagar with a Kodak Baby Brownie in the early 1940s. His father and uncles were into photography and their photographic establishment is still functioning in Delhi. 'In 1944, I took shots in my classroom with a Zeiss camera with a self-timer. I put the camera on a stool, started the self-timer and ran to take up position. I am still surprised that I did that.'

In 1954, he went to UK to be professionally trained at the Guildford School of Arts & Crafts where he was introduced to colour. Mahatta says he did industrial photography and portraiture, and architecture came only by chance when somebody brought architectural models to be photographed. That was in 1957, when all the architects who became renowned later needed their maquettes to be photographed. Mahatta's name spread by word of mouth and he ended up with a collection of negatives, which helped him mount his critically-acclaimed exhibition in 2012. But Mahatta, who wanted to become a master of all trades, admits: 'I never dreamt that an exhibition will be held.' Jayant Patel would perhaps have agreed with him. Mahatta died in March 2014. Mahatta is considered a pioneering Indian photographer along with Sunil Janah, T.S. Satyan, and Homai Vyarawalla.

Sunil Janah is one of India's best-known photojournalists and documentary photographers of the 1940s. His family was from Medinipur district in Bengal although he lived in Calcutta and studied English literature at Presidency College. The year 1943 was a watershed in his life. He left his studies at the behest of P.C. Joshi, general secretary of the Communist Party of India, who decided that while Janah would take photographs of the Bengal Famine, he would do the reportage.

However, Janah was distressed. He had shifted to the UK in 1978, and in 1998 in Wimbledon, he said in an interview: 'People were starving and dying, and I was holding a camera to their faces…It was a very harrowing experience, but I also felt that I had to take photographs. There had to be a record of what was happening, and I would do it with my photographs. Janah left behind a prodigious and seminal body of work that recorded famines, movements, peoples, and personalities unrivalled by any other Indian photographer. Their situations and forte may have been very different, but like any other photographer of consequence, Patel too recorded history.

T.S. Satyan from Mysore was known for his classic, contemplative compositions of people mostly from backwaters, who in spite of their poverty carried themselves with dignity. Even when he photographed well-known people, his lens searched for the human essence. He began shooting with a box camera at a very young age and his sole ambition was to get published in the print media. His photographs were published in *Life*, *The Illustrated Weekly of India*, and other prestigious magazines but he eschewed 'the speed and noise' of modern life and seriously believed that 'photography is history and life.' He always waited for the 'decisive moment' and felt it was his responsibility as a photographer to exclude what was redundant even in a chaotic situation.

Where his assignments and sensibility were concerned, Jayant Patel was closest to Homai Vyarawalla. She had access to all Indian leaders, including Jawaharlal Nehru, but she was not one to flaunt her clout. She had a high moral tone, and in spite of being so successful, she was against women giving up their families for the sake of their careers.

Vyarawalla was born in Navsari in Gujarat to a Parsi family in 1913, and her career covered three decades from the late 1930s to 1970. Both she and her husband, Manekshaw, who taught her to take photographs, worked for the British Information Services, and this enabled her to chronicle history as it unfolded in those turbulent times before and after Independence. She has left behind a rich archive of photographs. Like Homai, Jayant Patel too—rather his camera—had witnessed history in the making, if only it was for his assignments at Government House.

Jayant Patel's photographs can be categorised under certain heads—streets, statues, Government House, Dalhousie Square, Queen Elizabeth II's visit, Chiang Kai-shek's visit, and Durga puja. There are besides, stray, mostly one-off, photographs of Barrackpore Gandhi Ghat, Vivekananda Setu, Jinnah, Parshwanath Jain temple in Gouribari, Harrison Road, Nakhoda Masjid, Kalighat, Dakshineswar temple, Jadubabur Bazar, St Paul's Cathedral, and passport photographs of GIs, who were posted in Calcutta during World War II. Roland Barthes could have been speaking on my behalf when he wrote: 'With regard to many of these photographs, it was History which separated me from them. Is History not simply that time when we were not born?'

What all these photographs, taken at various points of time between the 1940s and 1970s, have in common is the city of Calcutta. And one has to scan them carefully to detect the changes wrought by time. The most obvious difference between then and now is that although the city was always overcrowded, in recent time the roads, pavements, and lanes have turned into a maelstrom of humanity and vehicular traffic. This stupendous crush was unimaginable in those days, even after the Partition. This truth is quite obvious from the photographs.

The prevailing sartorial style is striking. Indian men still wore the dhoti, although a handful of them had started slipping into trousers. There is an arresting shot of two Bangali babus in dhoti waiting in front of a sugarcane juice seller (p. 137). Arranged in neat piles on the platform on which the sugarcane crusher is installed is a neat pile of *bhands*, the earthenware cups. Now the juice is sold in glass tumblers which are dipped into a bucket of turgid water by way of washing. Or else in plastic tumblers meant to be thrown away. Behind them is the stately building of the Military Secretariat, which means this is happening in Curzon Park opposite the tram depot.

Few middle-class women were visible in public spaces. They were still housebound. The third point is the physical degeneration of the city and its buildings. In most of the areas which Patel had photographed, the buildings are almost all intact, but they look worse for wear. Even then, all the buildings were not in prime condition and the whitewash was not quite white.

If one begins one's journey back in time, one should start at Howrah Station itself. All the horse carriages (p. 90) disappeared years ago, and so did the double-decker buses. Trams, which once used to shake, rattle, and roll over the bridge, have gone the same way. Innumerable bus bays have been constructed in the space between Howrah Bridge and the station.

The gridlock of vehicles begins early in the day and continues till late night. The number of people trying to catch buses or walking across to the station has risen exponentially. Unauthorised eateries along its bank block the Hooghly from view. With the state government going soft on hawkers, pedestrians have lost their right to pavements.

Many of the houses and warehouses in these pictures along the river are gone, the most notable one to go in recent times being the gorgeous Strand warehouse. New Secretariat building designed by eminent architect Habib Rahman was constructed a few years later, and the old building of the State Bank of India had not been demolished yet.

There is one photograph of Habib Rahman's work. It is that of the celebrated Gandhi Ghat with a secular design of Indian origin on the Hooghly river bank at Barrackpore, composed of intersecting vertical and horizontal stone slabs. From afar, the vertical slab gives the impression of a Hindu temple with an Islamic dome on top, while the horizontal one forms a cross. It was inaugurated by Jawaharlal Nehru in 1949, when C. Rajagopalachari was Governor-General (p. 82–83).

Howrah Bridge has not changed but the river that flows beneath it has silted up so heavily that the ships you can see in Patel's photographs can never sail this far any longer. Nowadays, river traffic constitutes boats of every description, including steamers that ferry passengers from one ghat to another. The bore tide is not half as spectacular or violent as it used to be.

Some neighbourhoods were born sad. Harrison Road (Mahatma Gandhi Road) with its rows of grimy old houses with wooden louvres looked battered even when we used to pass it regularly in my childhood, more than 50 years ago, to catch a train in Sealdah Station. Our destination was my *mamarbari,* or mother's parental home, in Ranaghat. Trams still judder noisily down this road.

Parshwanath Jain temple with brilliant mirror work on its facade (it has lost many of the mirrors, and much of its sheen) was always a huge attraction for tourists (p. 96). This exotic jewel box was inevitably shot by foreigners who came visiting Calcutta. Ray Badridas Bahadur (1833–1913), a noted jeweller, philanthropist, and Jain social leader, constructed the temple in 1867.

Tipu Sultan mosque (p. 140) with its elegant minarets in Dharmatalla is easily identified in the photographs, but where are the shops and hawkers that hem it in today? Dharamtalla Street (now Lenin Sarani) itself was a bustling street with clanging trams (p. 138).

A little further down on Chowringhee are the cheaper and seedier hotels like Chowringhee Hotel and bars before one reaches Metro cinema and the Whiteaway Laidlaw department store. Two years or so ago these buildings were hidden behind giant billboards. Now that these screens have been removed, the skeletal iron frames of billboards, and the naked glory of these buildings, without the epidermis of plaster, lie exposed. A little further down is

Hotel Continental and its rows of windows with Gothic arches (p.150). It was demolished to build what is now Peerless Inn (Quality Inn in its earlier avatar).

Mark Twain stayed in this hotel in 1896 and thanked its owner, Senor Boscolo, for his comfortable stay there. Senor F.A. Boscolo, an Italian, was caterer and proprietor of Bellevue Hotel, which he left to take over Hotel Continental a year before Twain came to stay there. In spite of his 'thank you' note, Twain was down with bronchitis almost throughout his stay in this plush hotel, and had to miss both the public reception planned for him and the hotel's French cuisine for which it was famous till 1920.

It was a popular rendezvous among British Army officers visiting Calcutta, who preferred it over Mrs Monks' Hotel next door, or the expensive Great Eastern Hotel in Old Court House Street. During World War II, the hotel was used by American Red Cross as a club for enlisted men known as the Continental Service Club and Hotel. But it is said that even in 1944 the hotel lacked modern amenities.

Mrs Monk's Hotel later became the Oberoi Grand (p. 151). Its entrance on Chowringhee is large enough for several cars. The building covers a whole block. It was in the arcade of this hotel that Bombay Photo Stores had a branch. There are several shots of the hotel, and one from Lindsay Street, which leads to New Market. The grounds opposite the Grand were clear then. No open space now, what with the parking lot, Bidhan market and hawkers.

Patel took the photograph of New Market long before a fire razed the rear section in 1985. Cars are parked in front of what was Globe cinema then (p. 152–153). Since there was hardly any traffic, either human or vehicular, that was fine. Now there is an underground parking lot. But with an array of clothes, giant soft toys in pure colours, and lady's handbags usurping the pavements and streets, plastering the walls of the main market and hanging like strange fruit from trees, this neighbourhood has turned into a permanent bustling mela ground.

Patel had taken a panoramic view of glamorous Chowringhee with its rows of splendid buildings. Did he take it from what was known as Ochterlony Monument in 1969? The crumbling building on Corporation Street (now S.N. Banerjee Road) behind the Esplanade Metro station, which once housed the chambers of American orthodontists, was in mint condition then.

Patel had taken a panoramic view of Dalhousie Square with the tank, Laldighi, at the centre of it all (p. 118). The Dalhousie Square area is a heritage zone, although only built heritage is covered by the current laws. So even a historic waterbody like Laldighi which is older than the city itself, lies unprotected. Even worse, Writers' Buildings of 18th century vintage, standing out against the skyline, is apparently being 'restored' by the Public Works Department, not known for its expertise in heritage conservation (p. 114).

The Reserve Bank of India building on Netaji Subhas Road (earlier, the smart Clive Street) had already come up then. St Andrew's Church looks familiar enough (p. 111). There is a pre-Reserve Bank shot, too, where the dome of the General Post Office dominates the scene and Howrah Bridge can be seen in the distance (p. 120). If one inspects the photographs closely, one can detect small changes. The building of the Bengal Bonded Warehouse Association, which was the property of Carr, Tagore and Company, a failed enterprise started by Dwarkanath Tagore, was ravaged in a fire about two years ago when the section facing N.S. Road was destroyed. Its arched gateway is visible in a photograph (p. 115). And in Old Court House Street, Great Eastern Hotel has transformed into Lalit Great Eastern. All that remains of the heritage landmark is the facade (p. 124).

There is something missing in his photograph of Magen David synagogue at the junction of Brabourne Road and Canning Street (p. 108). The grand synagogue was built in 1884 by Elias David Ezra in memory of his father, David Joseph Ezra, a real estate magnate. There is open space in front of the huge porte-cochère where some people, presumably labourers or masons and carpenters, are waiting for people to hire them. Beyond that is the thoroughfare where people and rickshaws are going about their business, and a bullock cart is parked by the wayside. But where is the ugly white structure in front of the synagogue, which blocks this grand view from Brabourne Road? My inquiries at Nahoum and Sons, the Jewish bakery whose owner, David Nahoum, was the custodian of the synagogue before he died in 2013, drew a blank. Later, I discovered that the building we see today, came up in the early 1950s, obviously after Patel took the photograph.

Brabourne Road had already been laid out when Patel took a picture of the street which shows a section of the Cathedral of the Most Holy Rosary built in 1799, popularly known as Portuguese church or Murgihata church (p. 110).

While these photographs are more or less routine, there is one remarkable shot taken in front of what is now the HSBC bank building (p. 112). As a tram turns around towards the direction of the Dead Letter Office with its campanile, a Bengali and a Marwari cross the road from opposite directions. Both wear the dhoti but in different styles, and the Marwari is noticeable for his headgear, de rigueur among the business class in those orthodox times. Now Marwaris wear turbans only during ceremonies like weddings. A telling photograph indeed, for in a few decades' time north Indian culture would overtake that of the Bengalis', and although the natives of this state are still in a majority where numbers are concerned, they have a minority share in West Bengal's economy. As land prices skyrocket, Bengalis are gradually moving out of Calcutta to the suburbs. Power has slipped out of their hands, and they are not the ones who decide the fate of West Bengal any longer.

I met Saroj Mehera, who is in his late 80s and belongs to the Burdwan royal family, one afternoon while he was enjoying a drink at Calcutta Club. In the course of our conversation, I discovered that he had joined Finlays & Company Ltd, a branch of the company based in Glasgow, in 1949, and that tea was their principal business. *The Thacker's Indian Directory* of 1950 states that Finlays were agents for tea, transport, jute, sugar, shipping, and insurance companies besides being representatives for miscellaneous organisations. I wanted to find out from him what upper-class life was like at a time about which some people still speak only in superlatives.

Originally all the management staff was British, but Indian managers began to be recruited after World War II. Gradually more and more Indians began to be appointed on the same terms as those from the West, except that the latter received an overseas allowance. Clive Street had much less traffic and was less crowded, although hawkers were still present. The Europeans mixed freely with Indians, who, at the managerial level, were westernised.

The Calcutta Municipal Corporation had a fleet of Thorneycroft lorries, which had no pneumatic tyres. Instead, they had metal wheels with strips of felting. Trams had lights of different colours to indicate their routes. The noisy GIs, who were posted here, had deep pockets. So the Tommies were jealous of these Americans. Mehera took me on a round of night life in the city, which, as a fleshpot, was second to none. 'Firpo's was flourishing then and I used to be taken there as a kid by my parents. The flamboyant 300 Club on Theatre Road was patronised by the hedonistic Huseyn Shaheed Suhrawardy, who drove around his Packard.' Mehera even remembered its number—BLA 1. Suhrawardy was the last prime minister of Bengal when the British ruled, and after Pakistan became independent in 1947, he became a populist leader of East Pakistan and served as the fifth prime minister of Pakistan.

After the War, performances used to be held at Prince's at the Grand and Maxim's at Great Eastern. Male and female dancers performed at the 300 Club opened by the White Russian, Boris Lissanevich, himself a ballet dancer, hotelier, and restaurateur. His wife was a ballet dancer named Kira Shcherbacheva. He introduced the famous dish, Chicken a la Kiev, to Calcutta as a menu item at 300 Club and opened the first hotel in Nepal. Saroj Mehera said: 'Boris introduced fruit machines (for gambling) and these are still in operation in Nepal. Those who visited 300 Club had to dress formally—men in dinner jackets and ladies in saris.'

I asked him if the dancers were white or Anglo-Indians. Mehera replied: 'You couldn't tell.' Some famous foreigners performed at the Grand, including 'Hutch,' (Leslie Arthur Julien Hutchinson) the famous cabaret star of the 1920s and the 1930s, darling of high society (he was rumoured to have had an affair with Edwina Mountbatten), and known as much for his interpretations of Cole

Porter (Hutch and Cole were lovers) numbers as for his prodigious manhood (he was gifted a bejewelled Cartier sheath, allegedly by Lady Mountbatten).

I asked Saroj Mehera if he had witnessed any performance by Hutch. He replied (we used email for our correspondences): 'Yes, I saw Hutch perform. He made a hit singing 'The ladies of Calcutta…' set to a well-known tune of the time, which, I regret, I cannot recall. He was a great performer in London in his day and went down well in Calcutta. Duke Ellington gave a performance during a visit to Calcutta in the 60s or so.'

The mansion of the fabulously rich Jewish tycoon, David E. Ezra, was at 3 Kyd Street, and he was known for the open house he kept for the GIs and the Tommies. A photo feature in *Phoenix*, the Anglo-American magazine for armed forces, produced by journalist Frank Owen at the behest of Lord Mountbatten, describes 'Tea at Lady Ezra's': 'Civilians throughout India have been hosts of GI Joe and Tommy Atkins, but few can compete with the record of Sir David and Lady Ezra, prominent Calcutta couple, who have opened their doors to more than 40,000 servicemen and women of all branches of the Armed Forces…Lady Ezra started her open house long before the war—for the benefit of the British peacetime soldiers. When the war broke out, she added hundreds of pounds of tea and cakes to the weekly order and continued to play hostess to all ranks on a strictly informal basis, and rank actually is forgotten…For the Ezras, it's a lot of fun playing host to the men in uniform. They like to take guests around the grounds and show them the thousands of birds, imported from all countries in the world, as well as monkeys, deer, leopards, sheep and a mammoth turtle 300 years old, which hundreds of soldiers have ridden. After tea guests are taken to the drawing-room upstairs for a tea dance.'

In the photographs, David Ezra is a bald and corpulent old man, while his wife is a matron with a severe parting. They don't look like fun people. The caption of one of the photographs reads: 'Tea dancing usually follows tea and young ladies are always available as partners.' Well, Free School Street was only a few houses away, and it had a reputation then. Of course, this was all meant for the white GIs, racial segregation being strictly enforced by the American army.

Here is a first-hand account of the entertainment provided in five-star hotels. I met a cabaret artiste, who in her heyday was known as Luscious Lola (she was not a *firang*), on Facebook some time ago. She used to perform at all the big hotels in the 1960s, and when I asked her if the shows in Calcutta compared favourably with the ones in the West, she inboxed: 'They were up to the West, if not even better in class and style, in 5 or 4 star clubs and hotels.' Lola was famed for her sexy burlesque acts. Luscious Lola added that all the publicity shots for cabaret were taken at Bombay Photo Stores.

So that was the good life for you. While the hedonists were having a whale of a time, the cries of the poor and the hungry and the dying found voice in the popular songs of Kamala Jharia, like '*Shonre shon Bangla desher kangal chashi bhai*' (Listen, our wretched brothers, the farmers of Bengal) and '*Bhulona rekho mone Panchasher akal*' (Don't you forget, keep in mind, the famine of the Fifties), composed by Tulsi Lahiri, the man with whom she was said to have lived in sin. These two songs, recorded by Megaphone in 1946, bemoaned the lot of exploited farmers as World War II arrived in the Indian sub-continent. While the rich in their 'hat, boot *aar* suit' and hoarders of 'sugar, atta, flour, and rice' became richer, the farmers lost even bare essentials, notwithstanding a golden harvest. Kamala Jharia's plangent voice still reminds us of the grim war years.

Jayant Patel has left behind a valuable record of the statues of our colonial overlords that once stood at strategic points of central Calcutta. Long, long before the equestrian statue of Netaji was installed at the five-point Shyambazar crossing, the Maidan and Esplanade areas were dotted with the magnificent statues of those who ruled the country. These were taken down from their perches in 1969, and reinstalled either at the Flagstaff House in Barrackpore or in the Victoria Memorial Hall grounds. I had to seek the help of Kamal Kumar Sarkar's book on Calcutta statues and the nonagenarian Bhaskar Mitter, who was once Chairman of Andrew Yule in an executive position and a non-executive Chairman of CESC, to identify the British grandees.

The funniest photograph in the collection is that of Lord Outram's splendid equestrian statue with the horse's tail standing on end, and the English general, who helped quell the First Indian Uprising looking behind him (p. 173). Sir Jadunath Sarkar had written that once a Bengali gentleman bribed some Muslim urchins to chuck stones at the statue, and as they carried out his orders he began to clap his hands in joy. Another old Shia man got up on the horse and began to beat Outram with his shoes, shouting at the same time: 'You have snatched Oudh from our ruler Wajid Ali Shah.' Such were the passions that Outram roused. In Patel's photograph, a man, apparently mentally unstable, sits at the tailend with a crowd looking up at him. This statue stood at the crossing of Chowringhee and Park Street. It is now inside Victoria Memorial Hall. It was the model for Netaji's malformed statue at the Shyambazar crossing.

Calcutta's first equestrian statue was installed in the Maidan in front of the Ochterlony Monument. It was that of Lord Hardinge and it had the remains of a canon at its foot (p. 159). The third equestrian statue is that of Lord Mayo on Red Road (p. 161). The fourth horse rider is Lord Lansdowne (p. 172). His statue was on Red Road, and in Patel's photograph he is surrounded by a herd of goats, a common sight at the Maidan even today.

The one who really rides a high horse is King Edward VII (p. 171). His equestrian statue is on top of the gateway of Victoria Memorial Hall from the south. They were conceived of as Roman generals and they played their part rather well. The ponderous Queen sits on her throne in the midst of it all, and her gravitas and girth would impress any viewer (p. 170). The massive marmoreal mausoleum, Victoria Memorial Hall, was built in the sovereign's memory between 1906 and 1921 and is a popular tourist destination today.

Once in a while, Patel did stray into both north and south Calcutta. There is a shot of Kumortuli (p. 98). But it is not the Kumortuli cliché of Hindu deities. What we see here is a typical pitcher shop displaying pitchers of all sizes, from the giant *matka* to the much smaller ones. Long before the advent of plastic bottles, pitchers were the only vessels for storing water available to the common man. A huge tin roof covers the rows of shops.

Way before Kumortuli is Nakhoda Masjid with its three domes and slim minarets, on the same street, Chitpur, today's Rabindra Sarani. The mosque, Calcutta's biggest, was funded by Haji Zakariya and construction of the entire structure was completed in 1934 (p. 106).

Patel took two photographs of Jadubabur Bazar, and common to both is the shop front of Auddy & Sons, gold and silver merchants (p. 178–179). This is close to the Netaji Bhavan Metro station. There is hardly anybody around save some rickshaws. Where is the angry traffic?

He also moved further down to Kalighat and the famous temple after which Calcutta is said to have been named, if some learned men are to be believed. The temple (pg. 180–181) has changed drastically in the past few years or so. Now, as in many other places of worship, which have been renovated of late, the floors of Kalighat temple are lined with marble. All the old flagstones have been removed and now the floors are treacherously slippery. Marble (usually the synthetic variety) is the middle-class status symbol. So why should the renowned temple be denied?

More interestingly, Patel had taken shots of the Adi Ganga flowing by the temple side (p. 182–183). It is reduced to a filthy runnel now, but 60 years ago it was still navigable. The photograph of the bathing ghat is crowded as it usually is. Above the ghat are two buildings meant to shelter pilgrims. Another structure, presumably a gateway, stands in between. When I visited Adi Ganga, I noticed one of the houses was gone. There were two temples next to the surviving one, which was in need of repair. A lone angler, a small boy, was dipping the line in knee-deep water.

Patel's photograph shows the water in the canal flowing swiftly with a boat sailing midstream. Now, the bed was almost dry and lined with boats used by pedestrians to walk over to the other side. The most conspicuous graffiti on the building was an exhortation to keep the Ganga pollution-free.The pious, and few of them were there that day, did not mind sprinkling the stinking water on themselves. Some even bathed in it. The runnel was more like a sewerage outflow channel.

I have known Santipada Bhattacharya, chief ritual and scriptural advisor and head priest of the Kalighat temple, in his late 80s now, for a long time. He says in his boyhood, he almost drowned in the river when somebody pushed him into the water. Although the river is almost dry, during bore tide the streets still get flooded. During Durga puja, kalabou (a banana plant) married to Ganesh is ritually bathed in the river. The shops lining the path to the river are still owned by people from Odisha. Seventy-five years ago there were horse-carriage stands, close to the temple. Now vehicles are not allowed.

The temple of Bhabatarini in Dakshineswar on the eastern bank of the Hooghly was built in 1855 by the feisty Rani Rashmoni, who had taken charge of her zamindari after she became a widow (p. 84). The temple is famous for its associations with the mystic, Ramakrishna Paramhansa. Earlier, Panchabati, the sacred grove planted by Ramakrishna, used to be lonely and tranquil and a kind of hush pervaded the green zone. Now it swarms with people.

Patel seems to have been interested in Durga puja, Bengal's biggest and most disruptive festival. College Square is and always was a huge crowd-puller. Their puja is on a grand scale and they must be spending close to a crore or even more. But so do many other organisers, now that Durga puja, like Christmas, has turned into a huge corporate venture with the media being involved in a big way. The College Square Sarbojanin Durgotsav Committee has its own website and, as is well known, for years its stunning image was made by the famous Ramesh Chandra Paul of Kumartuli. The pomp and splendour of this puja, which was started in 1946, have increased manifold over the years. The 23 Palli Durga in Bhowanipur in the 'Oriental' style was supposed to have been the rage in ancient India in keeping with old sculpture and the cave paintings of Ajanta (p. 99). This particular puja does not need a clay image any longer. It has a shrine of its own, with a large image of Durga made of some alloy resembling burnished copper.

T.S. Jayan had said in an interview: 'Every photographer must have a sense of history. Photojournalism is undoubtedly the visual biography of man on earth… Photography is history and life. The major contribution of the photographer/photojournalist has been to preserve for posterity the memorable moments of contemporary history which, I think, is the everlasting effect of photojournalism. The photographer is a serious witness in the court of history. The better photograph ceases to be a thing of the past. It acquires a life of its own and remains perennially fresh and relevant.'

In his capacity as official photographer of Government House, Jayant Patel was witness to certain events that had far reaching consequences for the future of this nation. First let us take a peek into Government House through Jayant Patel's eyes as history unfolded. There are two shots of the Raj Bhavan gates facing Old Court House Street with a lion on top (p. 126–127). A part of the building can be seen through the archway while a lone car drives past the scene. The other is of the same portal taken in 1947. A crowd gathered outside it, perhaps waiting for the swearing-in ceremony, which concluded with attempted vandalism of the property by onlookers. Patel perhaps never left behind any record of these disruptive events and of others such as the endless rallies (often violent), graffiti and posters that went hand in hand with the freedom movement.

The nonagenarian Bhaskar Mitter, whose father was acting governor for some time, was there to recreate the past. When Patel was clicking away, R.G. Casey (he was in office from 1944 to 1946) and Frederick John Burrows were the men in charge till Independence, when Chakravarti Rajagopalachari took over. The dapper and moustachioed Governor Casey, an Australian diplomat and politician, in formal attire and a bow tie sits next to Gandhi in his office, 'which he described as being about the size of a tennis court,' at a time when the latter was on a vow of silence, that is *maunvrat*. In another photograph taken in 1944, a silent Gandhi is seen handing over a letter, written in reply to Casey's question (p. 190–191). Casey had to deal with the situation after the devastating famine of 1943, and the deafening demands for independence in India. An Occasional Paper from the library of Raj Bhavan, Calcutta, carries an extract from *Tides & Eddies* by Maie Casey, the Governor's wife.

Maie descended the 'concealed spiral staircase of iron lace' to meet Gandhi, and since it was winter, the latter was wrapped in a 'fine white Kashmiri shawl.' 'I could not keep away once I had met Gandhi and hurried down the little staircase to greet him before he left, on every occasion except on his day of silence when any exchange of thought was conducted by him on slips of paper.'

Maie was fascinated by Gandhi. She wrote: 'I was not the Governor. I was only his wife, therefore my conversations with Gandhi flowed in unrestricted freedom. His eyes behind thick lenses were shrewd and kind and comforting.'

She found 'Mr Gandhi's friend, who became his adversary' (Mohammed Ali Jinnah) equally fascinating. About Jinnah Maie wrote: 'When he visited us in Calcutta he was the idol of the vast majority of Indian Muslims, the torch, the flame of cold light, that was to lead them to the partition of India.' This is how she described him: 'Mr Jinnah was tall, pale, thin almost to emaciation although his frail body suggested the strength of coiled spring. He had piercing dark eyes and spoke with the cool precision of a lawyer. I thought him a little frightening until he gave one of his rare smiles.' But to Mr Jinnah later.

There is a portentous photograph from 24 April 1946 of the swearing in of the Muslim League minister, Mohammad Ali, by the then governor, Frederick Burrows, in the presence of Huseyn Shaheed Suhrawardy, who served as prime minister of undivided Bengal from 24 April 1946 to 14 August 1947. Burrows was a friend of Suhrawardy's, and he asked him to form a ministry (p. 193).

There is an ominous photograph of Jinnah in the Maidan in those penultimate days before the bloodbath—what is known as the Week of the Long Knife that started on 16 August 1946 (p. 192).

A wasted Jinnah sits on a chair with his legs crossed, uncomfortably perhaps. One arm rests on his knee and his right hand rests on the arm of his chair. He is, as always, nattily dressed in a suit and tie but wears a fez as a mark of his faith. Whether he was a devout Muslim or not is a different matter. His brows are knitted and his expression is angry or perhaps deeply disturbed. His aquiline nose accentuates that look of sultriness anticipating the storm that was about to break out.

Surrounding Jinnah are upper-class members of the Muslim League, distinguished by their well-cut suits, but they have receded into the background. Huseyn Shaheed Suhrawardy stands out on account of his spotless white clothes. So Jinnah is the man of the moment.

This was before Direct Action Day was called by the Muslim League Council on 16 August. The Muslim League having accepted the Cabinet Mission Plan of May 1946 later backed out claiming that the Congress was 'bent upon setting up a caste-Hindu Raj in India with the connivance of the British,' and demanded the immediate establishment of Pakistan. In order to bring this about, it called on the 'Muslim Nation to resort to direct action.'

I could understand why Maie Casey was fascinated by the man. After India was torn asunder, and Jinnah became Pakistan's first Governor-General, Maie met him for the last time in Karachi. He died not long afterwards. She wrote: 'Mr Jinnah reminded me of our conversation in Calcutta and said, 'You see, Mrs Casey, if I had not been a fanatic, there would have been no Pakistan."

Jayant was adventurous enough to go out on the incarnadined streets of Calcutta accompanied by his brother Kanu during the 1946 riots. Lila Patel was married nine years later, and she says her husband told her that the cataclysm happened after the Maidan meeting where he had photographed Jinnah. It was not an official assignment so they had no police protection.

After processing the rolls, the Patels realised the explosive nature of the shots they had taken of festering heaps of dismembered bodies, entrails, and body parts in certain sections of the city, and made sure the album was kept under wraps. For added measure they handed over the album to their mother for safekeeping. But it could not be found later. It had disappeared without trace.

There are happy times in his photographs too. After Independence. C. Rajagopalachari became the new Governor of Bengal, and Jawaharlal Nehru was the first Prime Minister of the new-born nation. Patel had taken several formal shots of both in Raj Bhavan, where Rajagopalachari and Nehru are seen waiting outside, to welcome guests among whom is Rajaji's daughter, Namagiri, a frail, young woman (p. 197). Their hands are folded in namaskar. Nehru and Rajagopalachari wait at the foot of the grand staircase of Raj Bhavan along with the staff (p. 198).

In the next photo the Prime Minister takes the salute as Rajagopalachari watches. Nehru inspects the troops at the north gate. The Chinese cannon mounted on a dragon is easily identifiable (p. 199). They sit in the grounds for a formal shot (p. 200). Seated along with the Governor and the Prime Minister are General Cariappa, Prafulla Chandra Ghosh, the first Chief Minister of West Bengal, and standing behind them is M.O. Mathai. Rajagopalachari chats with a smiling Nehru. Behind him, his assistant is also all smiles. The others look reserved. The staff of Raj Bhavan look impressive enough with their moustaches and turbans, and starched uniforms.

Viewers are allowed a glimpse of a banquet hosted by Rajagopalachari at Raj Bhavan (p. 201). He is engaged in a private conversation with Maharani Radha of Burdwan, who has her head covered with her sari, and next to him is Lady Pratima Mitter, whose attention has been caught by something outside the frame. How photographs can tease our imaginations! Opposite them is Nehru, his profile sharply etched by the brilliance of the flash. Behind them are the liveried footmen. Their uniforms have remained unchanged till today.

Lady Pratima Mitter happened to be Bhaskar Mitter's mother. Her husband was the barrister, Sir Brojendra Lal Mitter, Dewan of Baroda and later the first Advocate-General of India, and her father was Pramatha Nath Bose, the pioneering geologist. When Rajagopalachari went on leave for three months, Brojendra Lal, who belonged to the Mitter family of Darjipara, held the fort at Raj Bhavan in November 1947.

Rajagopalchari congratulated Sir Brojendra on his appointment in a letter on 9 November 1947. The former was appointed Governor-General of India replacing Mountbatten, so there was a need for an acting governor of Bengal.

I asked Bhaskar Mitter what Raj Bhavan was like in those days. He said: 'It was still very much British. Rajagopalachari did not change it much. The waiters were liveried, and the dinners were all sit-down. The food was a blend of Indian and Western, what was jocularly known as Ingo-Bongo. There was plenty of porcelain and crested silver. Raj Bhavan had a very good library.'

Raj Bhavan has always kept a good table and a quick look at the menus of some state dinners would give us an idea of the fare that was served. Some of these were pretentiously printed in French. Here is a sampler of the food served when Haile Selassie, Emperor of Ethiopia, and Ho Chi-Minh, President of the Democratic Republic of Vietnam, dropped by in Calcutta. One could choose between vegetarian and non-vegetarian and Indian and continental.

> NON-VEGETARIAN: Almond Soup, Bhecti Tirale, Roast Turkey, Mutton Kabab-Pilau, Alu-Methi Bhujia, Chutney, Cream Chartreuse, Croutes Victoria, Dessert, Coffee.
>
> VEGETARIAN: Almond Soup, Vegetable Tirale, Vegetable Croquettes, Green Plantain Kabab-Pilau, Alu-Methi Bhujia, Chutney, Fruit Salad-Cream, Croutes Victoria, Dessert, Coffee.
>
> ON ANOTHER OCCASION: Perles de Malossol aux Blinis, Petite Marmite Bouchere, Filets de Beckty a la Bonne

> Femme, Poulet a la Kiev, Salade, Kurma Curry de Mouton, Riz Pilau, Poires Belle Helene, Champignons sur Canape, Frandises, Café.

The French may not make sense to most but the Chicken a la Kiev certainly does. An orchestra used to play on such occasions, and again it was a judicious mix of Indian, including hits from the golden age of Bollywood (it was contemporary then), and Western compositions, what can be broadly described as 'lollipops.'

> MARCH: *Martial Moments* (Aubrey Winter), OVERTURE: *Poet and Peasant* (Franz Von Suppe), *Rag Ashavari* (Sete), VALSE: *The Golden Valse* (Aubrey Winter), *Rag Bahar* (Sete), SELECTION: *The Merry Widow* (Dan Godfray), WALTZ: *Tumna Jane Kis Jahan Men Khogae* (Sete), MARCH: *Old Comrades* (C. Teike), *Jaen to Jaen Kahan* (Sete), VALSE: *Invitation a la Valse* (J. Riviere).

After the Sino-Indian border conflict of 1962, the local Chinese were incarcerated at the internment camp at Deoli in Rajasthan, where they were held for years without trial. Thereafter, they destroyed all old documents in an effort to wipe out their past. So they hardly possess any documents related to the visit of Chiang Kai-shek (1887–1975) to Calcutta in 1942. Jayant Patel had indeed dutifully recorded it.

Chiang Kai-Shek was a Chinese military and political leader who led the Kuomintang (Chinese Nationalist Party) for five decades and was head of state of the Chinese Nationalist government between 1928 and 1949. His beautiful and bewitching wife, the ruthless, steely, and brilliant Soong May-ling (1897–2003), once hailed as the 'most powerful woman in the world', who acted as the Generalissimo's English translator (he spoke no English), secretary, and advisor, accompanied him to Calcutta.

The British were worried about the Non-Cooperation Movement launched by the Indian freedom fighters, and even more so because Japan had influence over Hong Kong, Thailand and Malaysia. They wanted Chiang Kai-shek to mediate with Jawaharlal Nehru on their behalf and talk him out of it. So the Generalissimo came on a secret visit to India on 4 February 1942, via what the Allied pilots called the Hump in World War II. That is the eastern end of the Himalayan Mountains over which they flew military transport aircraft from India to China to resupply the Chinese war effort of Chiang Kai-shek and the units of the US Army Air Forces based in China. Chiang Kai-shek crossed the border of his native land for the first time since 1931. The Marquis of Linlithgow was the Viceroy then.

The Generalissimo arrived in Calcutta on 5 February 1942, but the Brits were not happy with him for he supported autonomy during the talks in New Delhi with the British governor on 10 February. However, Chiang Kai-shek held talks with Nehru on three occasions—once in New Delhi and twice in Calcutta. But Chiang-Kai-shek wanted to meet Gandhi too. Gandhi had written to him, and on seeing the letter he was moved to tears. The British were against such an encounter, but when the Generalissimo put his foot down, they agreed to a meeting on 18 February. It was facilitated by Nehru.

Gandhi came from Bombay to Calcutta with a *charkha* and a goat and stayed at the luxurious home of Ghanshyamdas Birla, who was his staunch supporter. He gave Chiang Kai-shek some yarn he had spun, and Madam the weaving wheel. Nehru announced: General Chiang Kai-shek discussed all matters regarding India, China and the world. The meeting lasted four-and-a-half hours.

The Birla ladies (all with their heads covered) and other members of the household posed for several shots along with Gandhi, Nehru, the Generalissimo, and Madam Chiang Kai-shek. Nehru in black appears in all of them and so does Madam. In the lone photograph with Gandhi, the Mahatma stands between the Generalissimo and his wife, who wears a flowered qipao in a dark shade and a garland of jasmine round her neck. The Generalissimo is also in black and Gandhi is in his usual garb. Behind them is visible the face of another Chinese man, probably a member of the entourage. At the far end is Nehru. The Birla ladies are all in plain cotton saris. All those photographed are beaming (p. 188).

In a second shot, the Birla ladies have stepped outside the shadow of their house into a pathway with bushes on both sides. Nehru stands next to them, and in their midst is Madam Chiang Kai-shek wearing a khaddar sari with the pallu demurely covering her head. She wears a vermilion bindi on her forehead, applied by Mrs Birla (p. 186). In a third shot, the guests and the Birlas are all having lunch together sitting on the floor of a large hall (p. 189). Marwaris were proud of their traditions then. Nehru sits between Madam and her husband, and the two seem to be having a chat, the Generalissimo not knowing any English. The Chinese 'official' sits next to her. However, this being a long shot, the faces of those having lunch are not clearly visible. According to *Life* magazine, which covered the visit, 'the low tables carry a beaker of water, four silver bowls of curry, a plate of rice and one of whole-wheat pancakes (chapati).'

There is a more interesting and intimate shot—perhaps the most intimate in this archive. It shows Madam Chiang Kai-shek and Nehru enjoying each other's company inside a large mirrored room (p. 187). Both sit on sofas and Madam still wears the garland. Nehru holds a sheaf of papers in his hands. His feet are bare. He had taken off his shoes for lunch. Their confabulation was about India's war effort.

Here are excerpts from *Life's* report. 'Gandhi looks like an Asiatic but he is really a Hindu lawyer from South Africa. Like all India's Hindu leaders, he is loaded to the eyebrows with the patter of English university education. His idea of being foxy today is to wait to see whether or not this war abolishes the British Empire. He was therefore opposed to coming to any agreement whatsoever with an Empire that may possibly be on the skids. To Chiang Kai-shek, the soft-spoken man of action, this brand of thinking was blankly mysterious, but he was exceedingly polite to all India's leaders.'

And in the concluding paragraph: 'It is significant that the pictures in the following pages of Chiang Kai-shek and Madam Chiang in India were all taken in the house of India's greatest capitalist, Gandhi's chief backer, a man willing to do business with anybody. It is hard to imagine what China's Generalissimo, hardened by awful sacrifice and heroism, made of this soft world of the Indians.'

In a letter dated 14 June 1942, Gandhi wrote to the Generalissimo: 'I can never forget the five hours' close contact I had with you and your noble wife in Calcutta…have told you of my faith in nonviolence and of my belief in the effectiveness of this method if the whole nation could turn to it. That faith in it is as firm as ever. But I realise that India today as a whole has not that faith and belief, and the Government in free India would be formed from the various elements composing the nation…'

There are two photographs of Sardar Vallabhbhai Patel (p. 194–195). In one he is being received at Dum Dum airport on 3 January 1948, the occasion on which the 'Iron Man of India' made his famous speech at a public meeting. Patel spoke about Kashmir, Junagadh, Pakistan, and the partition. In the second photograph, he is confabulating with Nehru and Ghanshyamdas Birla. Patel is known to have been close to the Marwari industrialist, although Nehru with his socialist ideals looks askance at the capitalist.

A kid though I was, I remember Queen Elizabeth II's visit to Calcutta in 1961, the frenzied excitement it generated, and how we stood by the statue of the Unknown Soldier in the Maidan as the young queen and her husband drove past, she waving at the jubilant crowds that had gathered along the route of her motorcade.

I recently discovered from Pathé footage that although the Queen drove down Chittaranjan Avenue, the delirious crowds had spilled over onto Bentinck Street, blocked the road and sat on the roofs of stationary trams. The other reason why I remember the visit is that soap manufacturers had announced a competition requiring children to fill in with paint a line drawing of the queen in an evening gown. I did paint a few of these, and although I did not win a prize, I did receive a large box of fragrant soaps.

Shooting the Queen was not an official assignment but Jayant Patel chose to cover it nonetheless, perhaps because it was a once-in-a-lifetime opportunity for him.

I tried the British Deputy High Commission for a list of events she attended while in Calcutta. But in vain. They did not have one. So I mailed my friend, historian Rosie Llwellyn Jones, in London and she readily agreed to help me. Her workplace is close to the palace.

On 21 September 2013, she wrote to Buckingham Palace, seeking the Queen's itinerary during her Calcutta visit. There was no reply even after several months, and so she sent them a reminder on 13 January, the next year. She used to assure me that they were slow but sure. Sure enough, she received a reply exactly two days later, from Christopher Sandamas, chief clerk. The letter was dated 15 January 2014.

This was her programme:

> THURSDAY 16 FEBRUARY: Arrive at Panagarh; Visit by HRH the Duke of Edinburgh to Jorhat Sports stadium; Reception held by ISCON and UK citizens.
>
> FRIDAY 17 FEBRUARY: Visit to the steel plant; Visit to Cinnemara tea gardens and Tocklai Experimental Centre; Drive around Durgapur township; Reception at the Jorehaut Tea Company's cricket ground; Luncheon within the Minister of Steel, Mines and Fuel; Reception ceremony in Calcutta.
>
> SATURDAY 18 FEBRUARY: Rally of UK children at Raj Bhavan; Visit to the National Agricultural Fair; Visit to the Victoria Memorial; Attend Race Meeting; Reception at the Royal

Calcutta Turf Club, given by the UK Deputy High Commissioner (Paul Henry Gore-Booth).

SUNDAY 19 FEBRUARY: Attend service at St Paul's cathedral; Farewell ceremony; Travel to Madras.

My friend, Amal Sircar, was a young man when the Queen visited Calcutta. He had taken some wonderful shots of the visit. I had requested him to write an eyewitness account of the visit. Here it is:

'Queen Elizabeth II and Duke of Edinburgh arrived in Calcutta on 17 February 1961. It was a sunny morning. Padmaja Naidu, then Governor of West Bengal, and Dr B.C. Roy, Chief Minister, received them at Dum Dum Airport as they flew in by a special BOAC aircraft (p. 202). Hundreds & thousands of people lined up along the route of the royal entourage from Dum Dum Airport to Raj Bhavan. Those days there were two routes from the airport to the city. One was via Jessore Road, Nager Bazar, Chiriar More-Shyambazar. The other route was Dum Dum Airport, Jessore Road, Nager Bazar, Belgachhia, and Shyambazar. The royal convoy was escorted by sergeants in white uniform on motor-bikes on the second route via Belgachhia.

'I was young and fresh from college. I had a small Agfa Clack camera. I wanted to take photographs of the royal entourage from a vantage point. It was impossible to take photographs from the pavement because thousands of people had lined up to have a view of the Queen since the morning. I took up a position on the balcony of a mansion near Shyambazar five-point crossing, which covered a wide area. Many reputed photographers, including press-photographers, were there with still and movie cameras.

I still remember Benu Sen, the eminent photographer, looking at my small camera with amusement.

'When the convoy reached Shyambazar, there was a crescendo of cheers from the public. The Queen was in an open car, standing and waving at the crowd. Padmaja Naidu sat beside the Queen. In the second car, there was the Duke of Edinburgh waving at the crowd. Dr B.C. Roy was seated by his side. I was able to take shots with my box camera of both the Queen and the Duke in two separate cars.

'On 18 February, I was present at the Calcutta Race Course. I was at the Grand Stand. The Queen and the Duke were received by Maharaja of Burdwan, the Royal Calcutta Turf Club's Senior Steward. Hundreds of pigeons were released when the Queen was at the Royal Box. She visited the paddock and showed keen interest.

'To the utter surprise of everyone, the favourite, ridden by Lester Piggott, who won the Queen Elizabeth II Cup, was overtaken by a rank outsider, Pa Bear, ridden by jockey Swinburne, owned by Mrs Billimoria and trained by Mac Gaulstan.

'Even after five decades, I remember Queen Elizabeth II's visit to Calcutta. Raj Bhavan, CESC Building, The Statesman House and many other buildings were lit up for the royal visit.'

Jayant Patel's photographs revealed some details of the Queen's visit (p. 202–220). Padmaja Naidu introduced her to dignitaries and the members of the consular corps in Calcutta at the airport. According to Buckingham

Palace, the British High Commissioner at the time was Paul Henry Gore-Booth. We see the crowds cheering her as the convoy drove down to Raj Bhavan where a banquet was organised on their behalf by Padmaja Naidu. Gates were erected along the route. Prince Philip was gifted a scarf by the Royal Princess of Bhutan, while the Queen, Vijaya Lakshmi Pandit, and Padmaja Naidu looked on. There is another photograph of the Queen in an evening gown and a gleaming tiara accompanied by Prince Philip at a Raj Bhavan reception. In another frame, she is with Paul Henry Gore-Booth. Next to them is Ivan Surita, a bureaucrat, whose brother was Pearson Surita, the famous cricket commentator. They were Anglo-Indians.

The Queen visited St Paul's Cathedral and Victoria Memorial Hall (p. 210). Queen Elizabeth II is the male-line great-granddaughter of Edward II, who inherited the crown from his mother, Queen Victoria, in whose memory this monument was constructed. To the latter destination, she was accompanied by Padmaja Naidu. There she was introduced to the board of trustees and she posed for a photograph with them.

She visited the National Agriculture Fair where she was greeted by Minister Ajoy Mukherjee and Tarun and Tushar Kanti Ghosh, who owned the newspapers, *Amrita Bazar Patrika* and *Jugantar*. Clay models of villages in Bengal were on display at the fair. Another destination was the Durgapur Steel Plant. The vibrant economy of what was then a fast-developing West Bengal was being showcased. Nobody had an inkling of how the dream would turn into a nightmare in 10 years' time.

As has always been her practice, Her Majesty wore elbow-length white gloves, and she always proffered her arm first before a handshake. But the

Queen was not the touch-me-not type. As the photographs show, whatever the occasion and whatever the hour, she always smiled radiantly. And she did not mind having chats with people she met. I have heard from the late Rajib Gupta that his father, Ranjit Gupta, who was chief secretary when the Queen came visiting, had gone to Durgapur to receive her. In the car, Ranjit Gupta talked about his days in Cambridge. Her Majesty talked about her children. 'It wasn't difficult,' Rajib Gupta remarked.

A high point of the Queen's tour was her programme on 18 February. On that day, she visited the Royal Calcutta Turf Club races in the Maidan (p. 218). RCTC was founded in 1847 and became the pioneer racing organisation in India and held sway over almost all the courses of the sub-continent. When King George V and Queen Mary visited Calcutta in 1912, they too enjoyed the races.

Queen Elzabeth presented the Queen's Cup trophy to Mrs Billimoria, whose steed 'Pa Bear' was the winner. Racing enthusiasts broke into tumultuous applause. As the Queen congratulated Mrs Billimoria, her husband, Ardershir, Pa Bear's trainer, Mac Galstaun, and jockey Wally Swinburn joined in the celebrations. The latter said he felt 'elated' and 'We received a great reception.'

Wally Swinburn (born 1937) was a callow young man when this happened. I was able to establish contact with him through my friend and colleague, Pravesh Gupta, and Sharan Kumar, who writes on horse racing. I made a lightning call at his home and got his email ID from his wife. I sent him an email. He took some time as he was on holiday. But once he was back he mailed his succinct replies. He said he was 19 when he arrived in Calcutta in 1956. At the time, the big horse owners were the Maharajas of Burdwan, Cooch Behar, Paralakamedi, and quite a few in Bombay like the Maharaja of Baroda and Gwalior, Dr R.M. Ramaswamy and many Indian and European business people.

I have heard from a relative of Ardershir Billimoria that he loved horses but sadly never won when he owned Pa Bear. So he gifted it to his wife Naja. He was all over the moon when it won, and the day after he got up early in the morning, bought a garland and garlanded the horse while still in his pajamas.

Uneducated he may have been, but he knew how to deal with people, and enjoyed one-to-one relationships with all the worthies. So when J.R.D. Tata could not get an appointment with Dr B.C. Roy he had to turn to Billimoria. He would stand in the lobby of Great Eastern Hotel and arrange for reductions for guests. He would not let them go to other hotels. Later he became managing director of the hotel and stayed there most of the time. When he became paralysed, he sold his shares and shifted to Jamshedpur, where he lived in a single room.

Jayant Patel's album of photographs of Calcutta ends here. If cities had memories, perhaps they would have resembled photographs, for both are inextricably linked. Jayant Patel's photographs of Calcutta belong to the category of 'memory photographs' similar to the ones of the dear departed we cherish so much. This Calcutta may still be alive in many memories, but time swallowed that fabled city, and it can never return.

—Soumitra Das

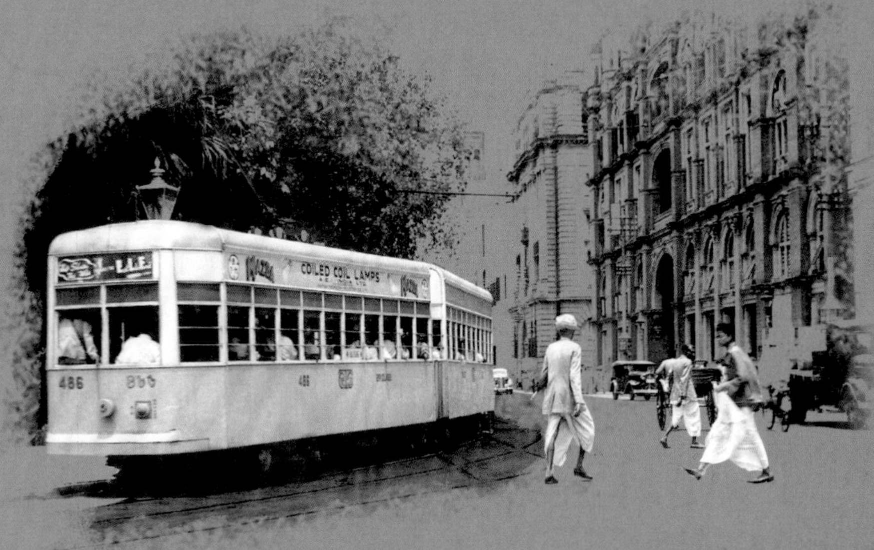
COILED COIL LAMPS
486

Places

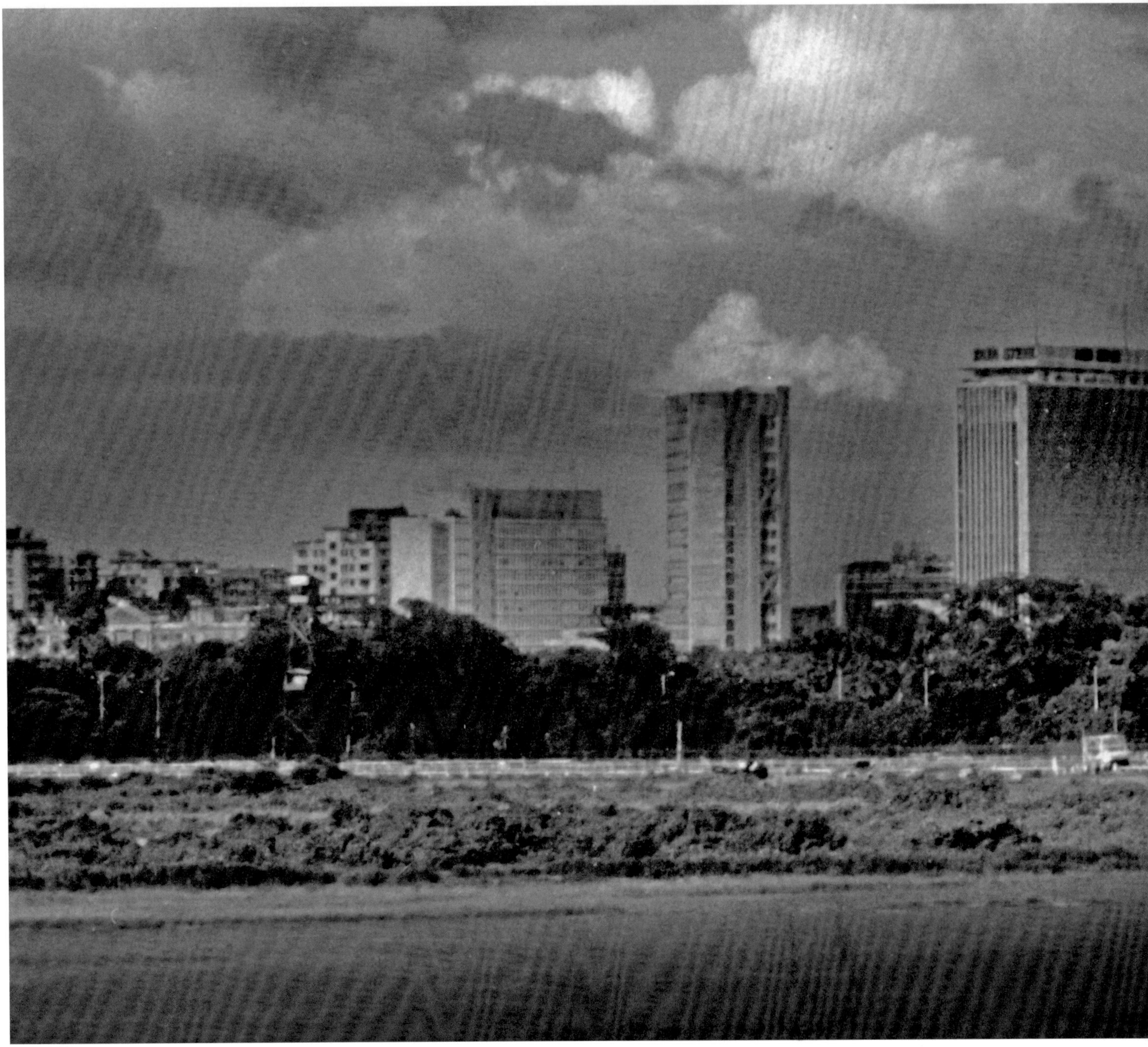

c. 1970

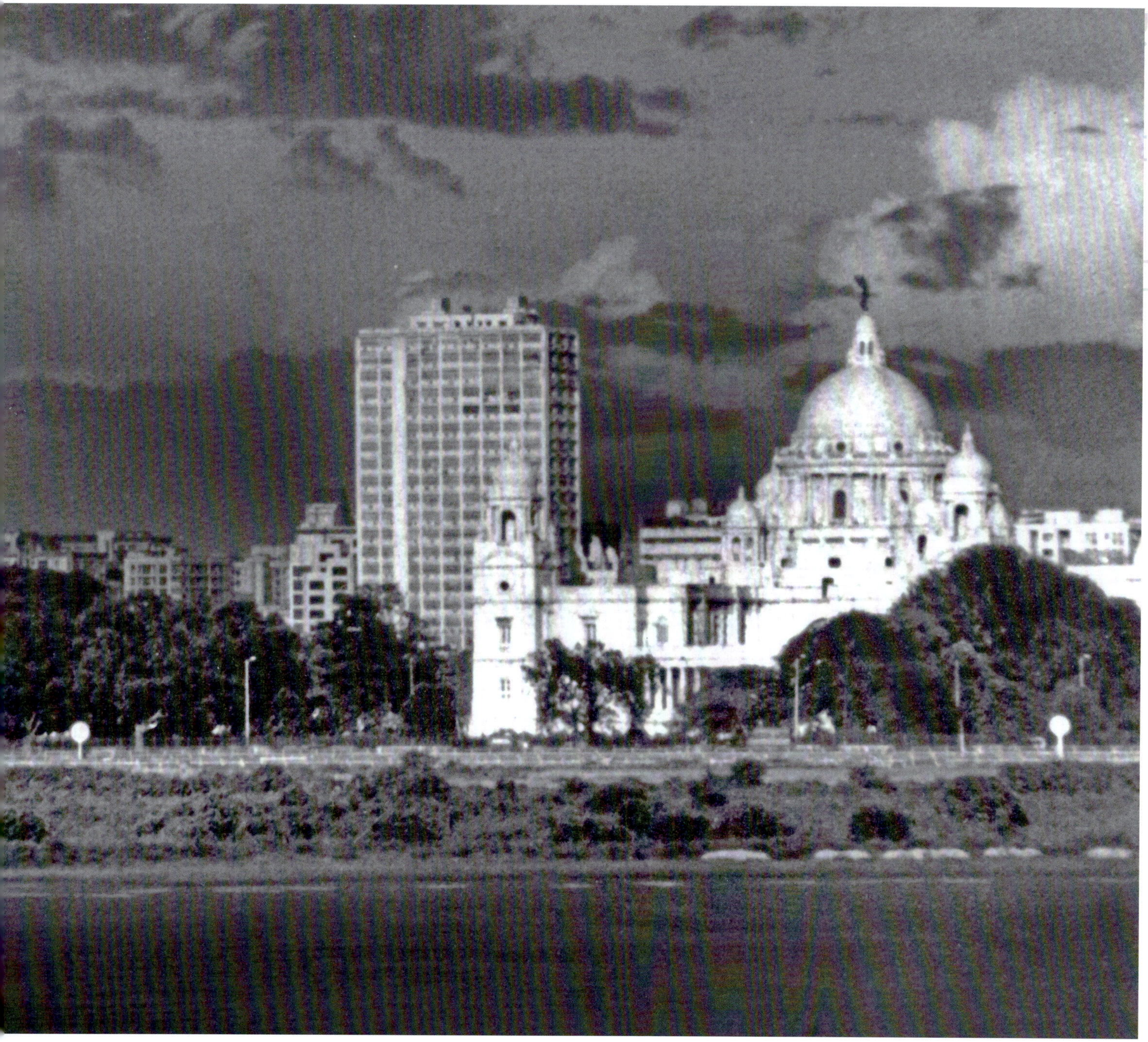

Late evening view of Victoria Memorial along with the skyline from the Maidan

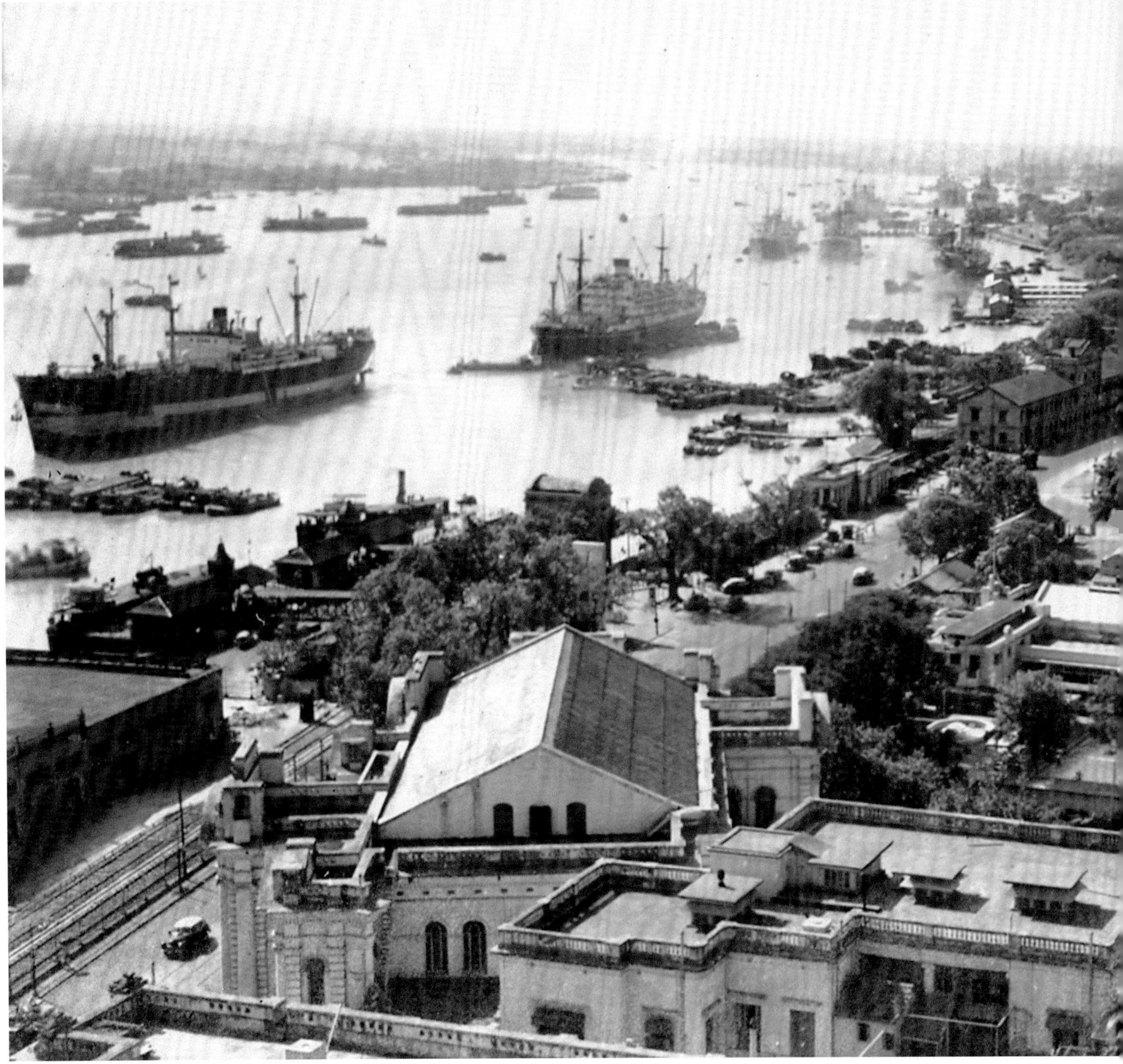

c. 1945

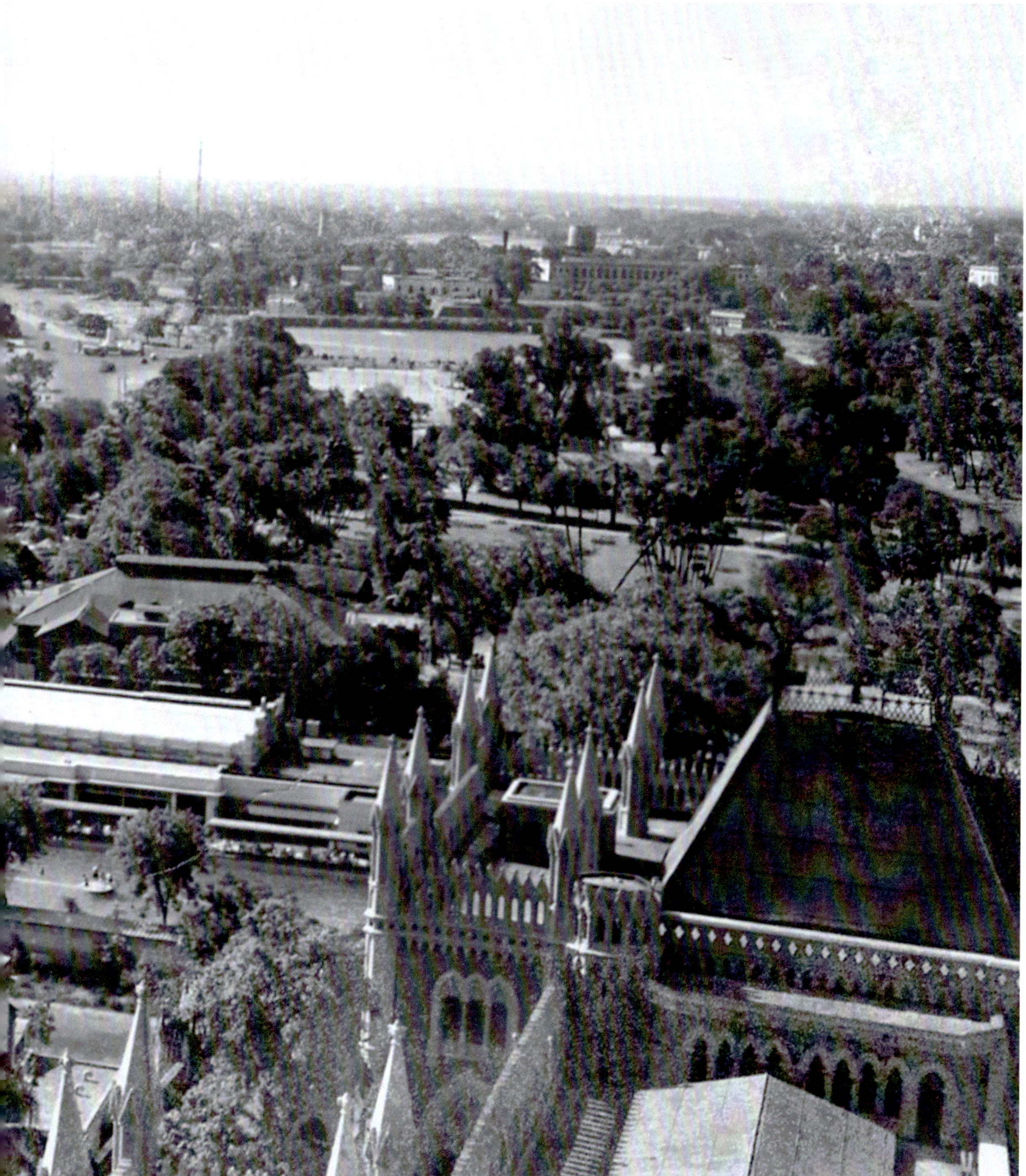

River Hooghly, an arm or distributary of the Ganges, providing access to Calcutta from the Bay of Bengal

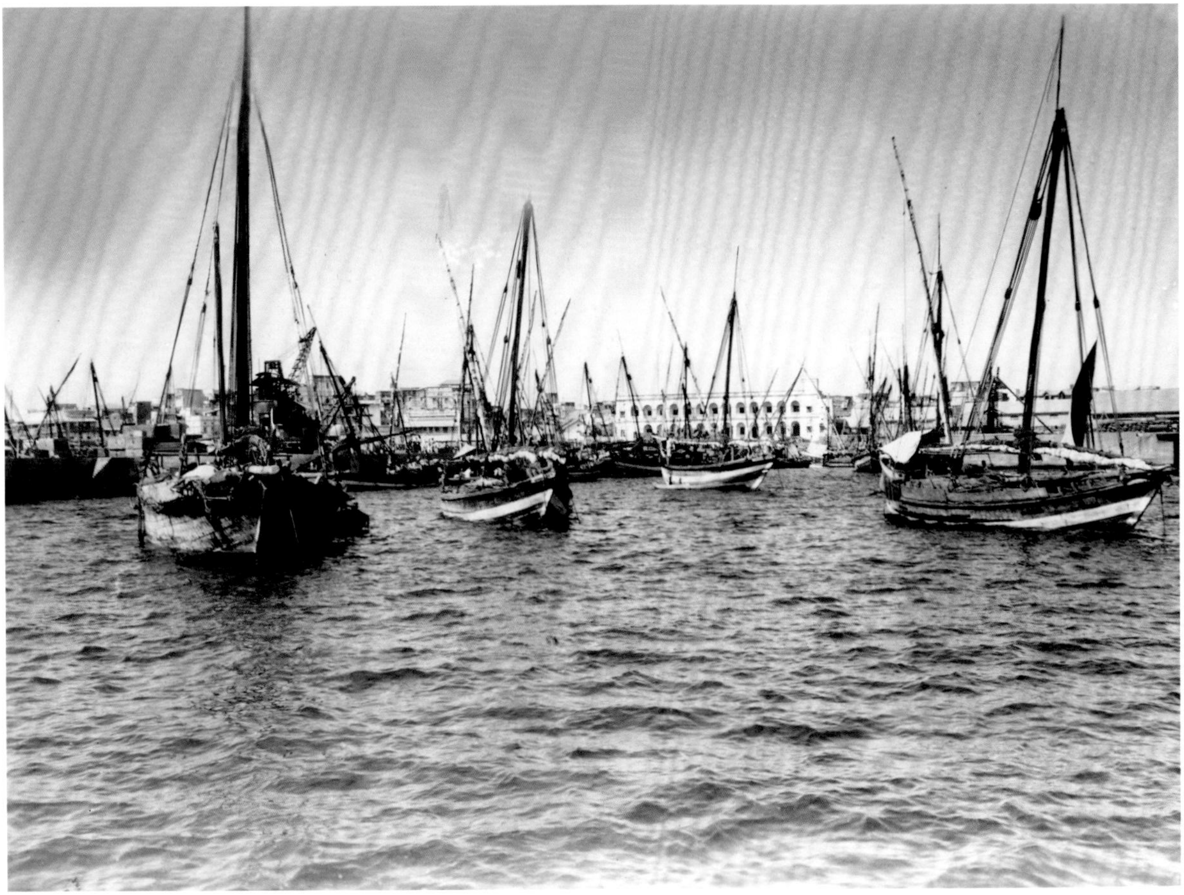

Hooghly River

c. 1944

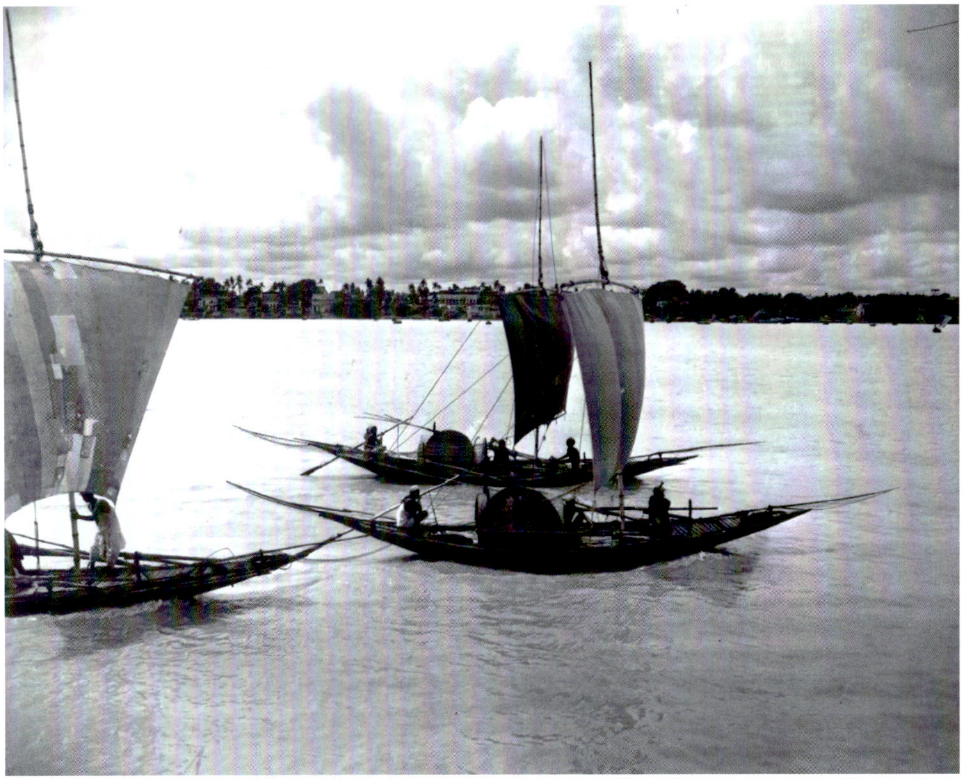

Dinghies or small boats, used for transportation and fishing on the Hooghly

c. 1945

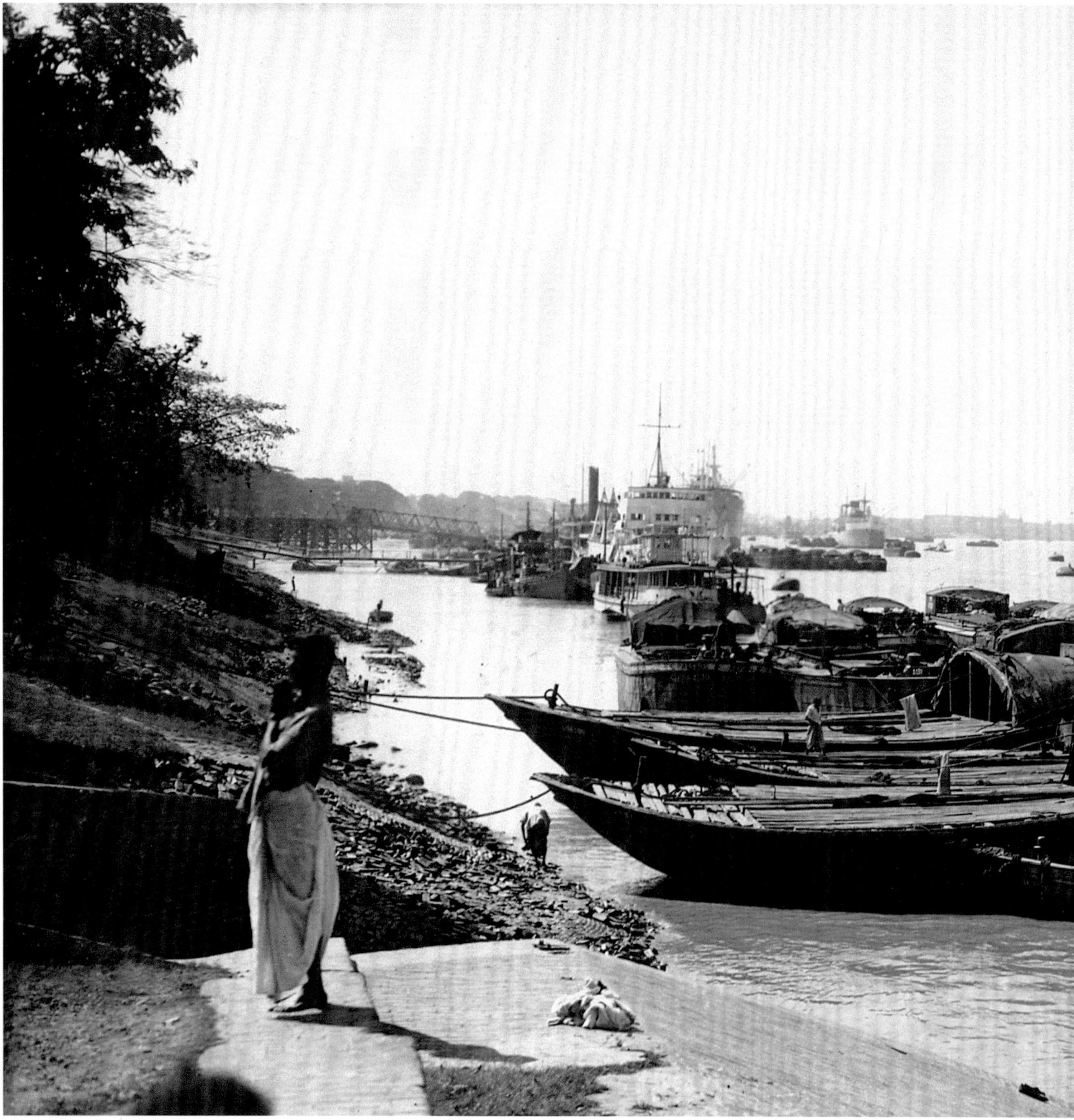

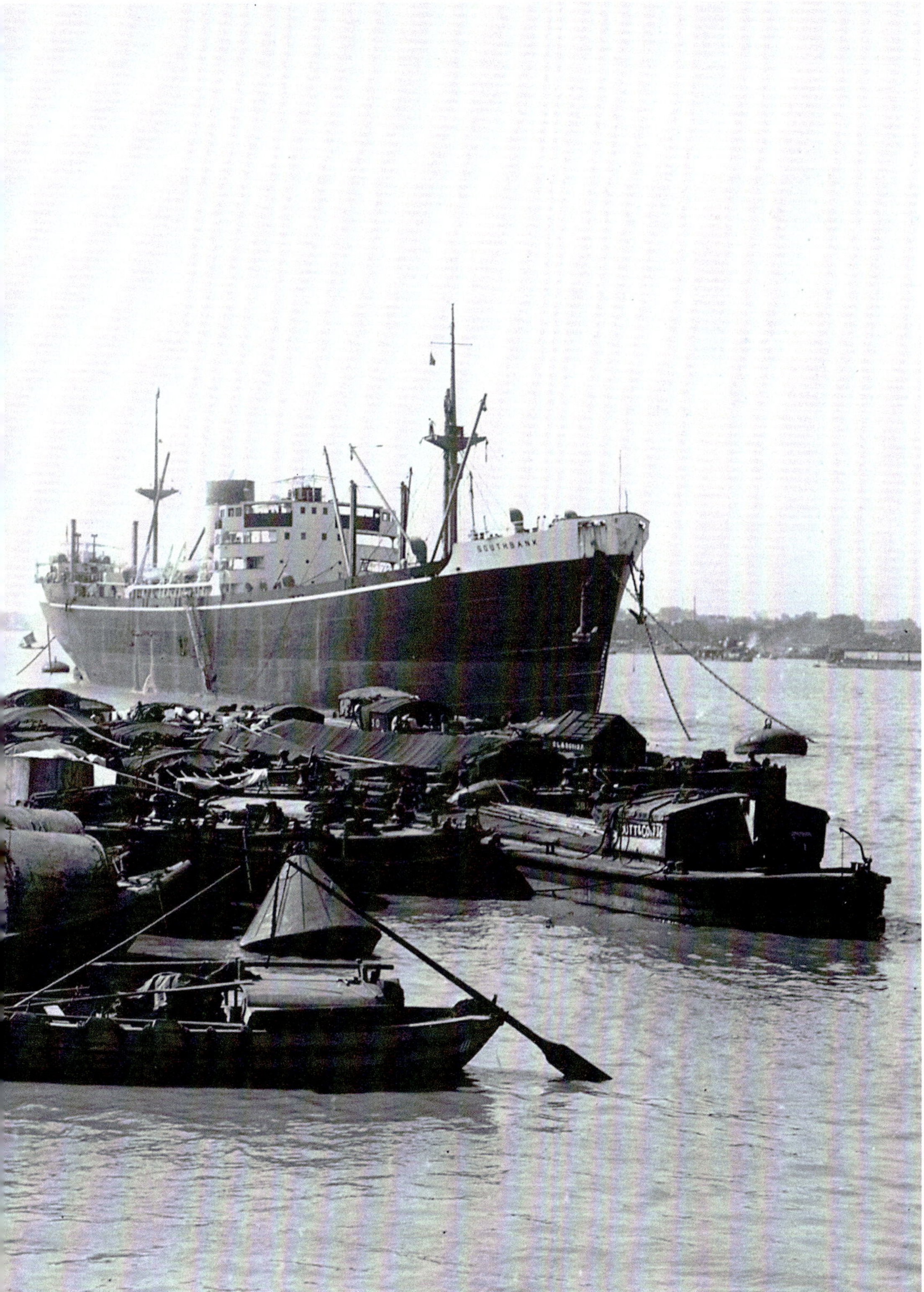

View of Hooghly from Outram Ghat

c. 1943

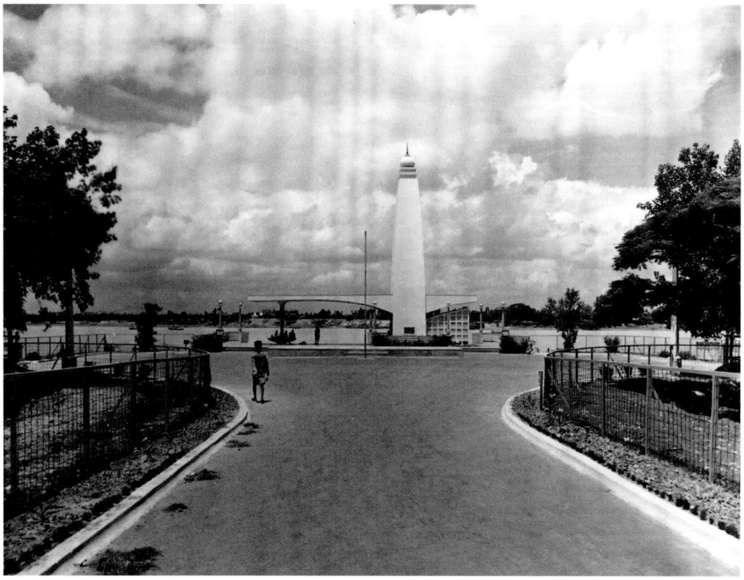

Gandhi Ghat built in memory of Mahatma Gandhi in Barrackpore. It was designed by architect Habib Rahman

RIGHT Gandhi Ghat as seen on a cloudy day with tourists

c. 1956

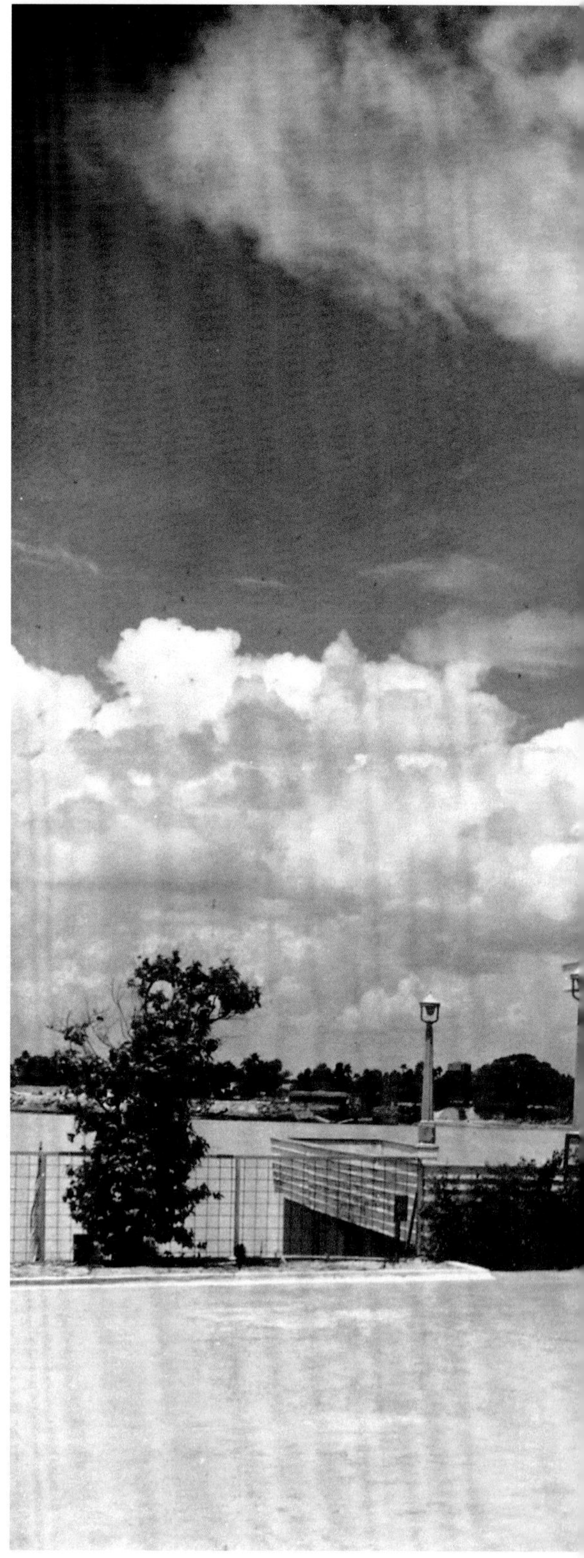

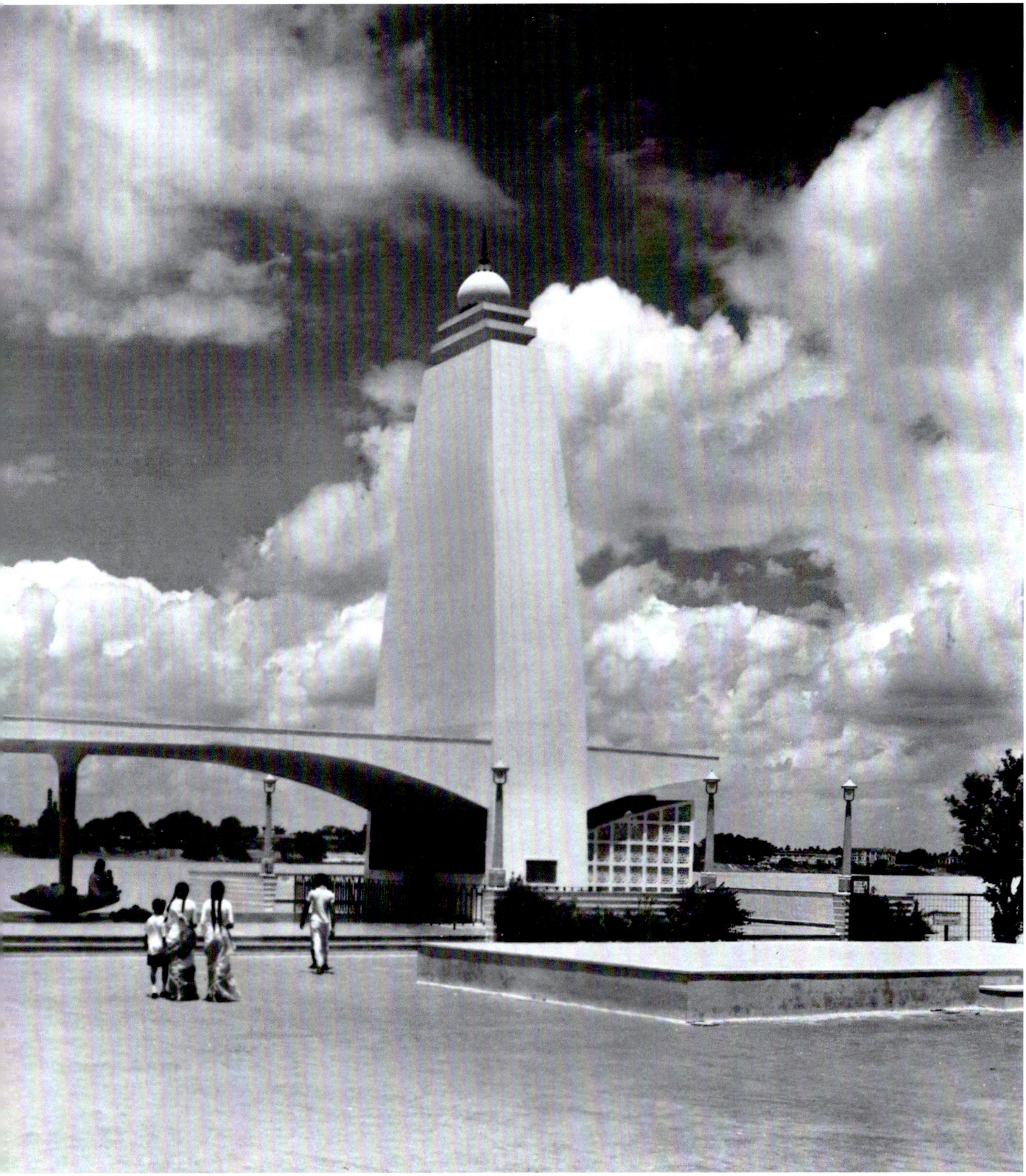

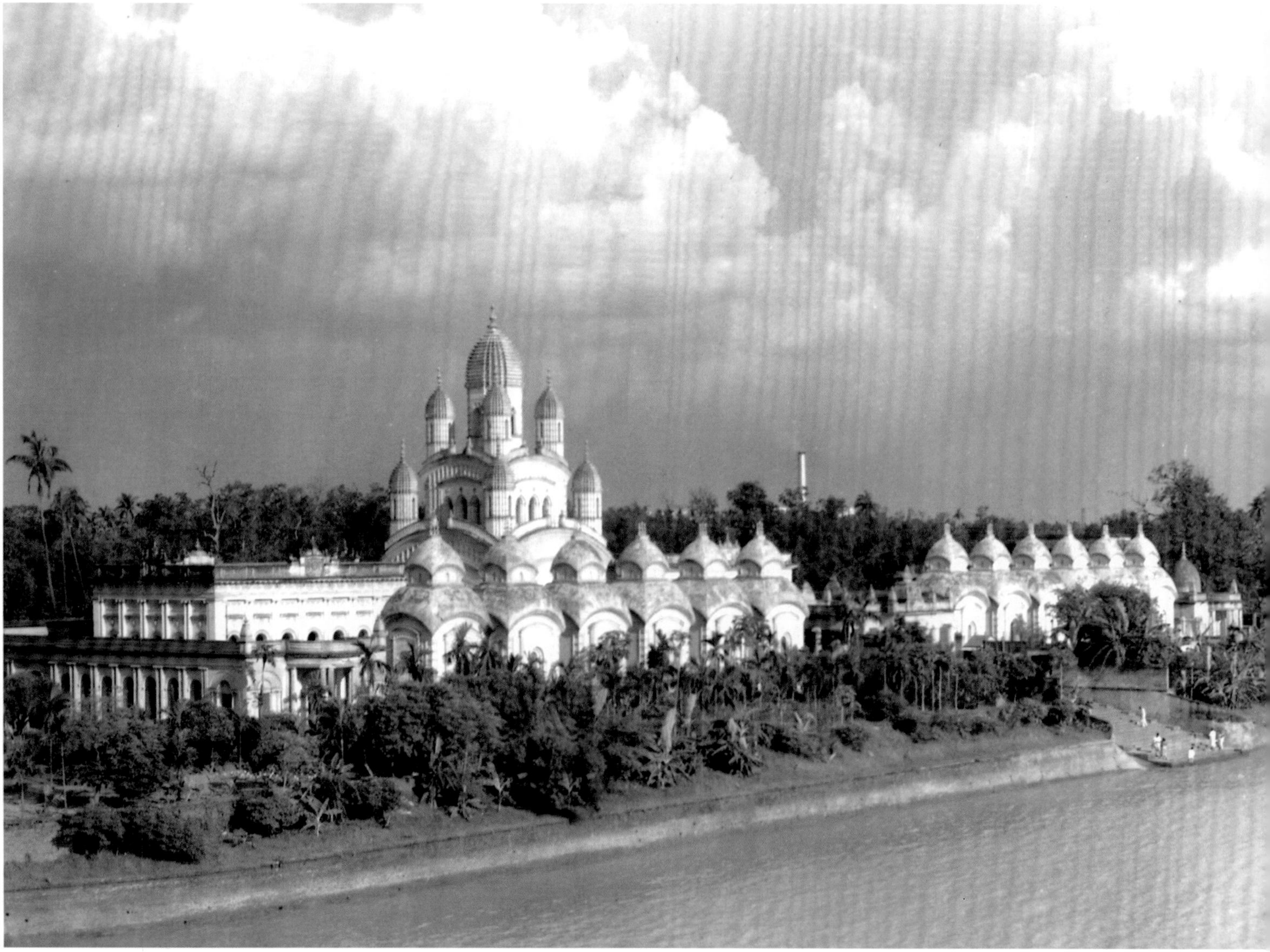

Dakshineshwar temple of Bhabatarrini or Kali. Built in 1855 on the banks of River Hooghly by Rani Rashmoni, who was ordained in her dream by Goddess Kali to build this temple and install her Idol. Ramakrishna Paramhansa served as the priest here

c. 1952

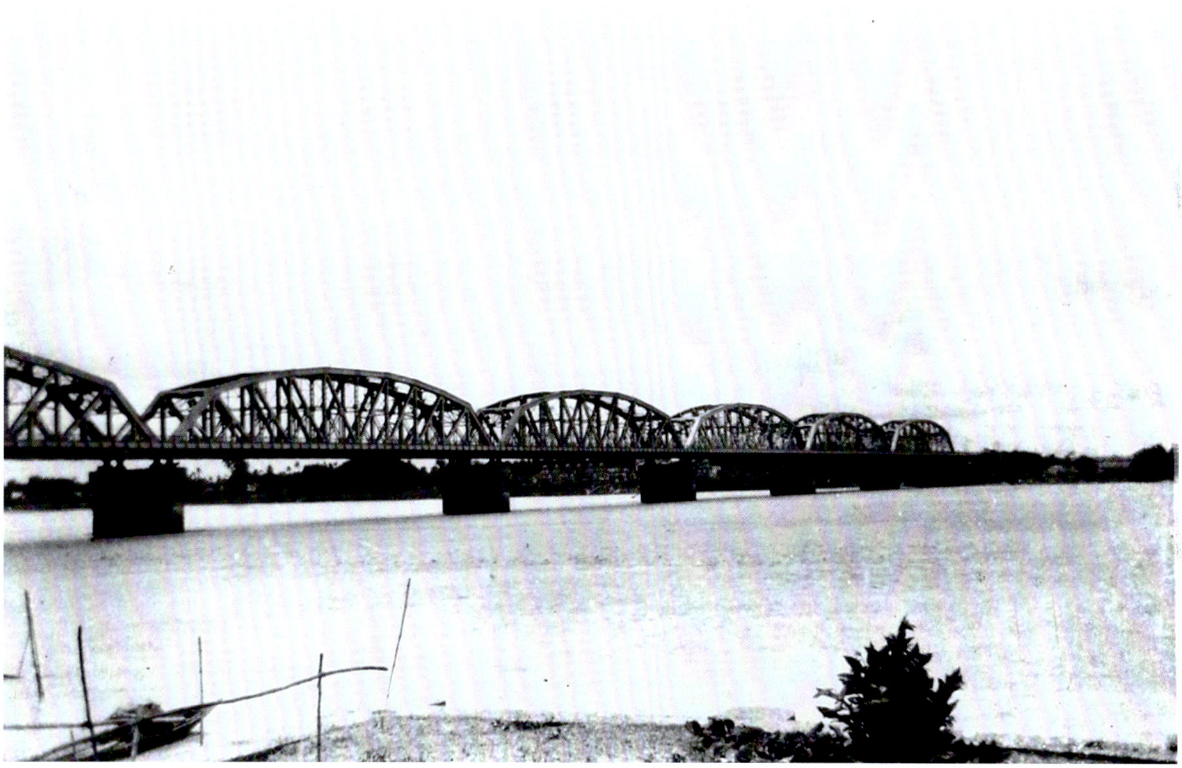

Bally Bridge was named Willingdon Bridge, when it opened in 1931, after the then Governor-General of India. Today it is known as Vivekananda Setu

c. 1945

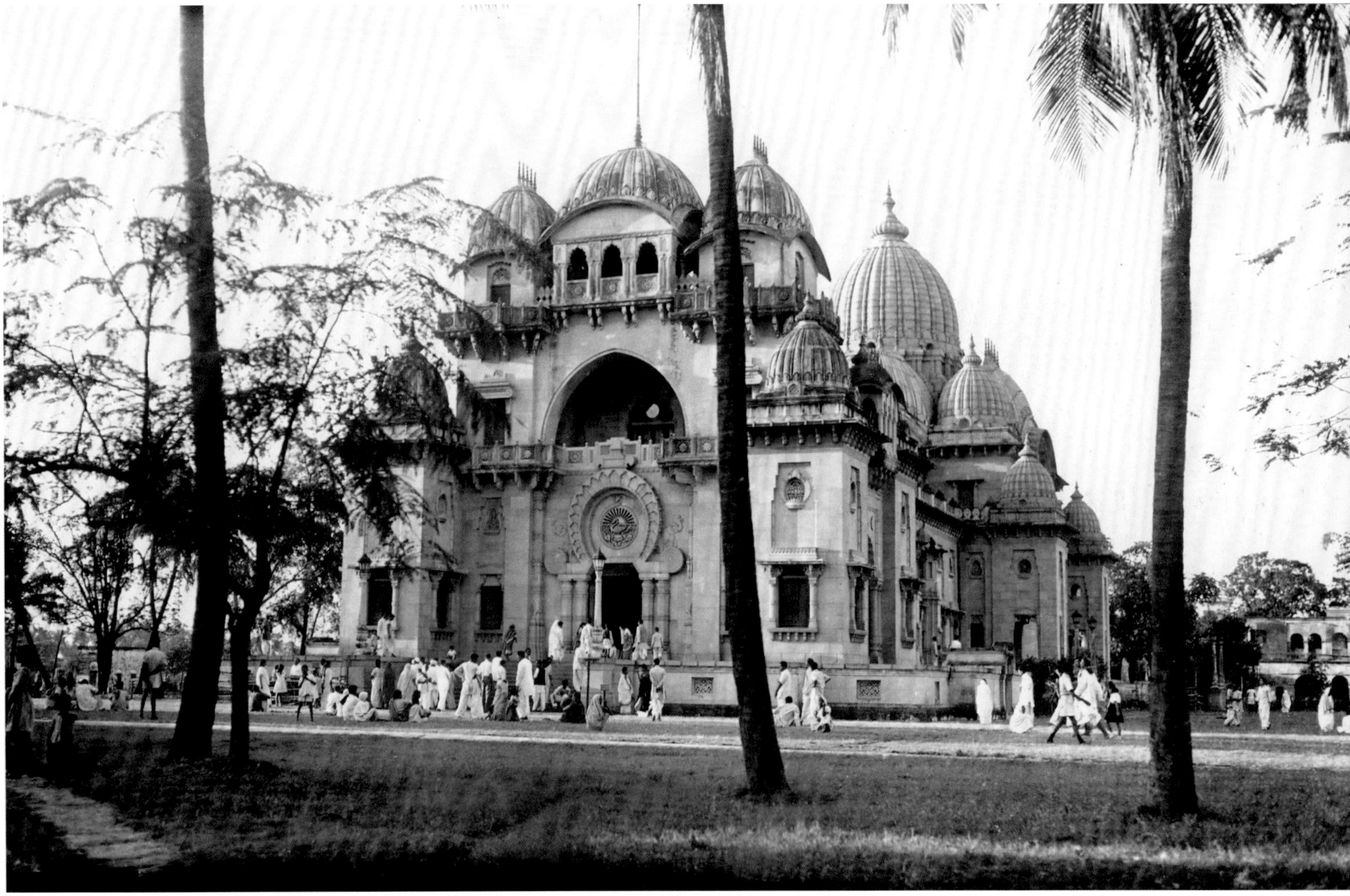

Ramkrishna's temple at Belur Math on the western banks of the Hooghly. It includes temples dedicated to Sarada Devi and Swami Vivekananda

c. 1954

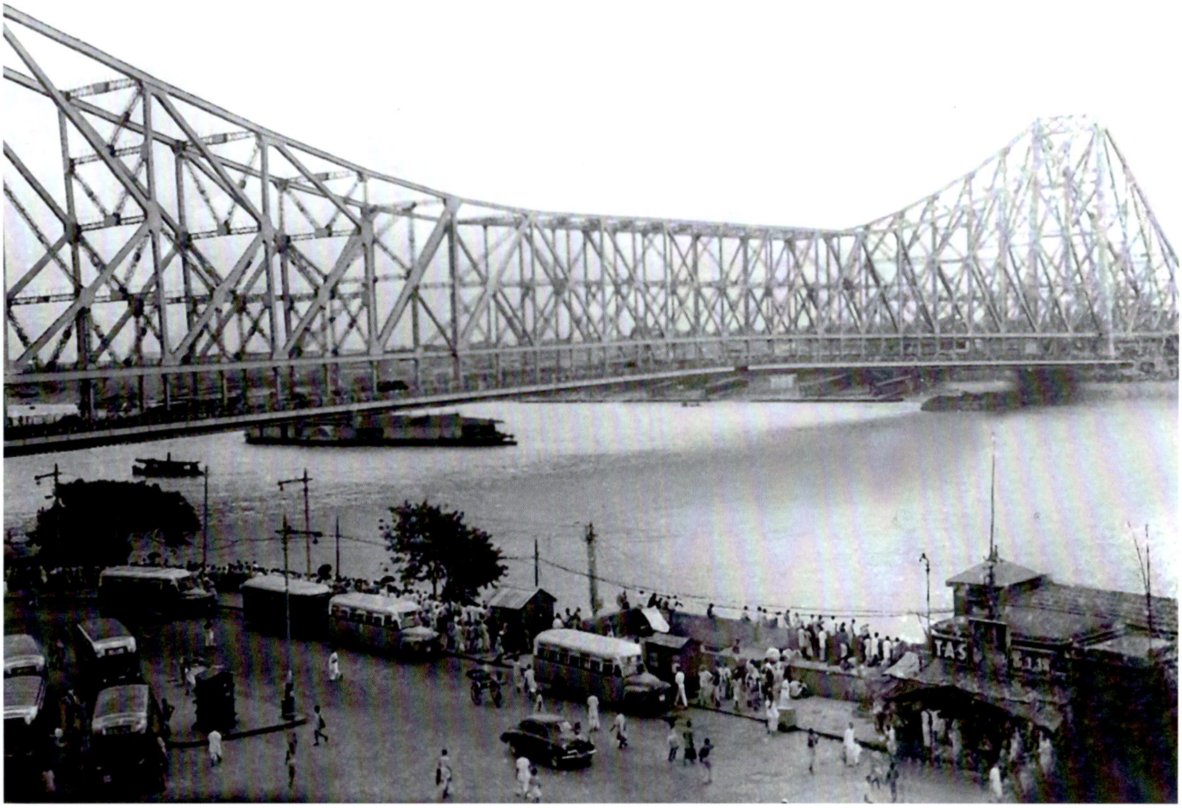

Howrah Bridge as seen from the Howrah side. There were no encroachments along the bank then

c. 1950

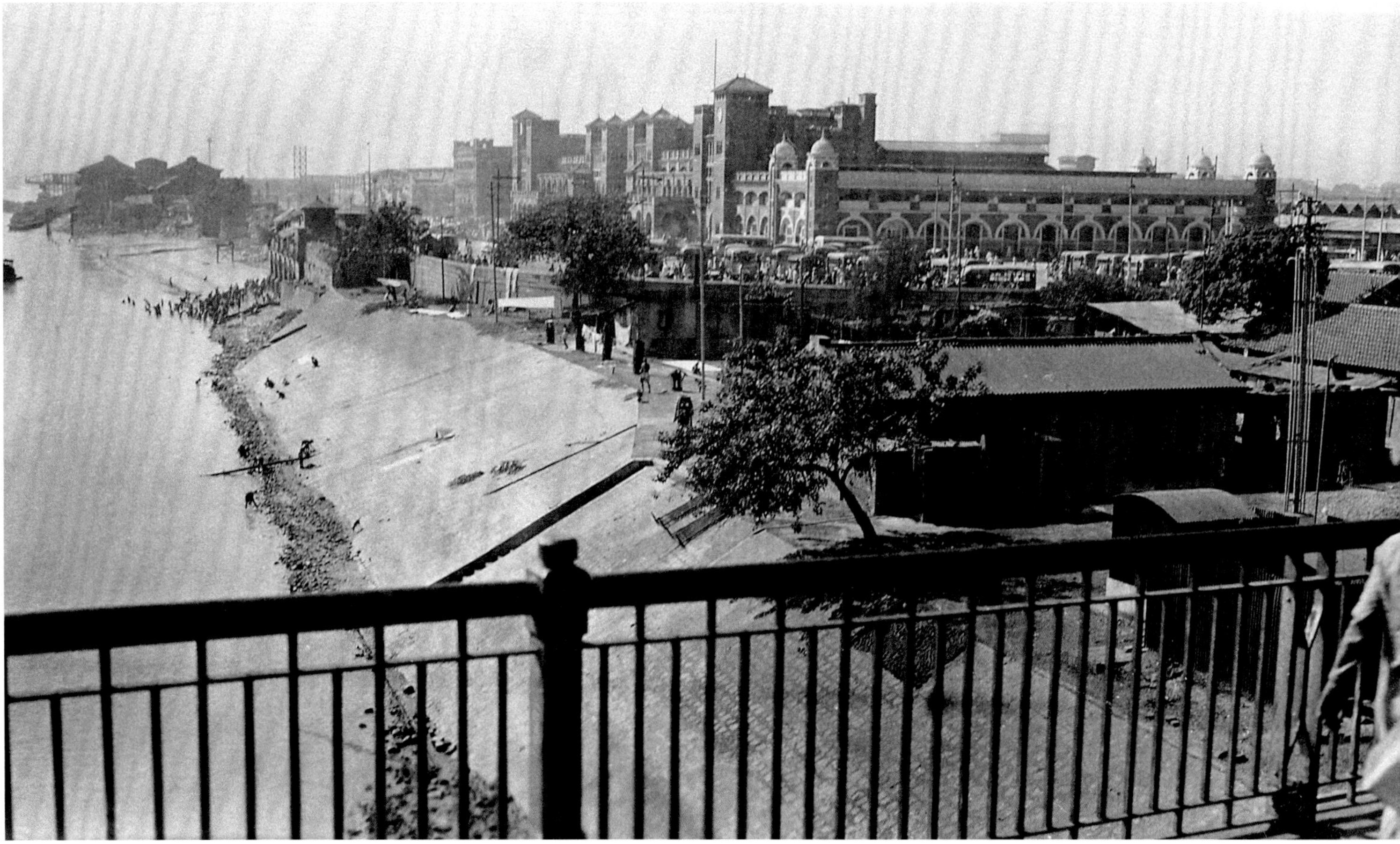

View of Howrah Station, taken from Howrah Bridge

c. 1945

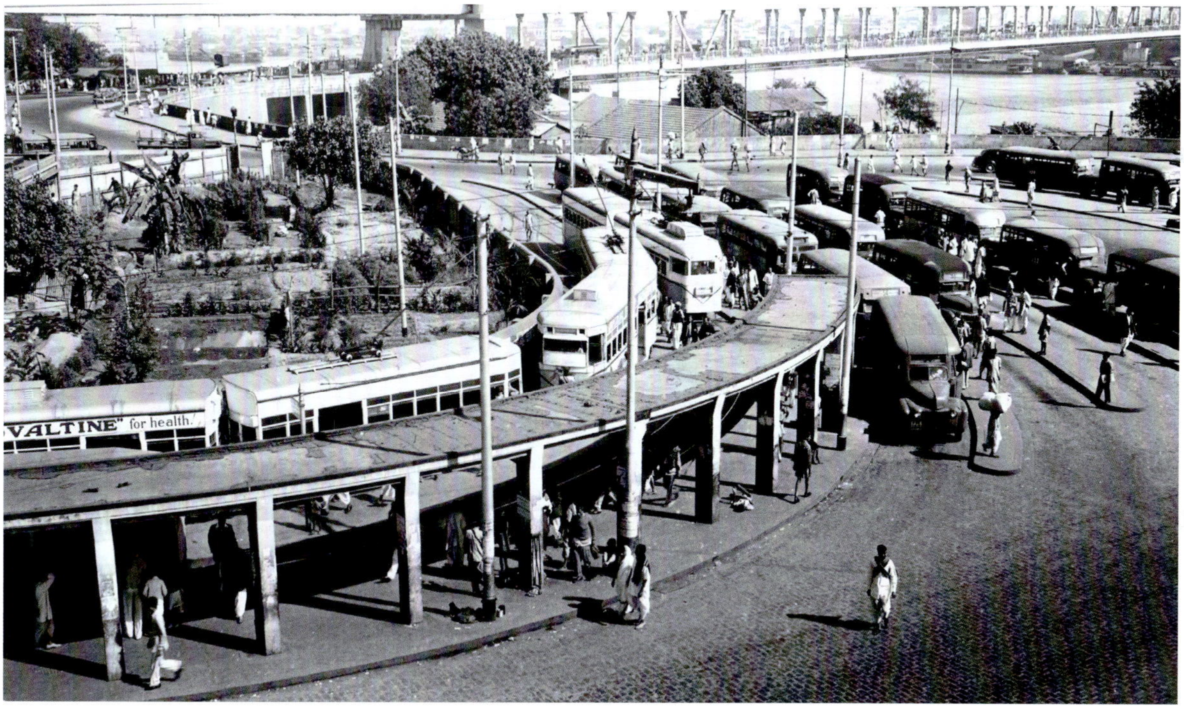

The bus and tram terminus facing Howrah Station. Now the trams are all gone. Bus bays have been built in their place

c. 1950

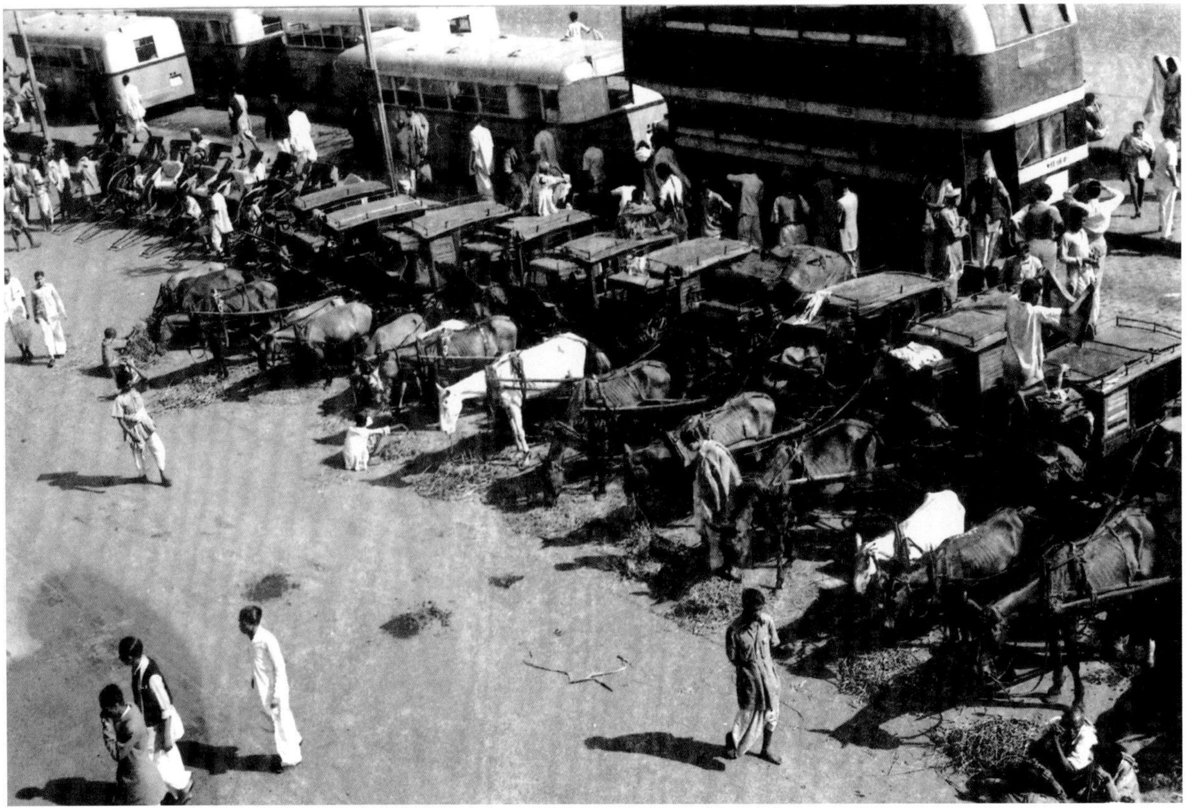

Hackney carriages outside Howrah Station. These were in use till mid-20th century. Behind them stands a double-decker bus, which first started plying in 1926. They were phased out in the late eighties and they disappeared from the streets of Calcutta thereafter

c. 1948

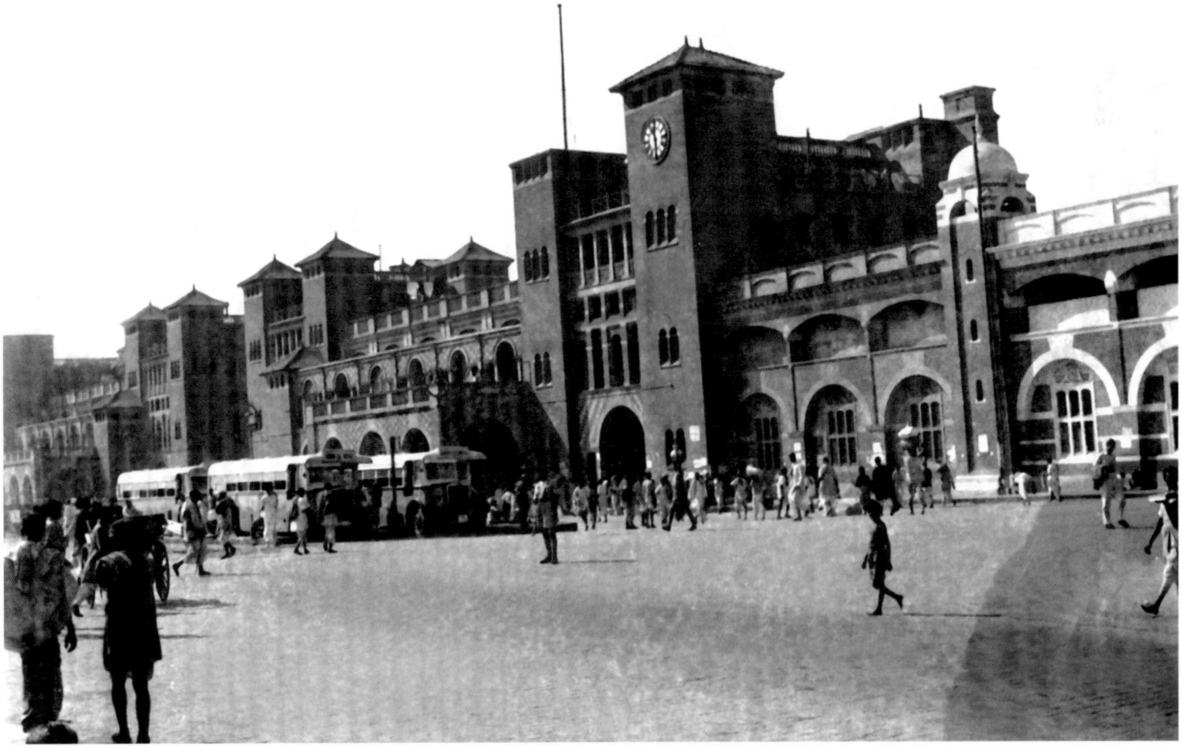

Entrance to Howrah Station with buses waiting for passengers. Howrah Station is the largest and oldest railway station in India

c. 1950

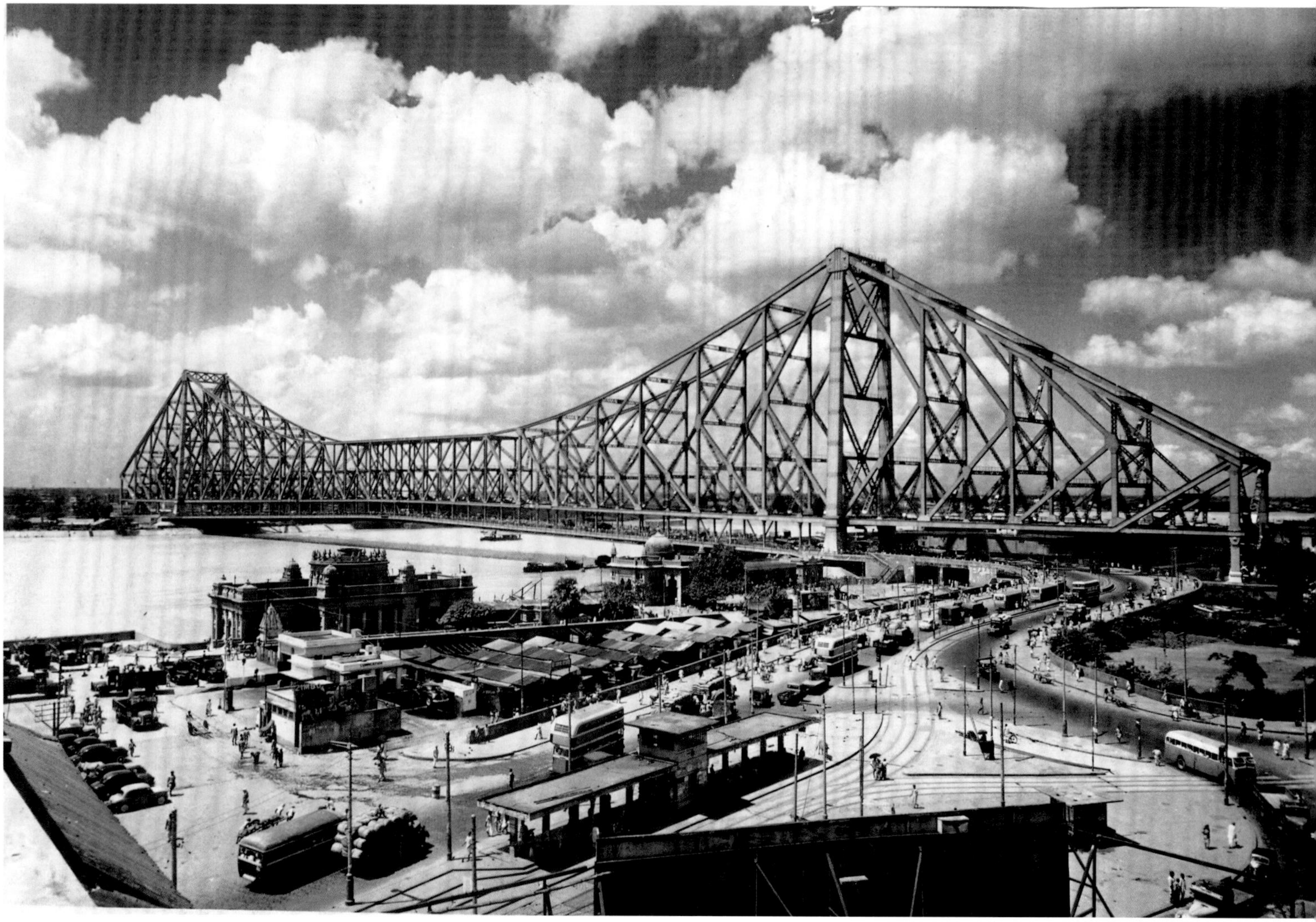

Howrah Bridge as seen from Strand Road

c. 1948

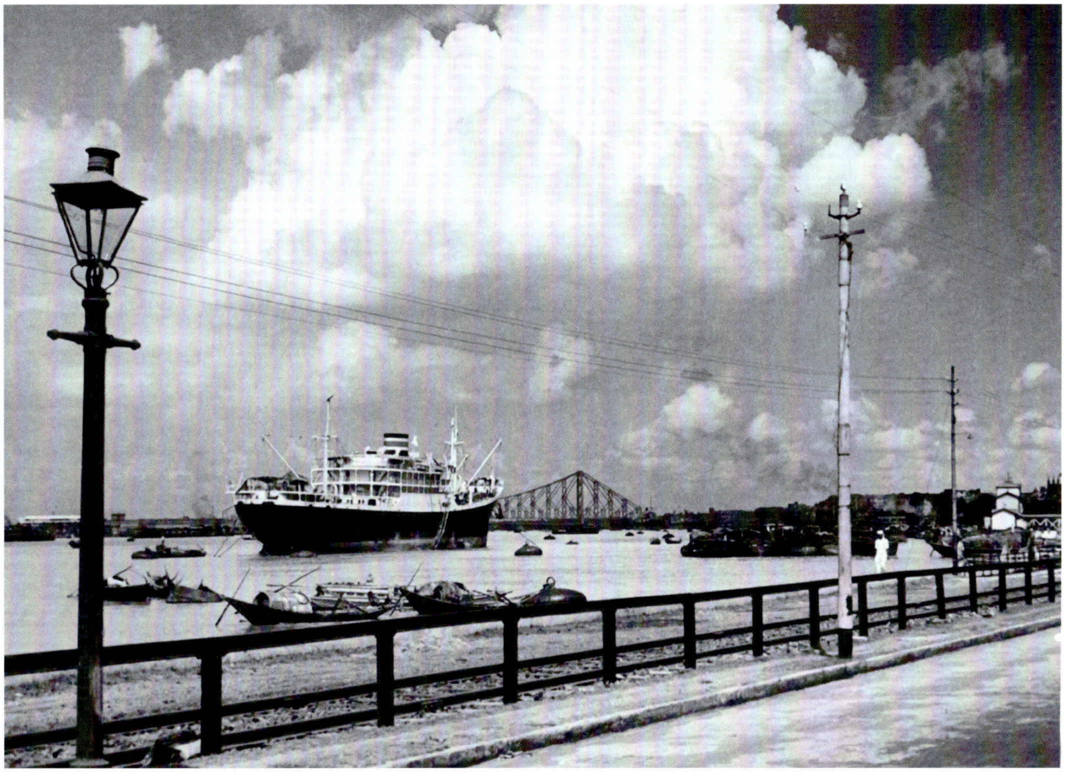

Ship anchored in the Hooghly, along Strand Road

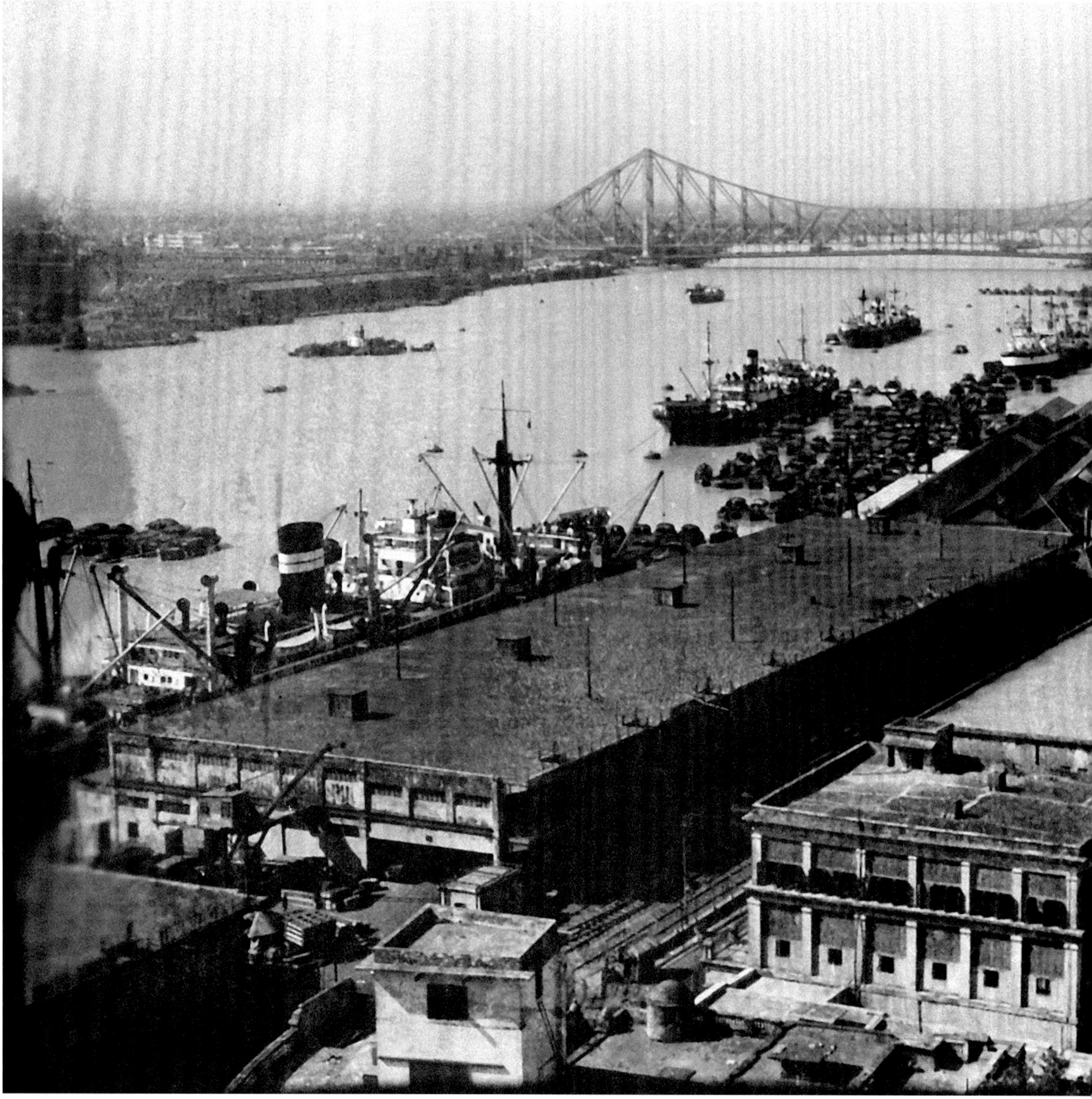

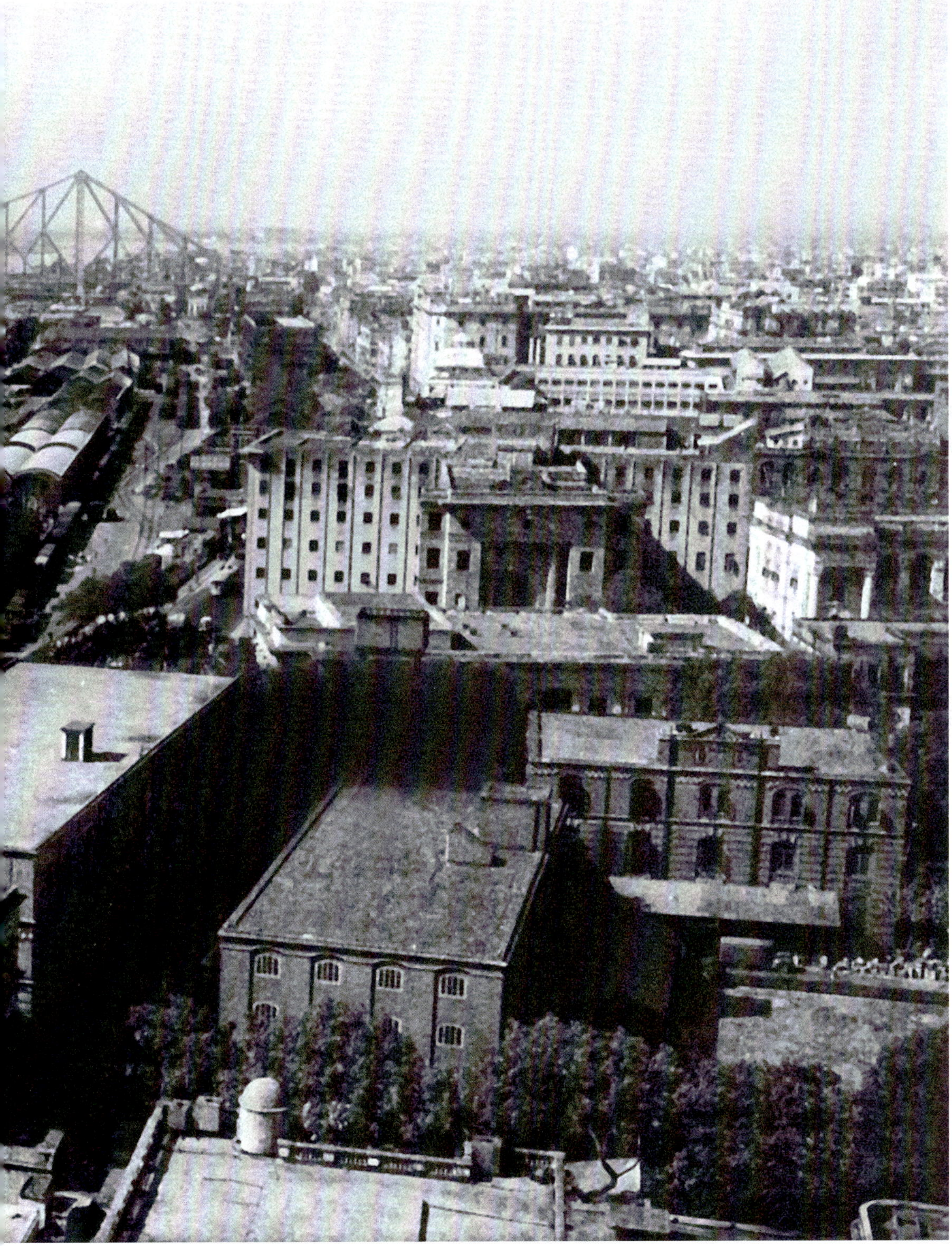

Howrah Bridge,
commissioned in 1943,
as seen from Strand Road

c. 1948

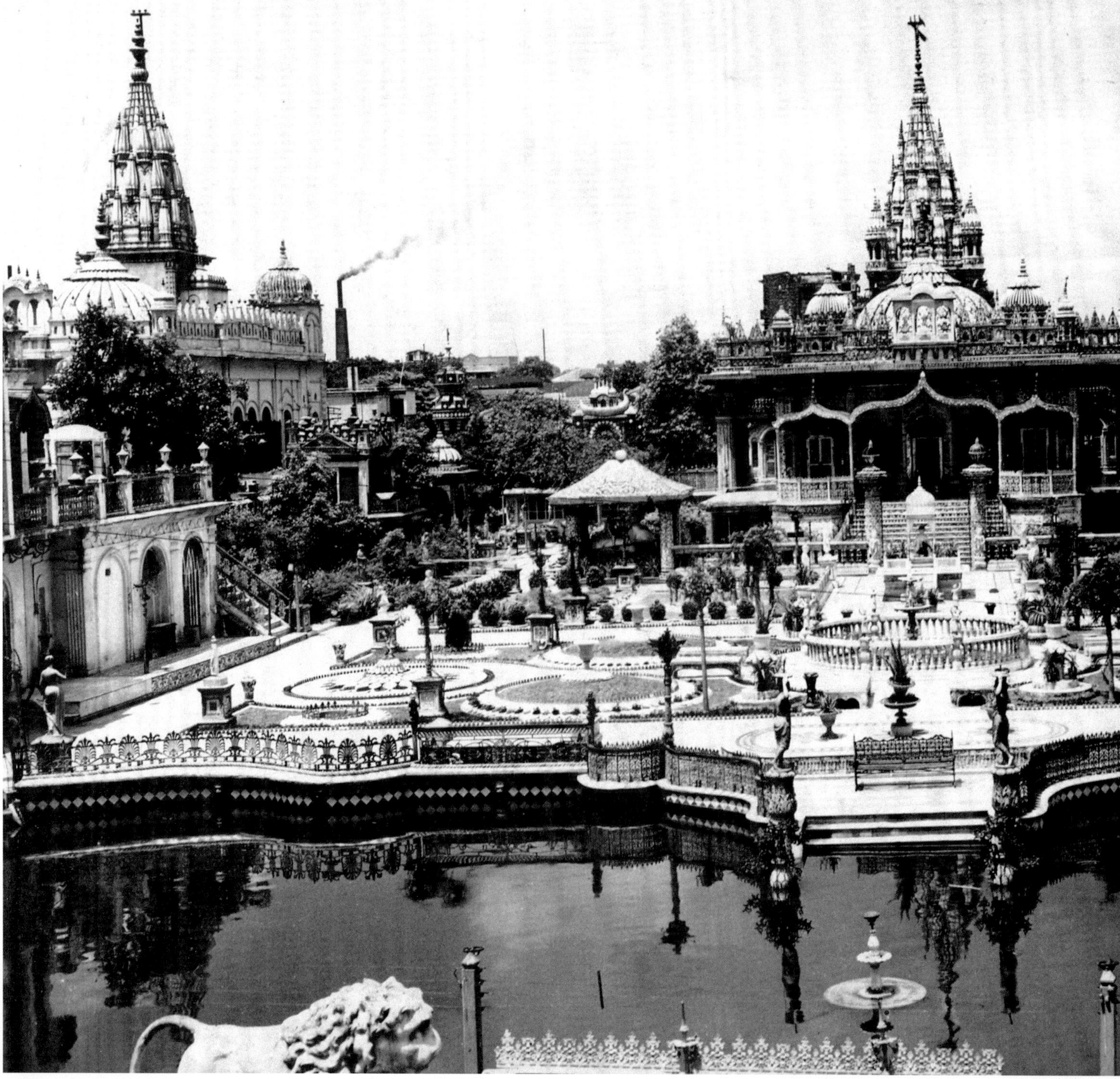

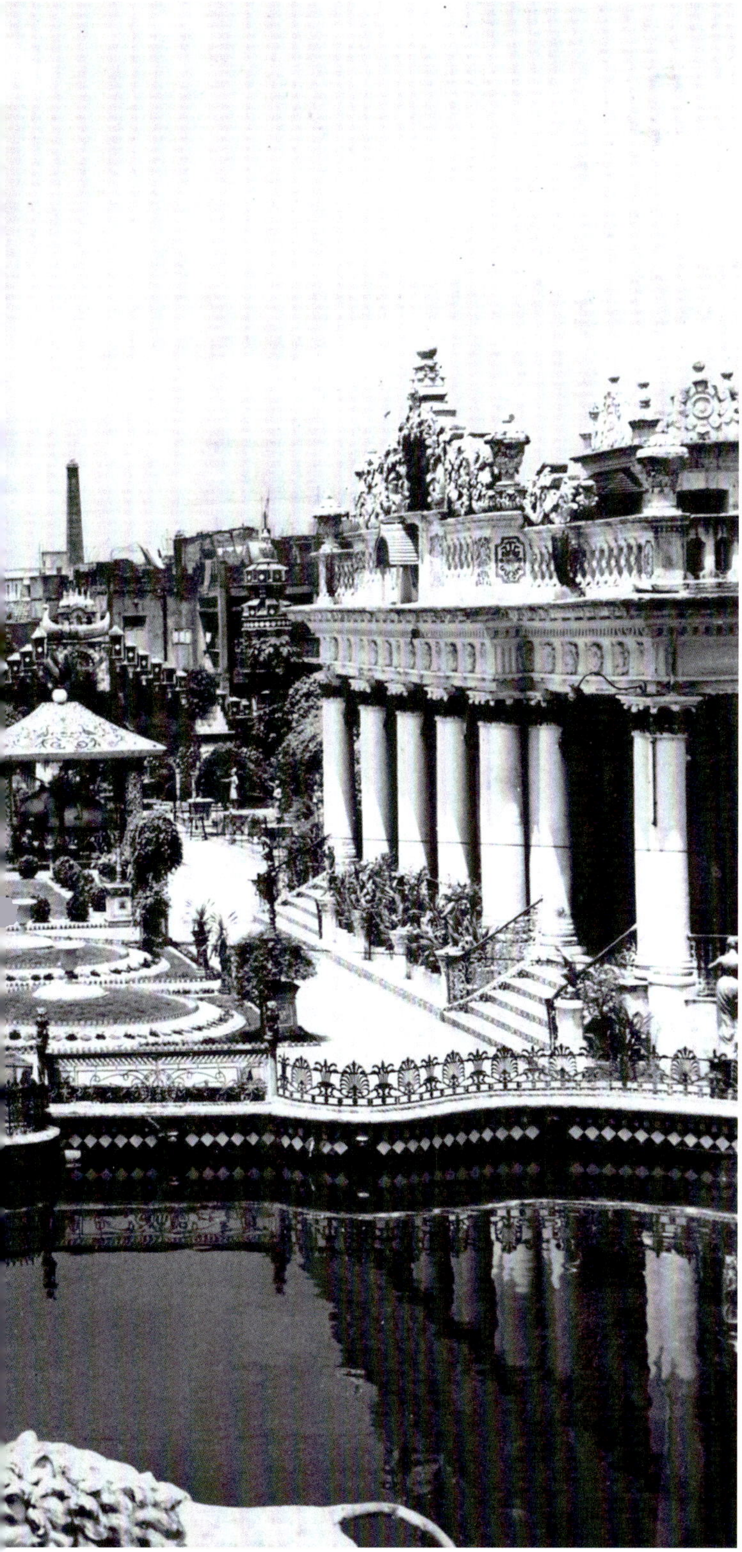

Maniktala Jain Temple, also known as Paraswanath Temple, with the Idol of Shitalnathji installed in 1867 AD, by Rai Badridas

c. 1950

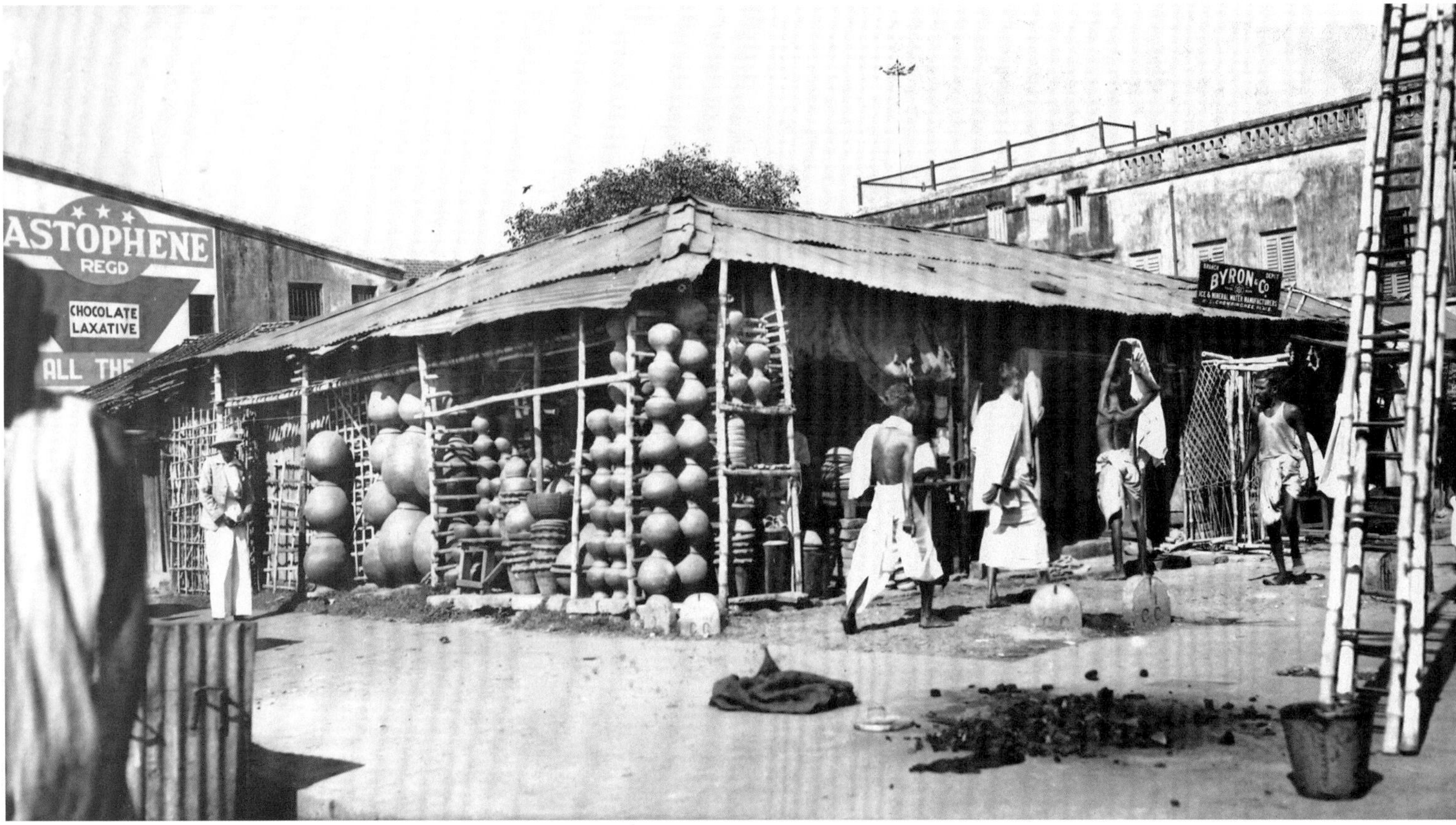

Kumortuli, a traditional potters' quarter, where pots and pitchers made with silt from the Hooghly are made. It is famous for its clay models of Hindu gods and goddesses

c. 1948

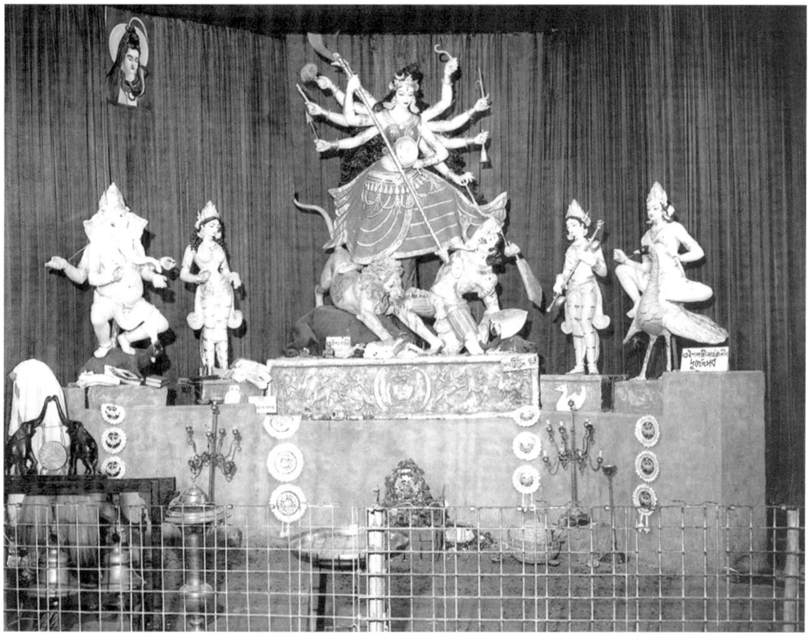

Durga Puja, showing idols of Ganesh, Lakshmi, Durga, Sarswati, and Kartik, in a pandal. Durga puja is the biggest festival of Bengal

c. 1960

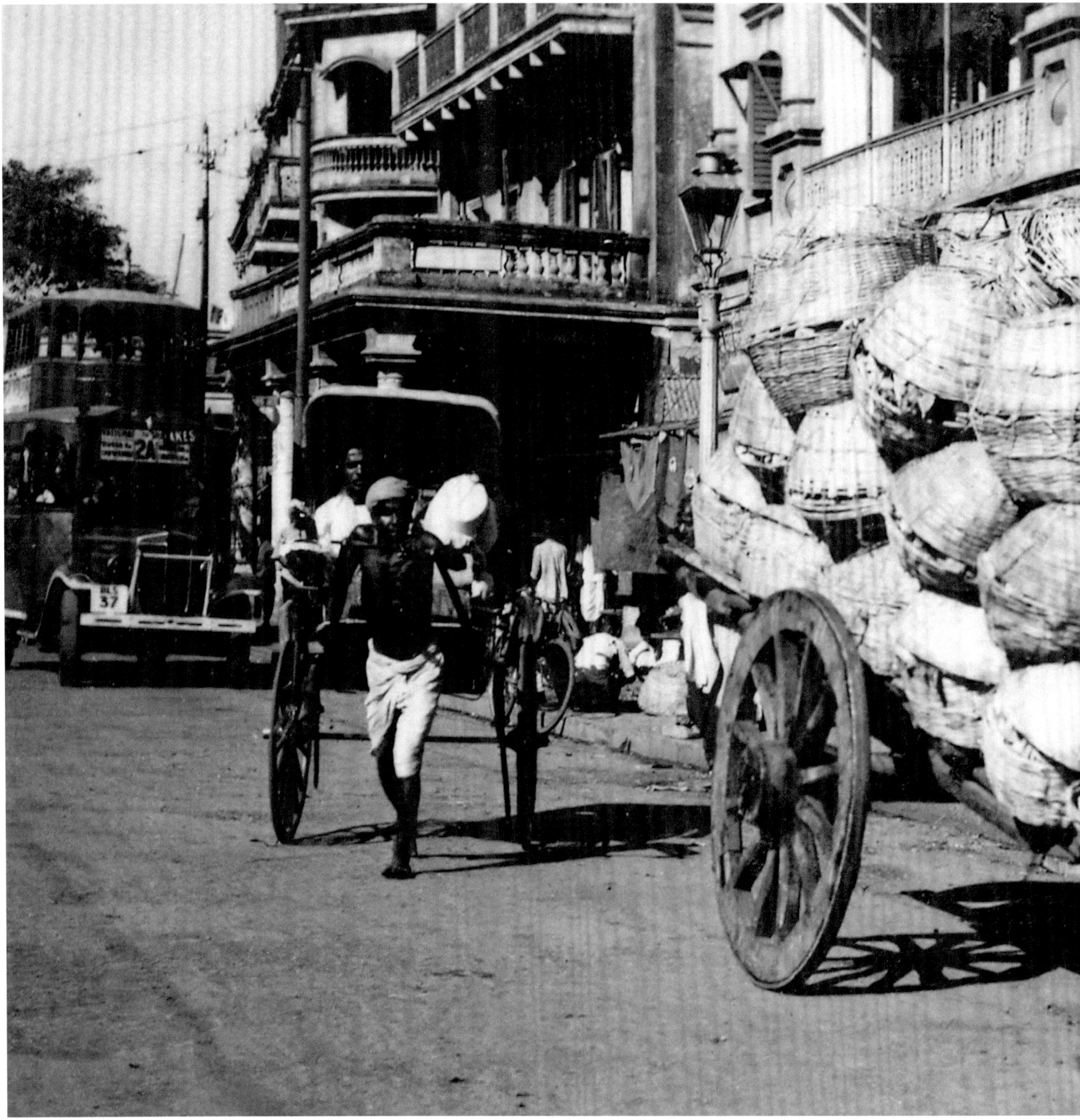
2A
37

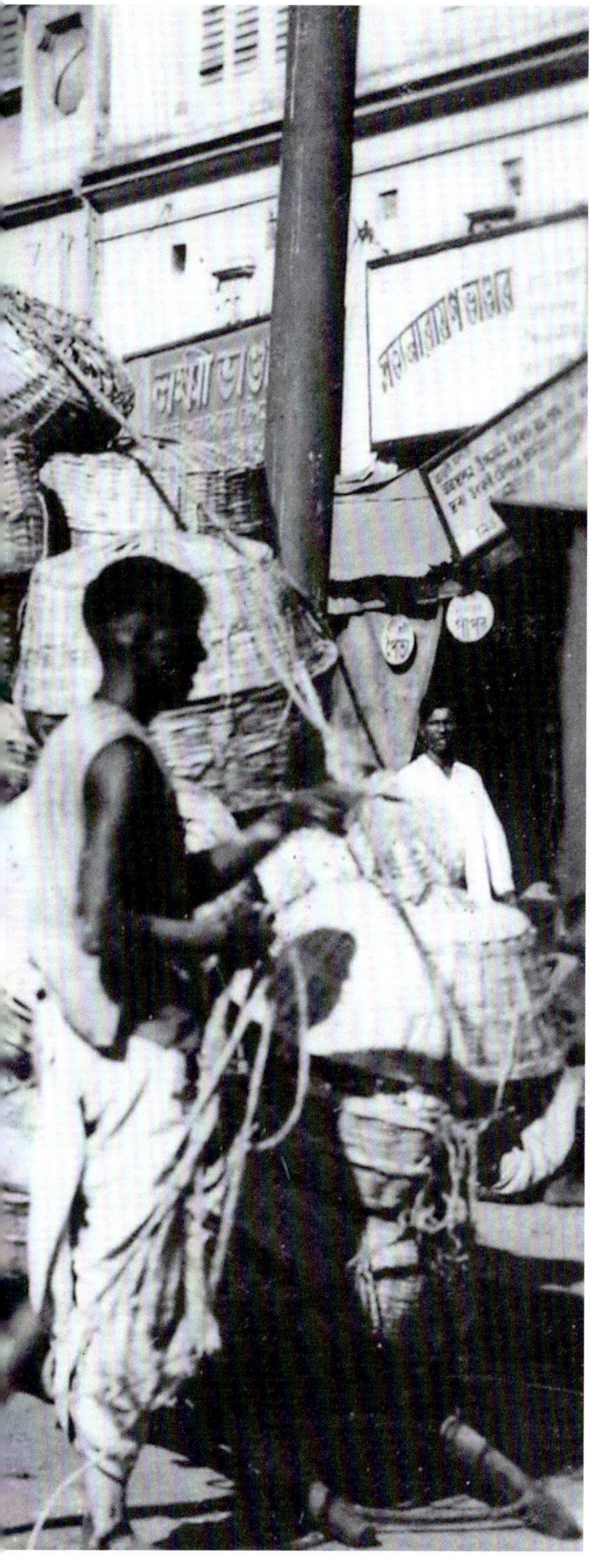

Posta Bazar, once a trading hub dominated by Bengalis, now a wholesale market

c. 1945

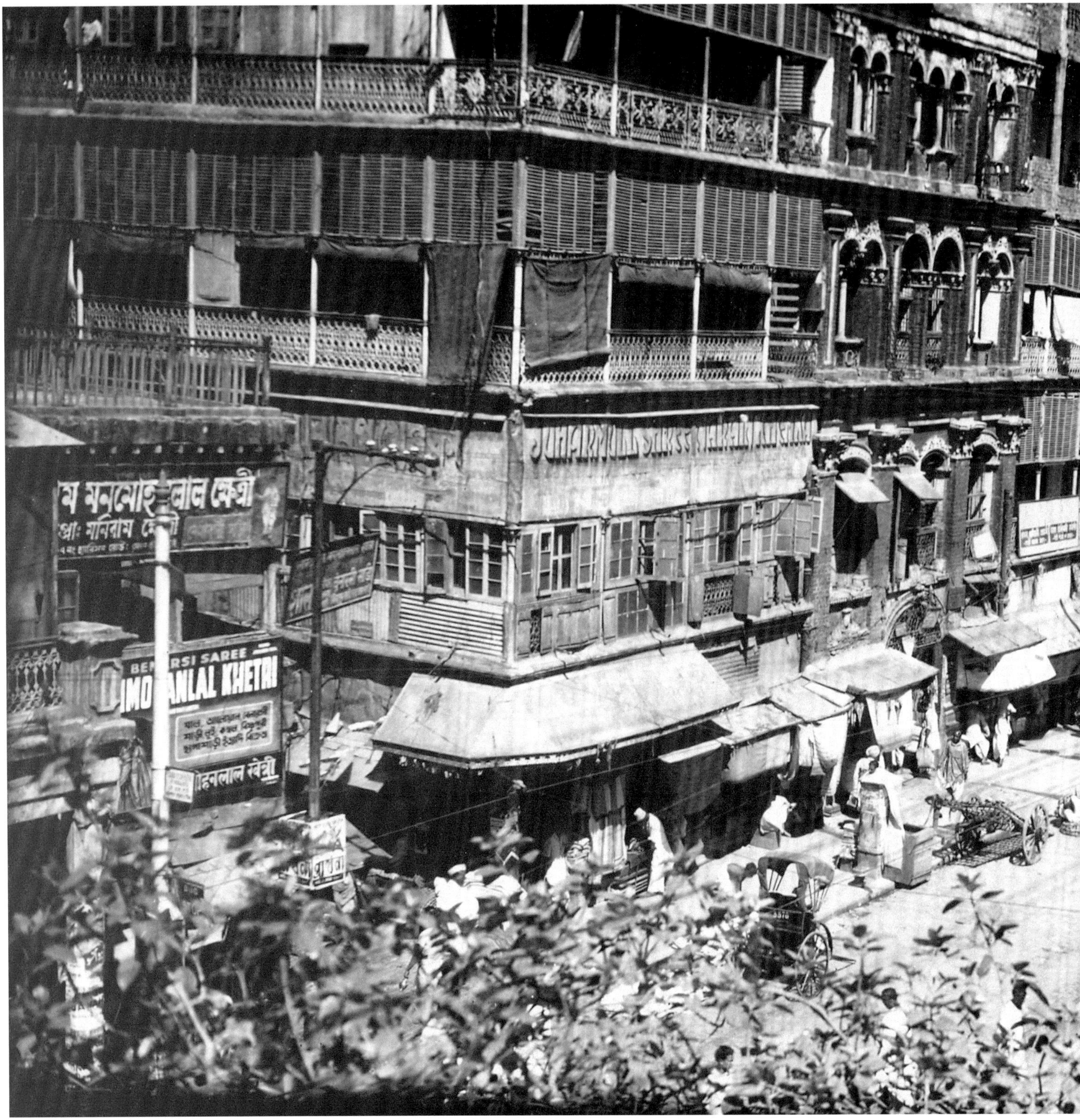
RSI SAREE
ANLAL KHETRI

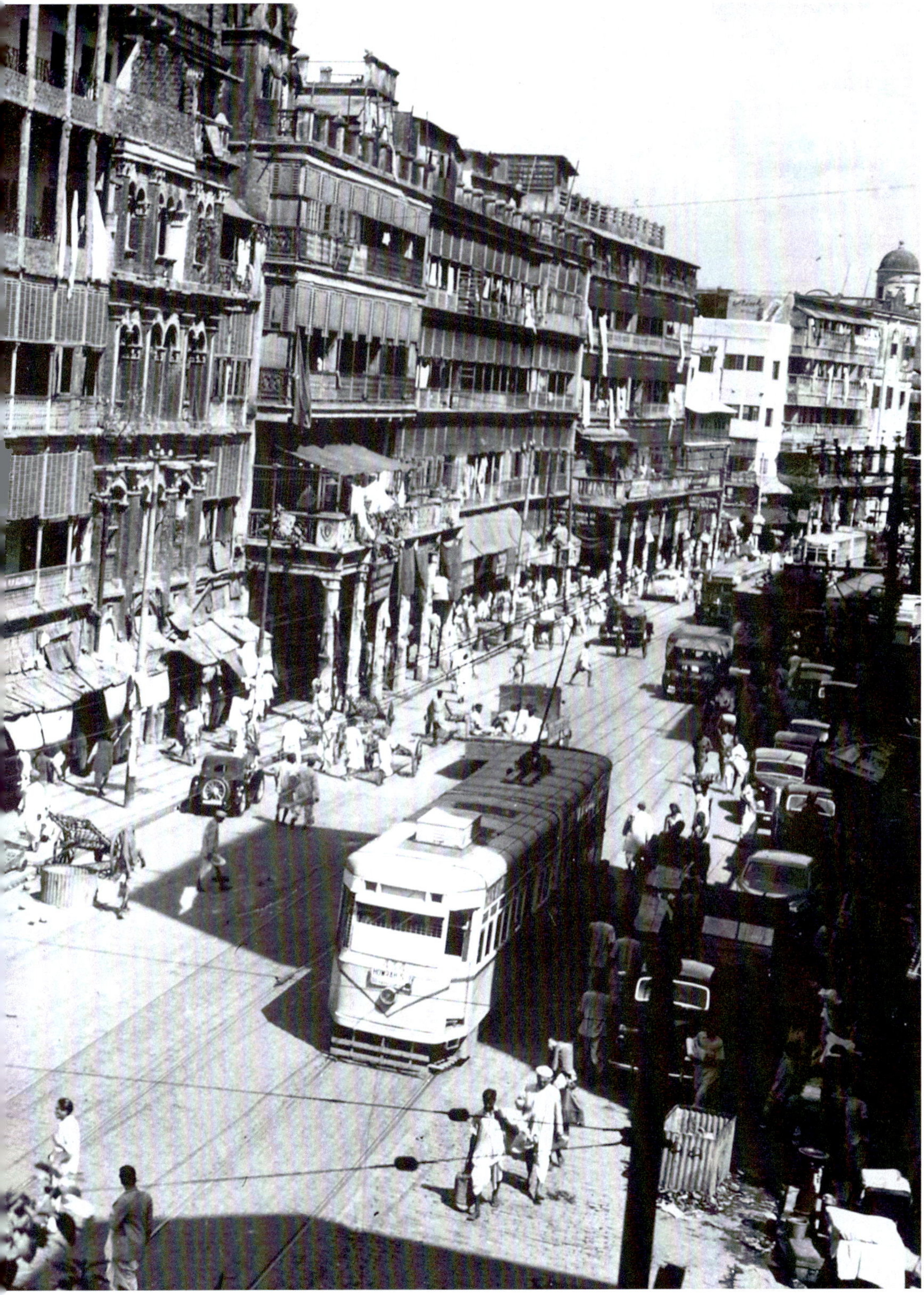

Harrison Road, now Mahatma Gandhi Road, has remained unchanged

c. 1952

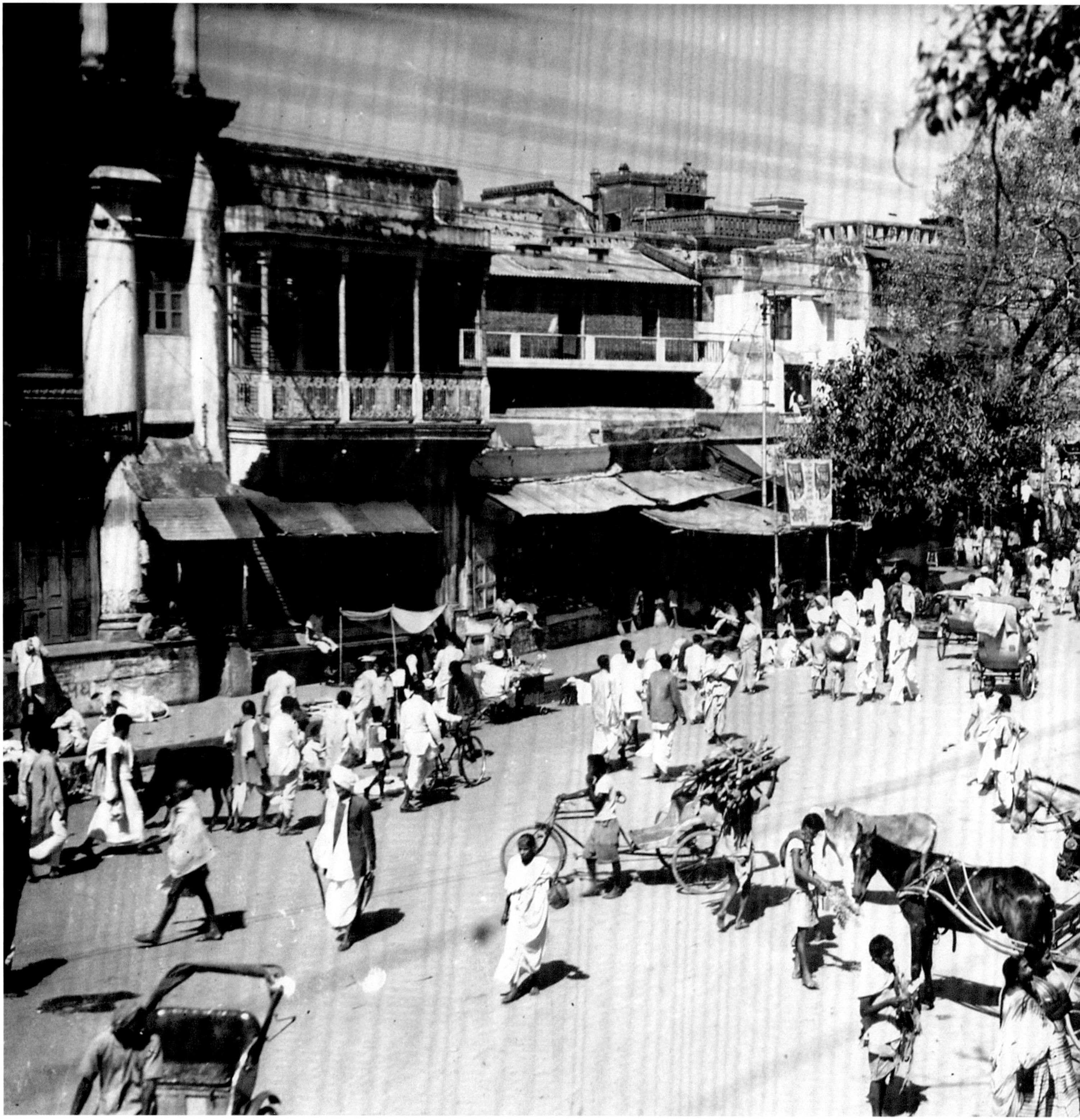

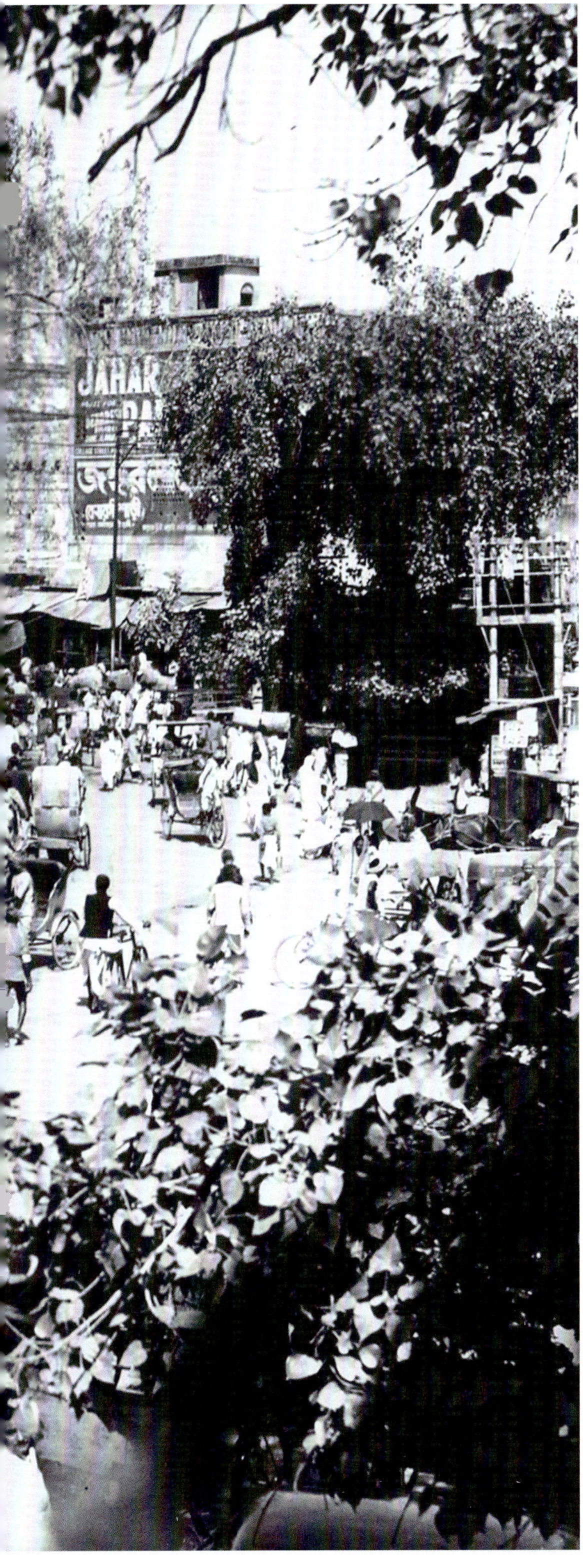

Burrabazar, a busy commercial hub, once a citadel of the Bengali aristocracy, today dominated by Marwaris

c. 1948

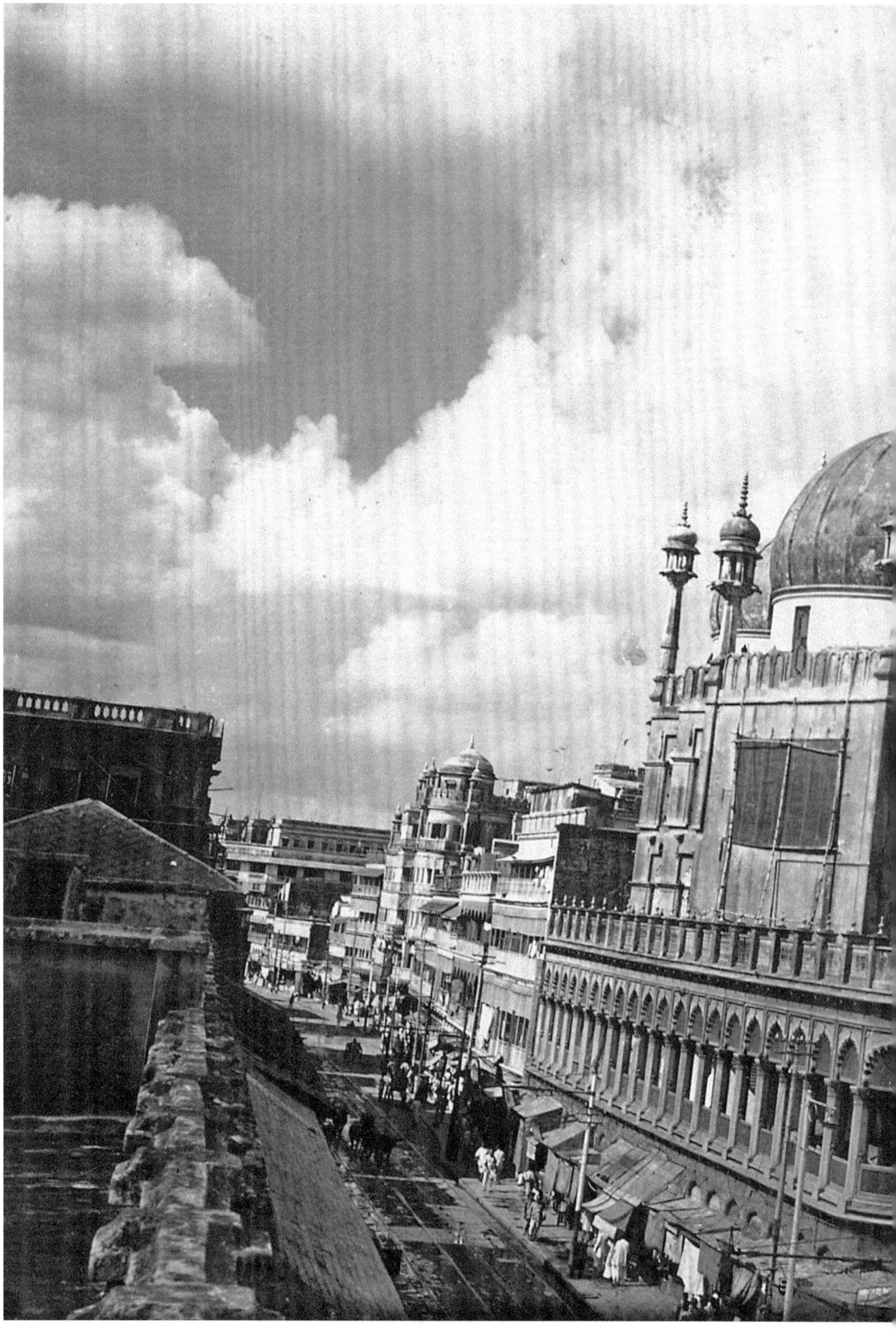

Nakhoda Masjid, biggest mosque in Calcutta on Chitpur Road, renamed Rabindra Sarani. The foundation stone of the Masjid was laid on 11 September 1926

c. 1952

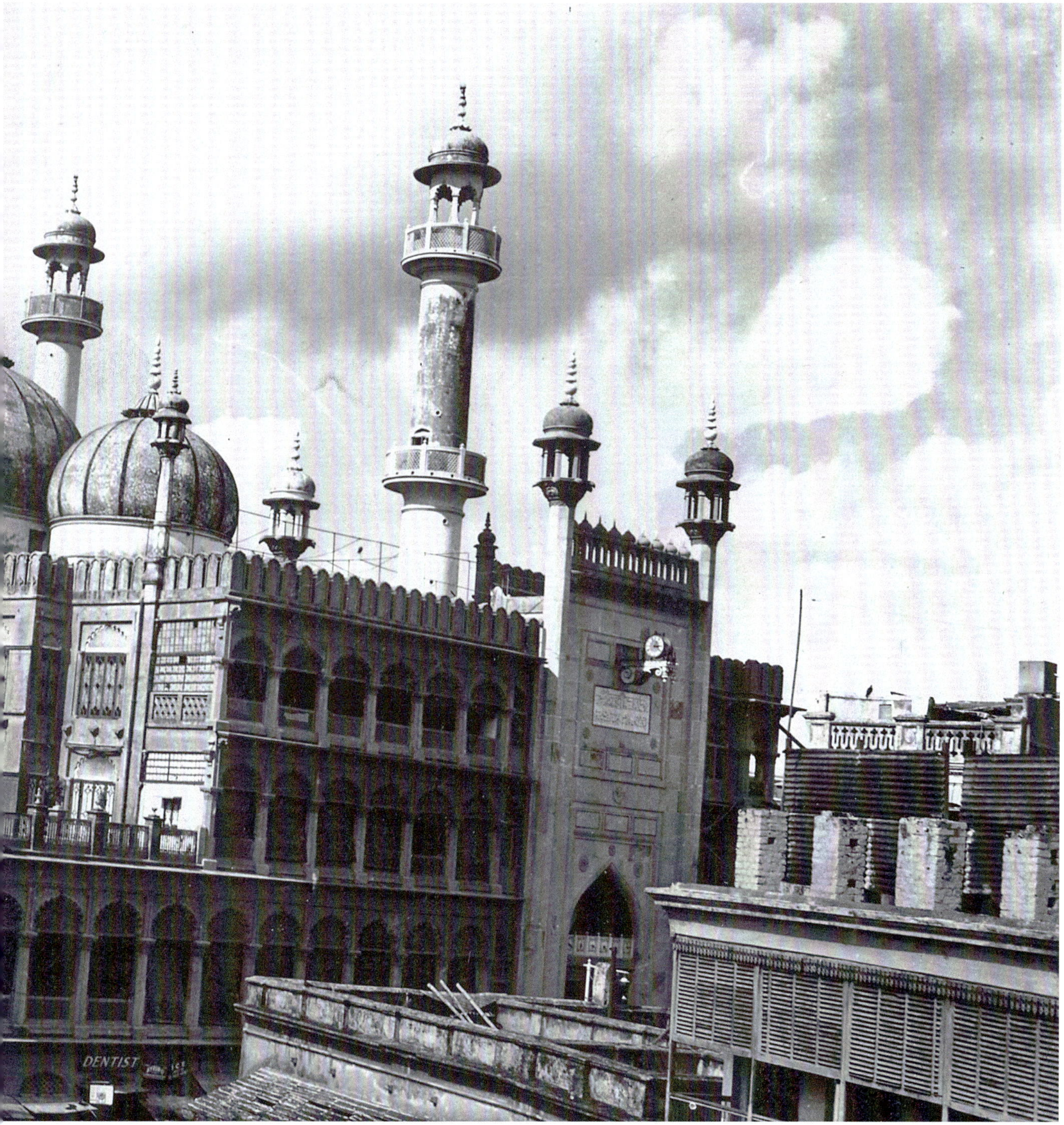
DENTIST

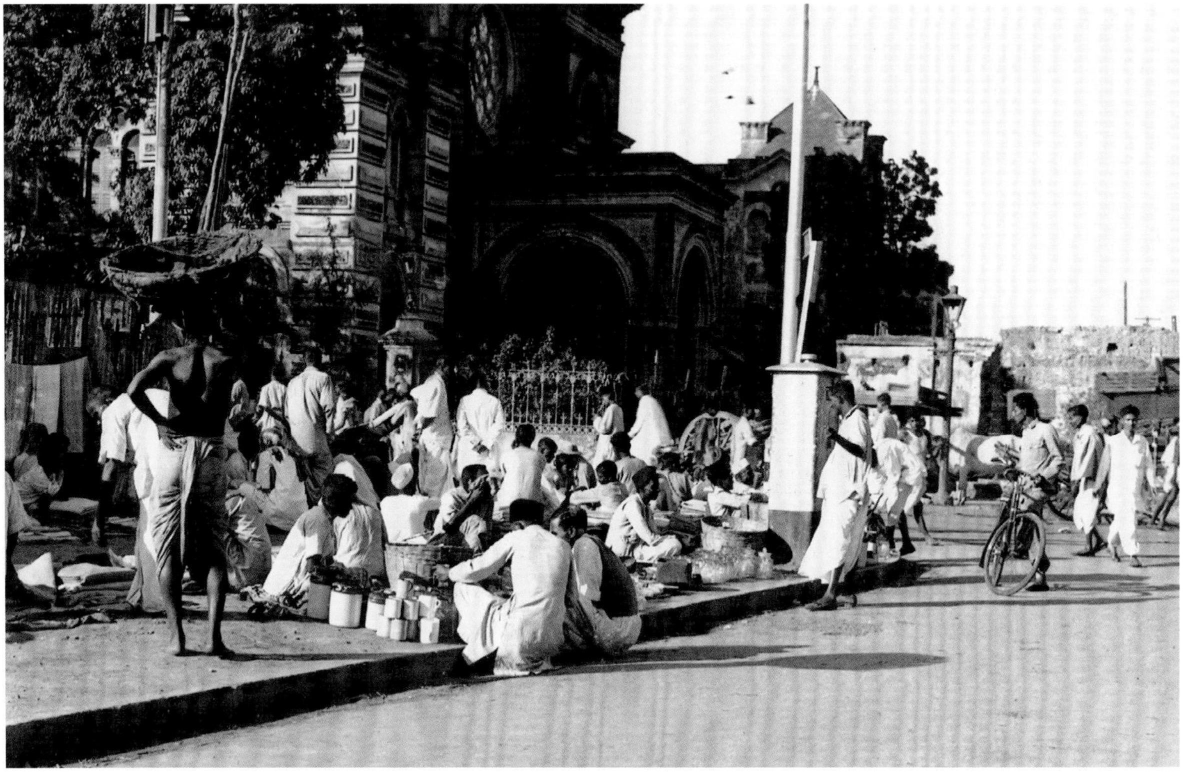

Labourers, masons, and carpenters, sitting outside Magen David Synagogue, at the crossing of Brabourne Road and Canning Street, waiting to be hired

c. 1948

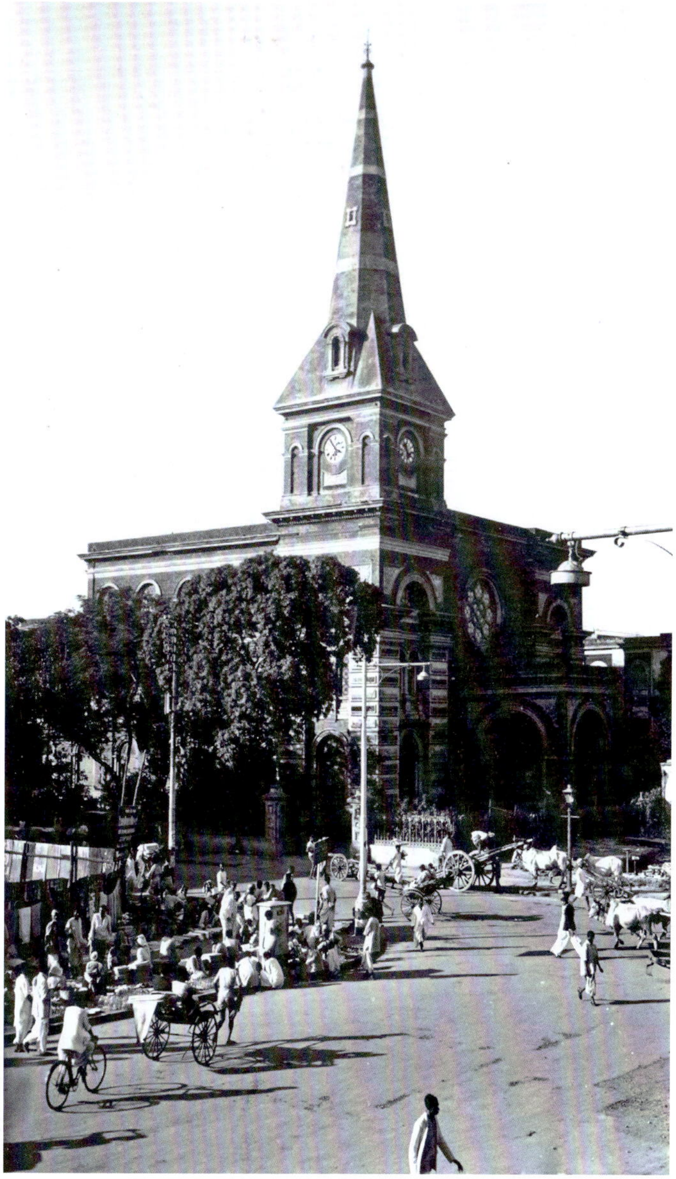

Magen David Synagogue, before a building, constructed in the 1950s, obstructed this majestic view

c. 1948

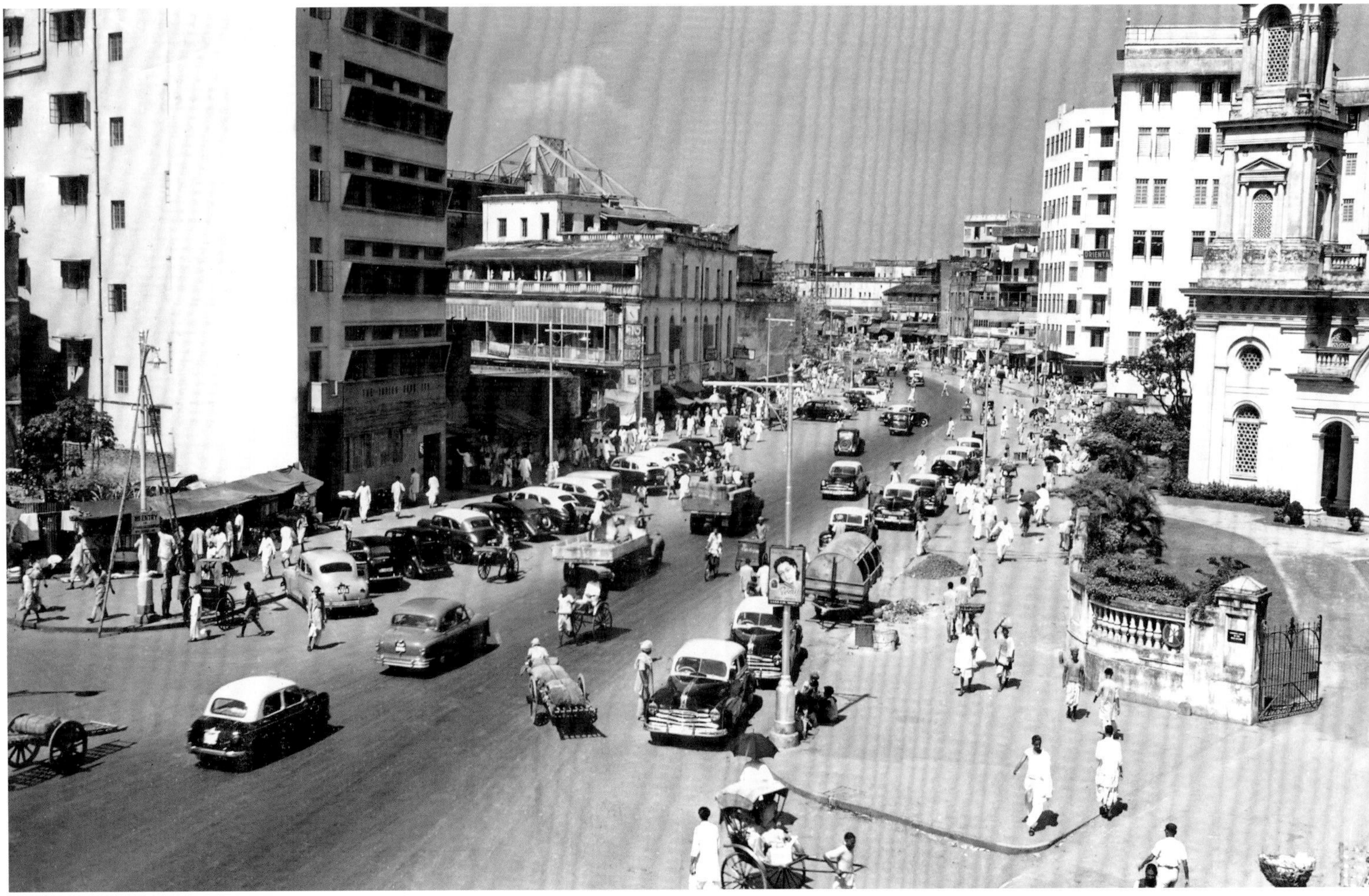

View of Brabourne Road with the Cathedral of the Holy Rosary, commonly known as the Portuguese Church, to the right

c. 1958

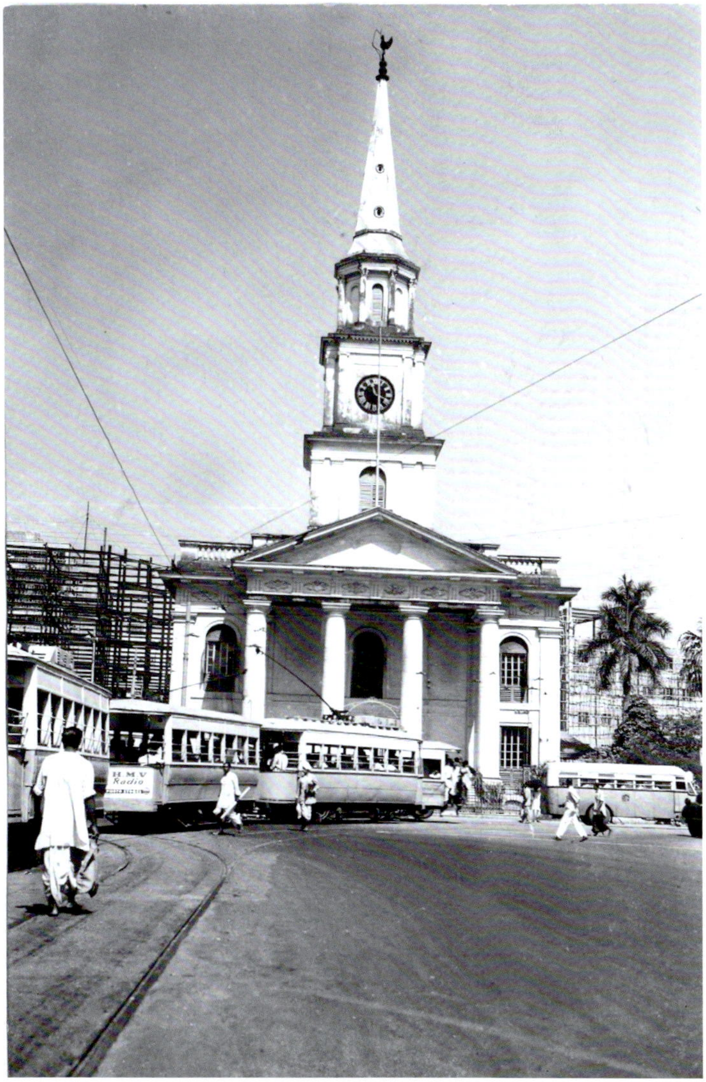

St Andrew's Kirk, built in 8 March 1818, the first Scottish church of Calcutta

c. 1950

Dalhousie Square was till recently the administrative hub of Calcutta. On the right are the Standard Assurance building and what was then the Hongkong & Shanghai Banking Corporation Ltd, the stone-clad Hongkong House

c. 1948

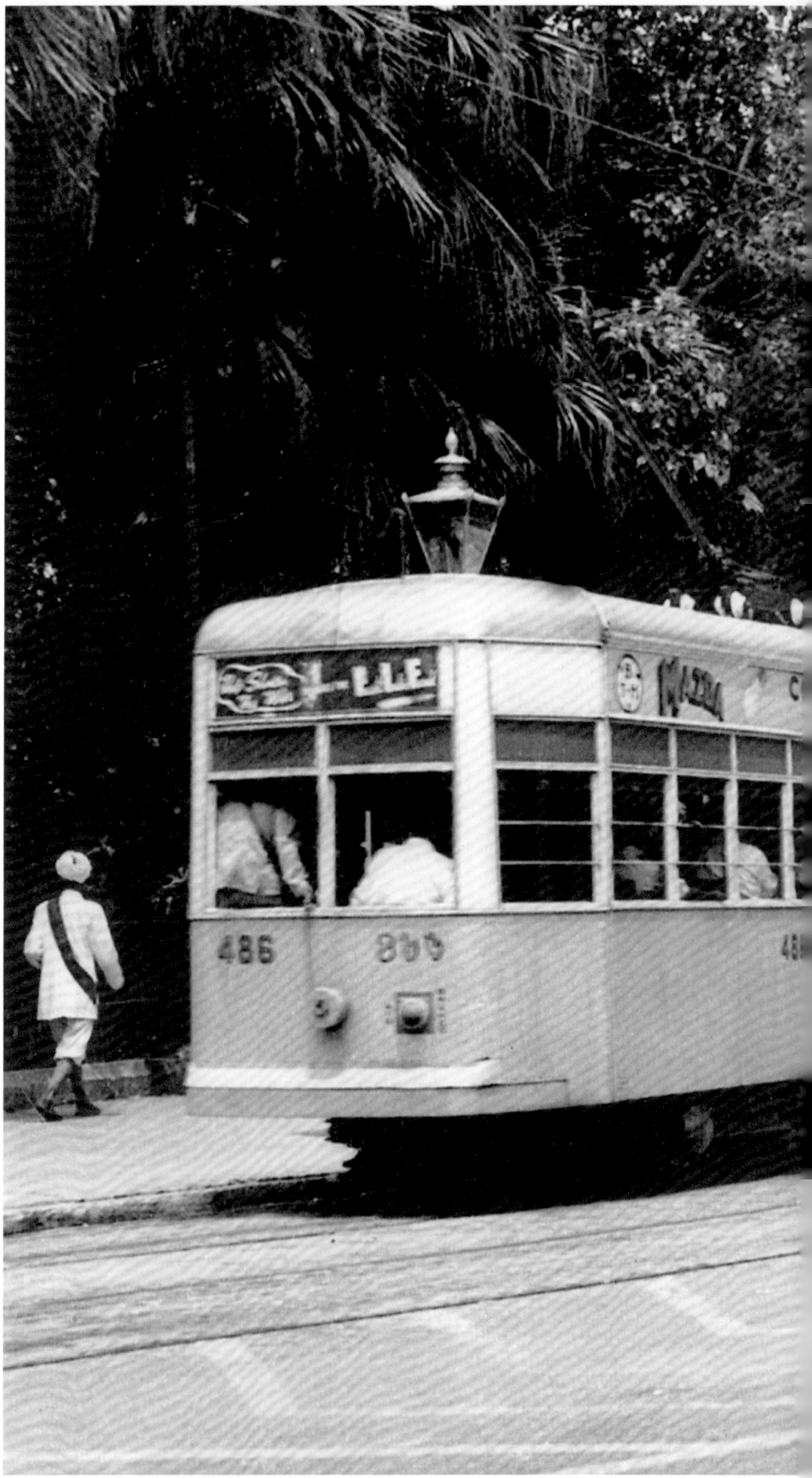

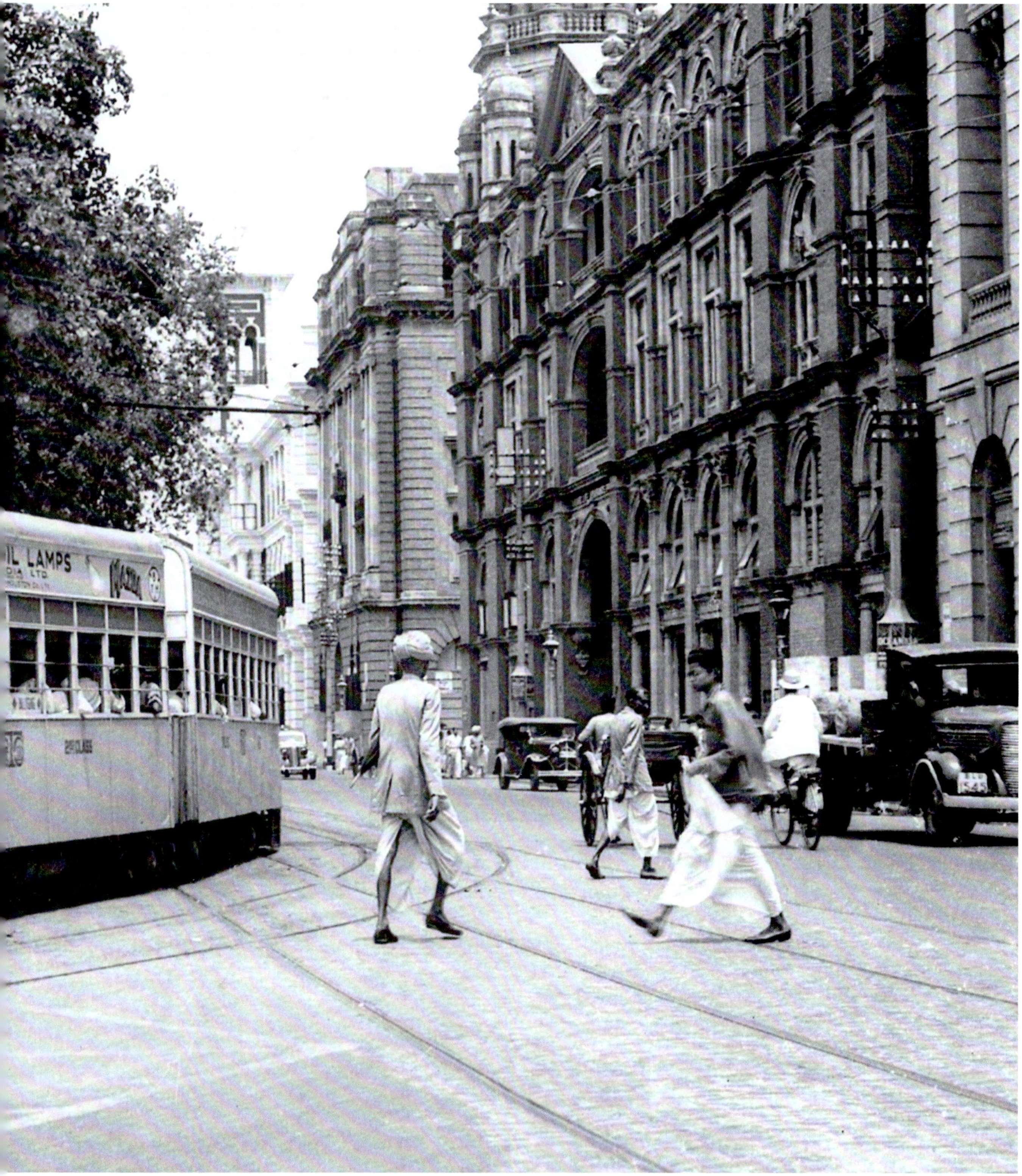
IL LAMPS

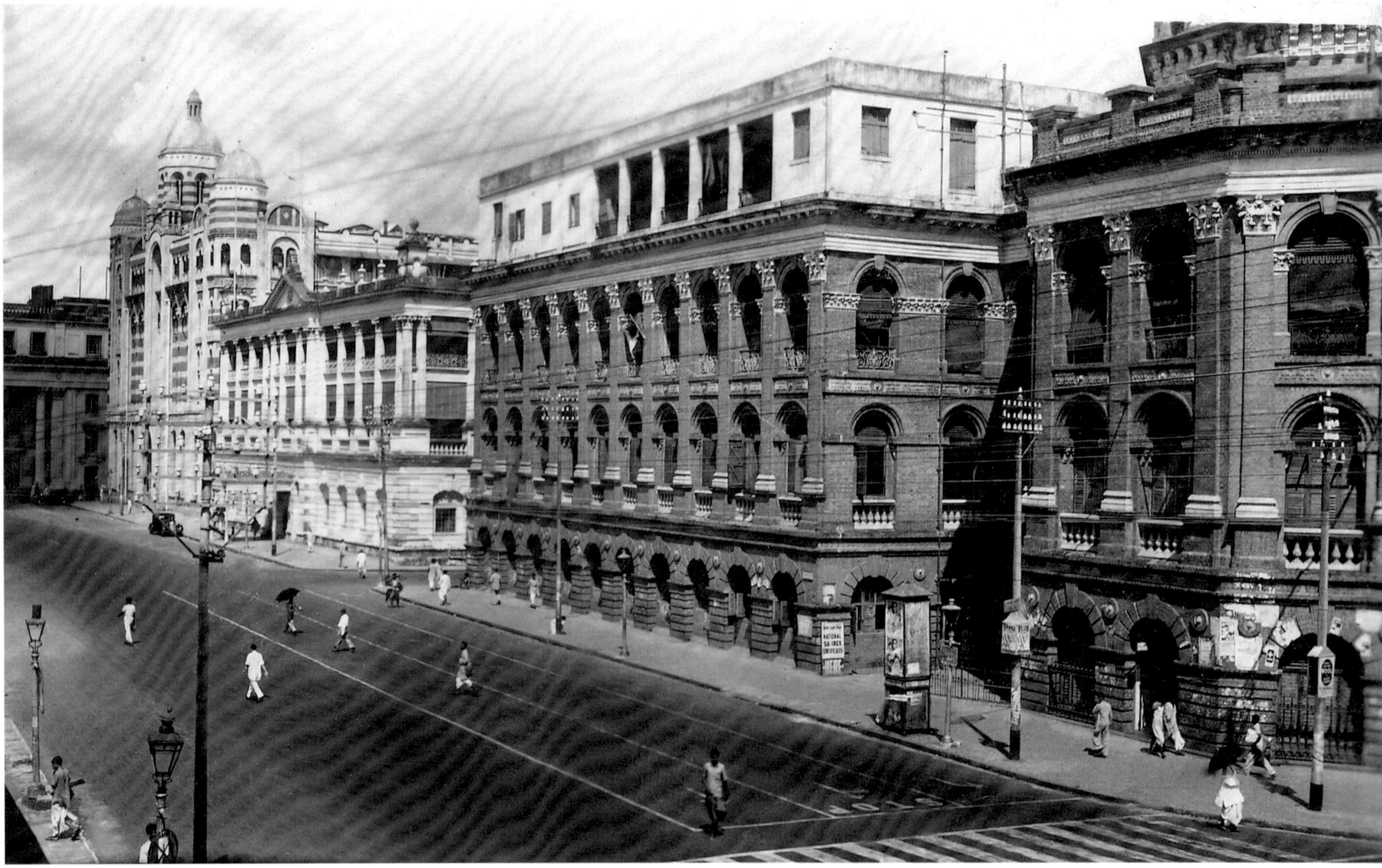

The domed of the Chartered Bank building with the Allahabad Bank next to it. Earlier the Allahabad Bank building belonged to Finlay & Compnay. Next to it is Writers' Buildings

c. 1945

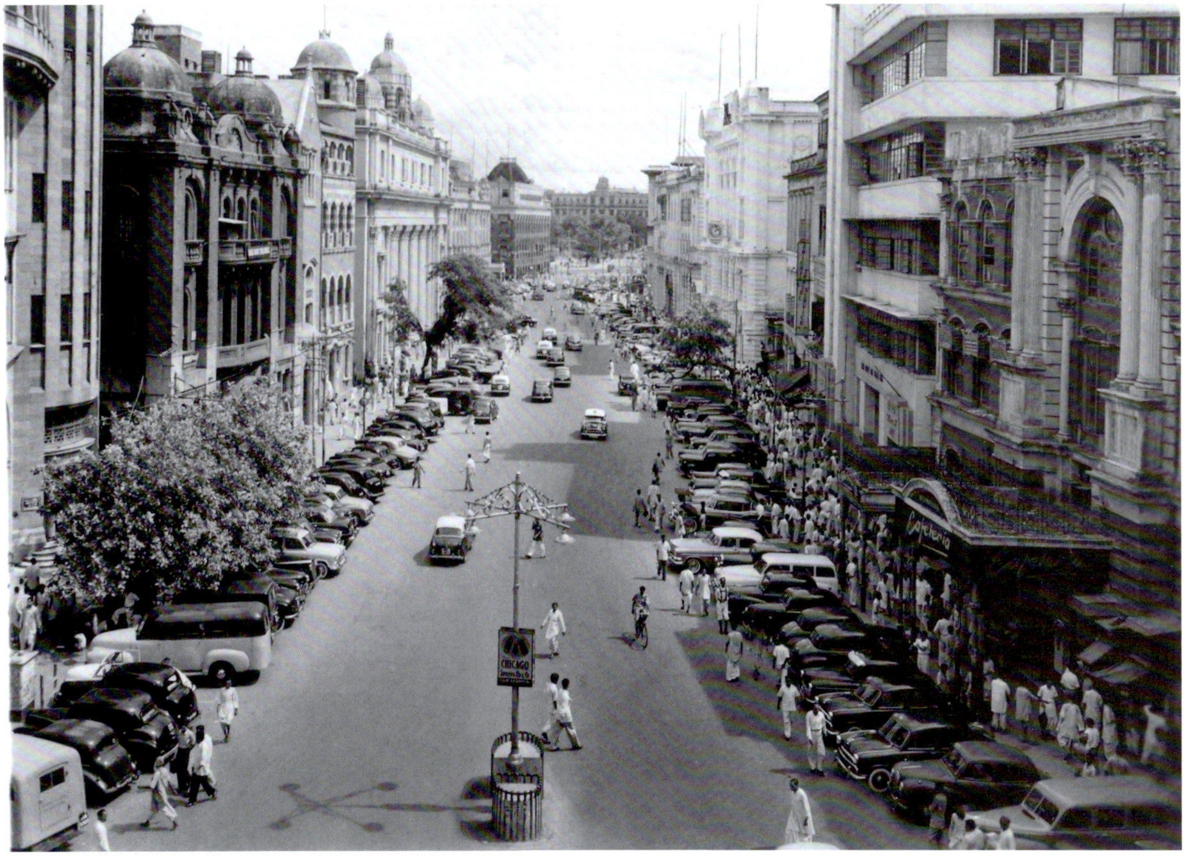

Looking south, down N.S. Road; Writers' Buildings at the far end

c. 1948

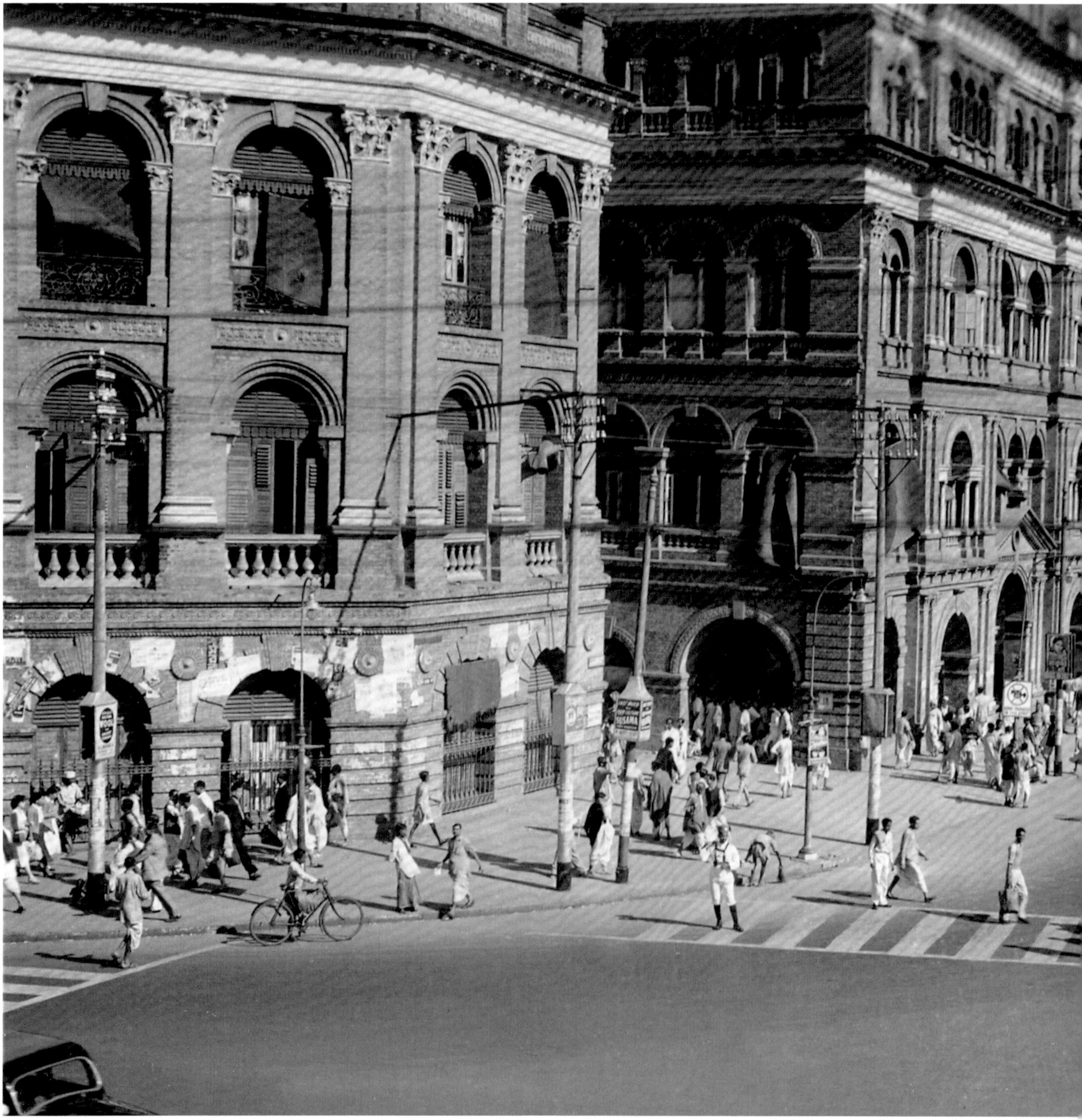

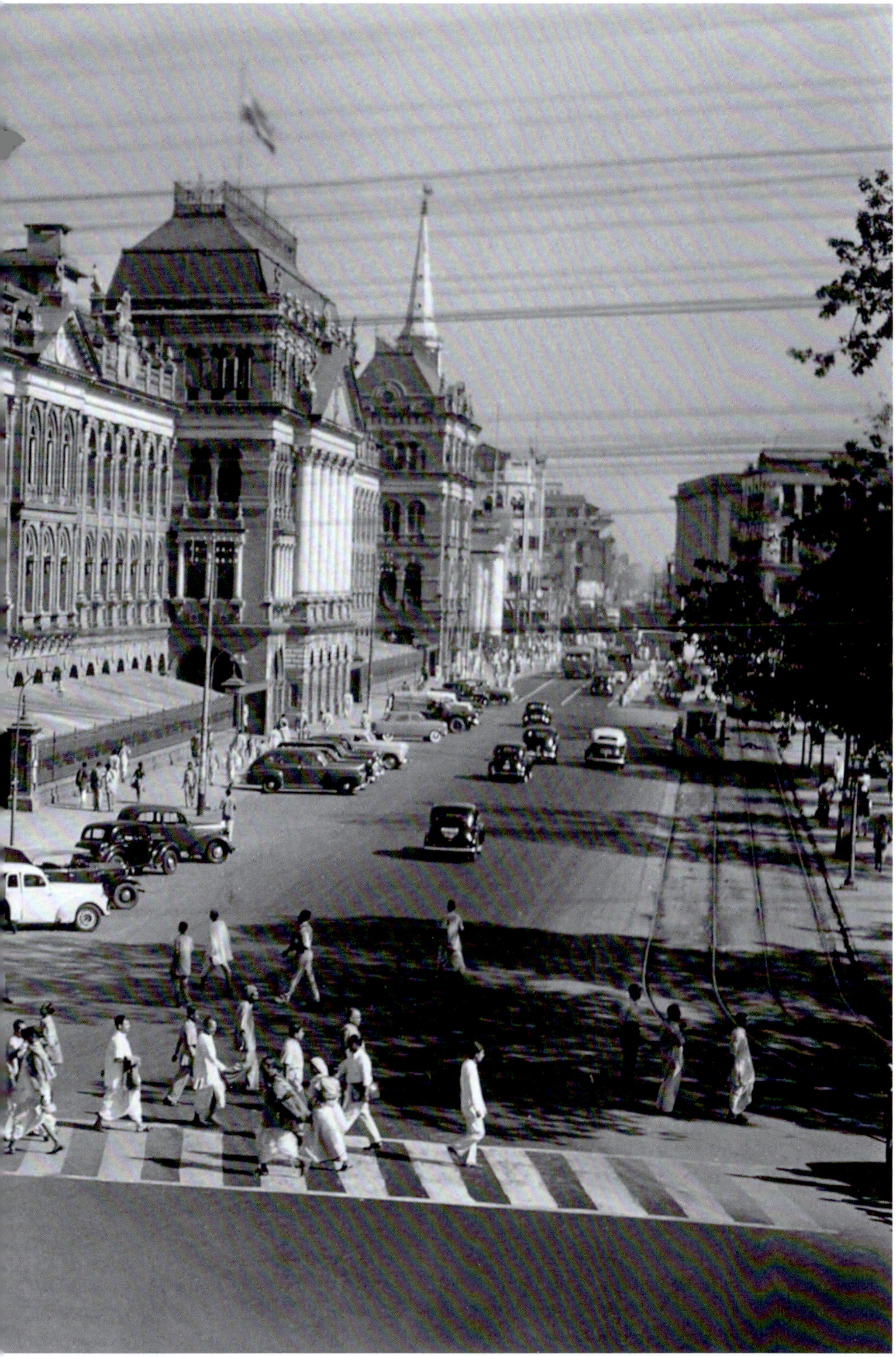

Writers' Buildings as seen
from the corner of Clive Street

c. 1950

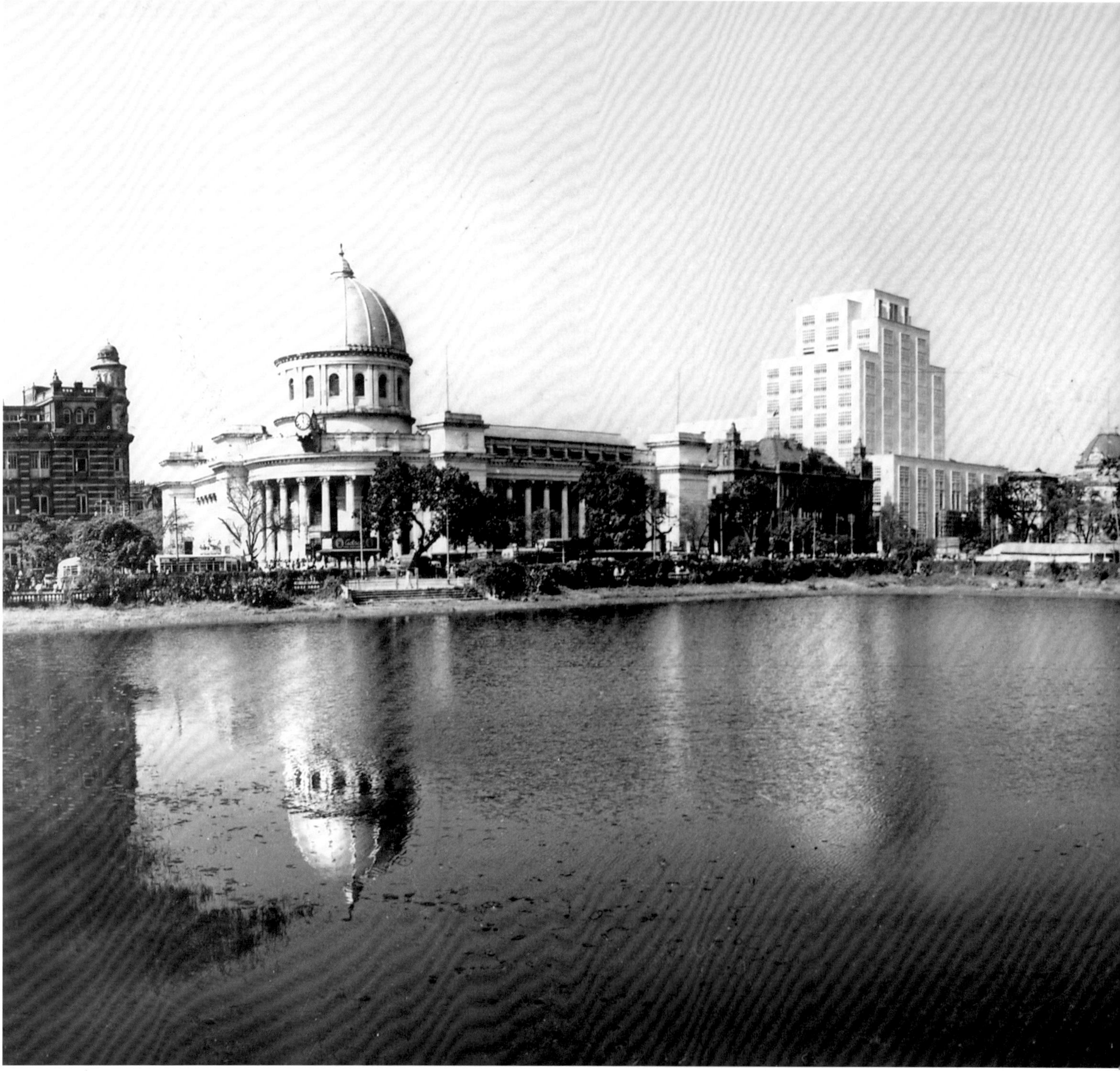

c. 1959

A panoramic view of Dalhousie Square built around a tank known as Laldighi, surrounded by the General Post Office, the Reserve Bank of India and Writers' Buildings

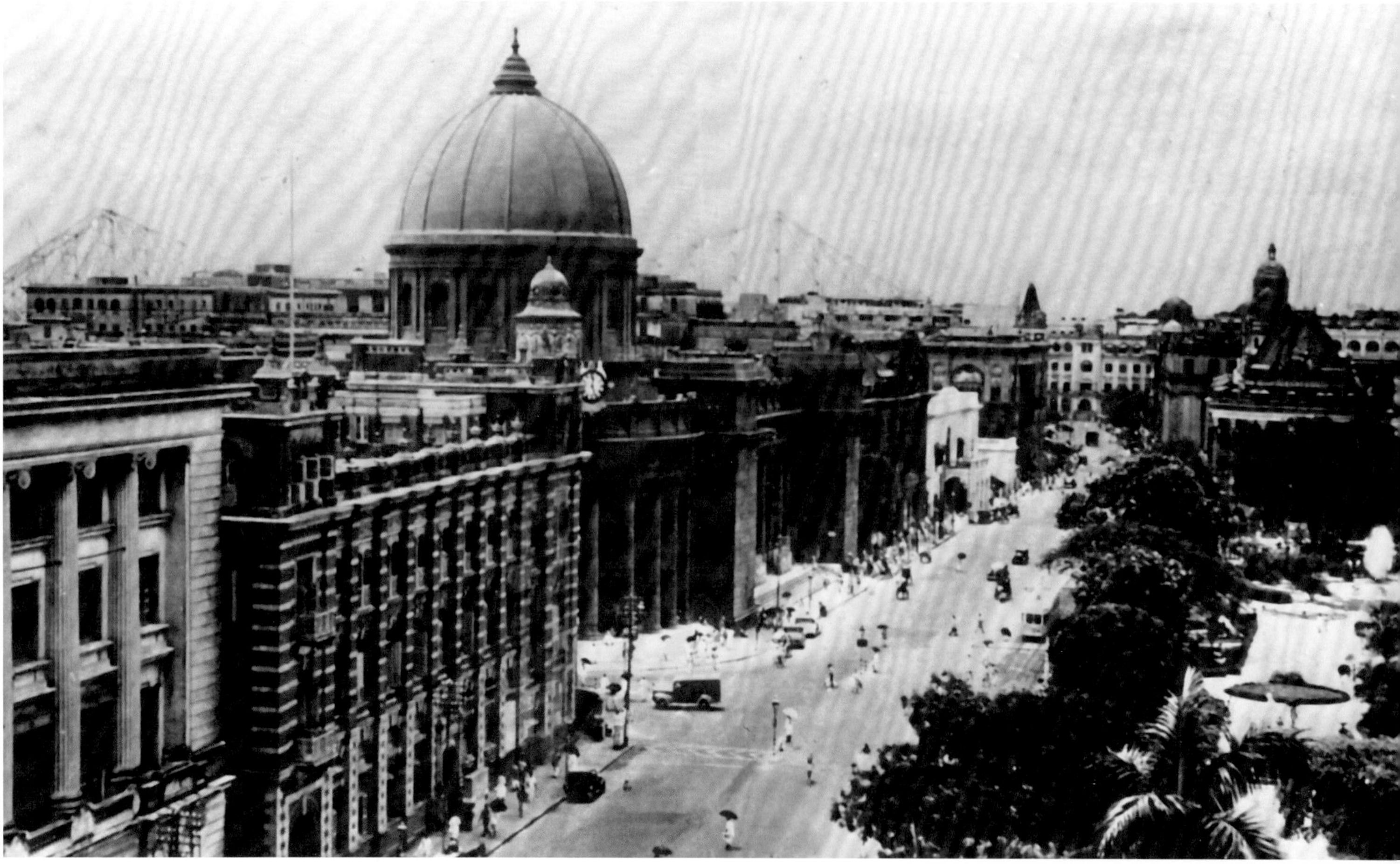

Clive Street, now known as Netaji Subhash Road, long before the Reserve Bank of India came up

c. 1945

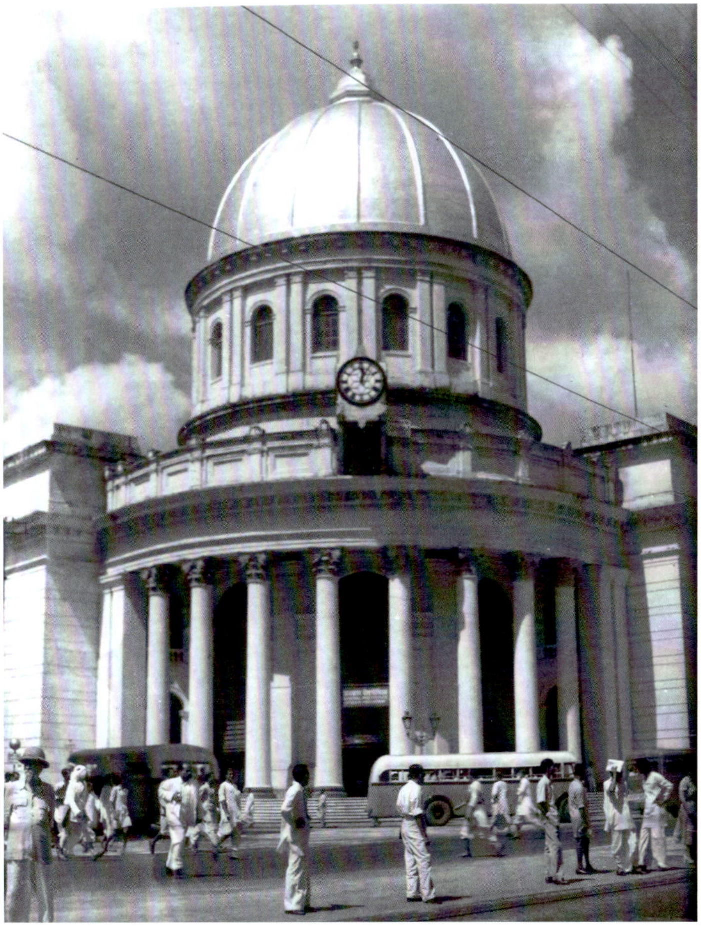

General Post Office, built in 1864, a majestic structure with a 220 ft dome, supported by Corinthian pillars. Its magnificent dome dominates Dalhousie Square

c. 1954

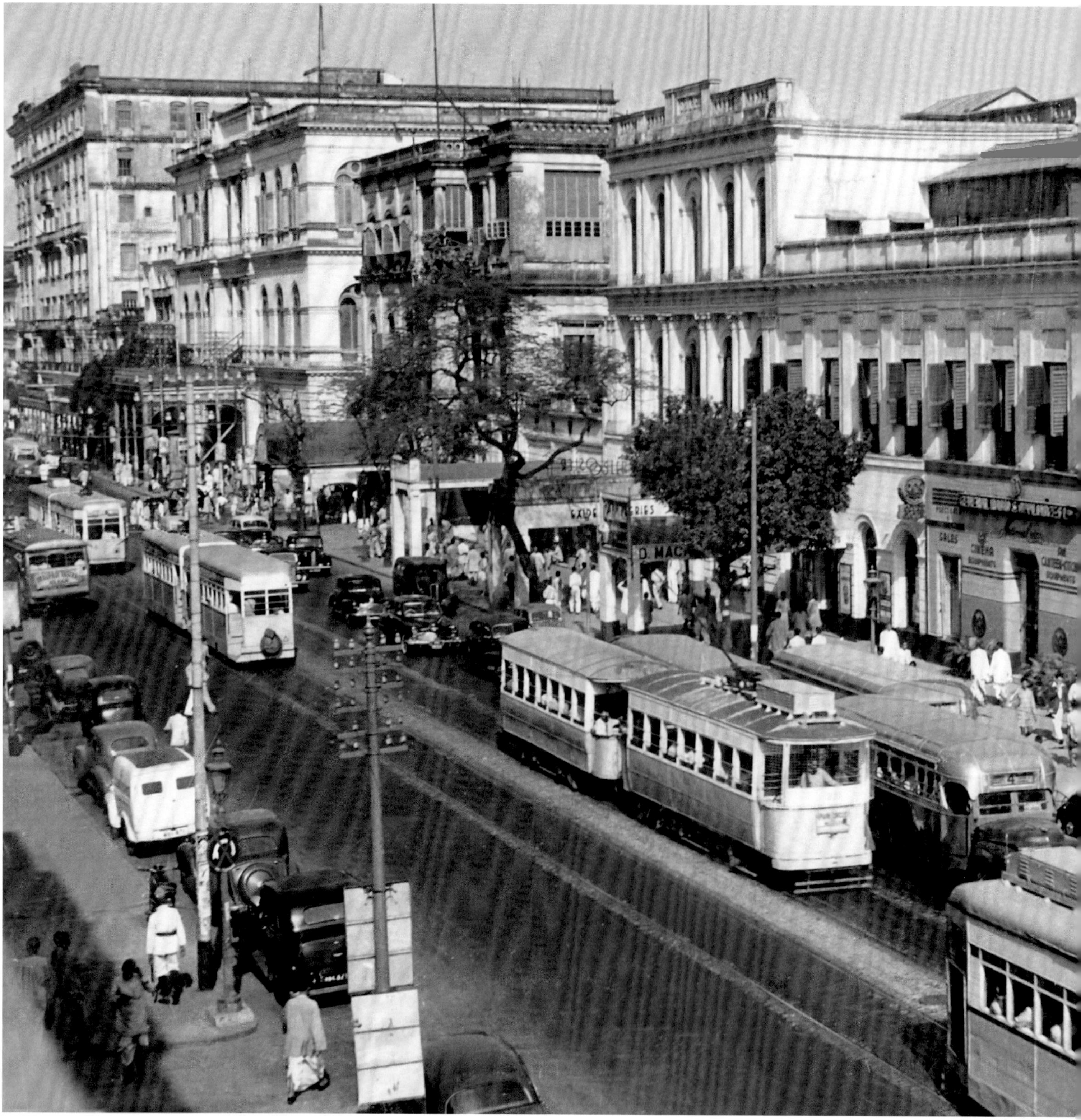

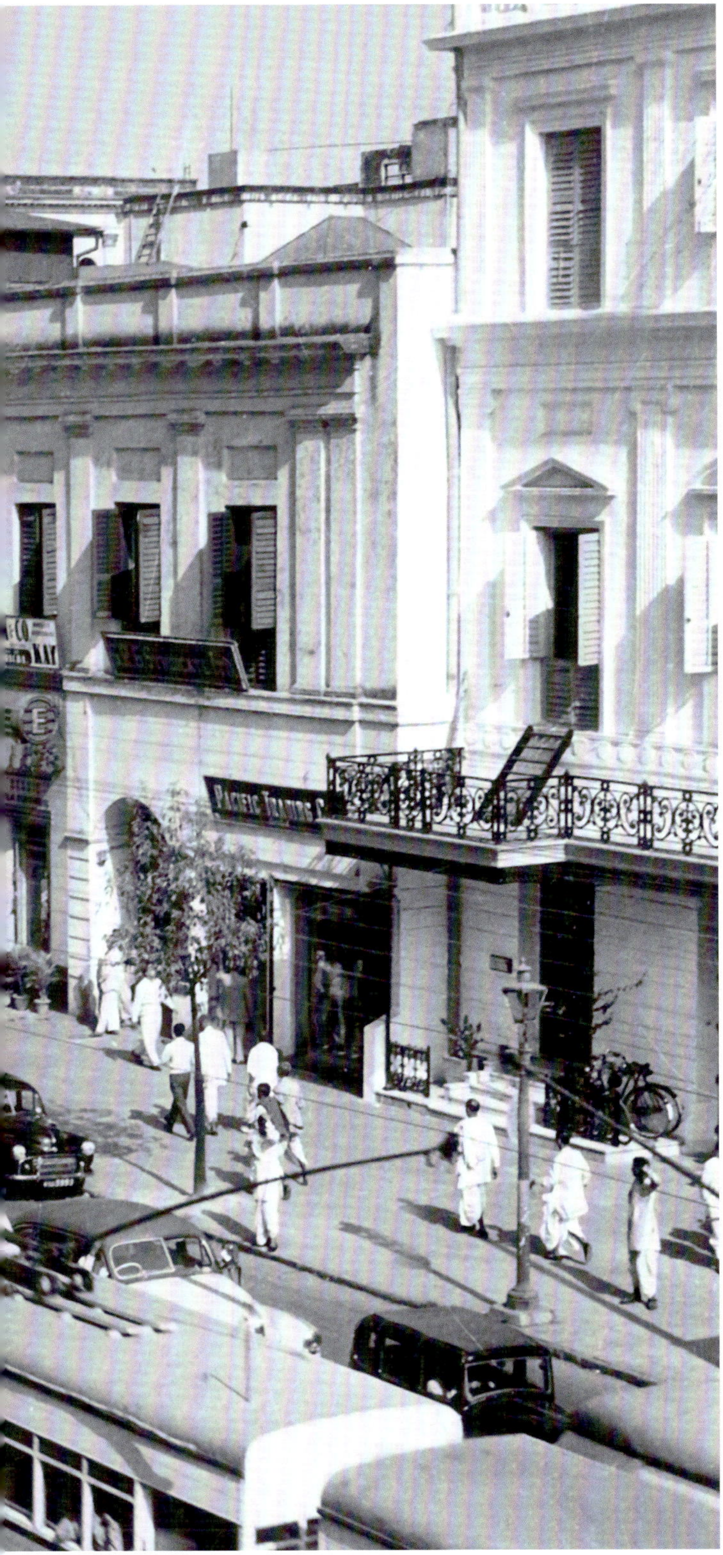

Old Court House Street
was a shopper's paradise

c. 1945

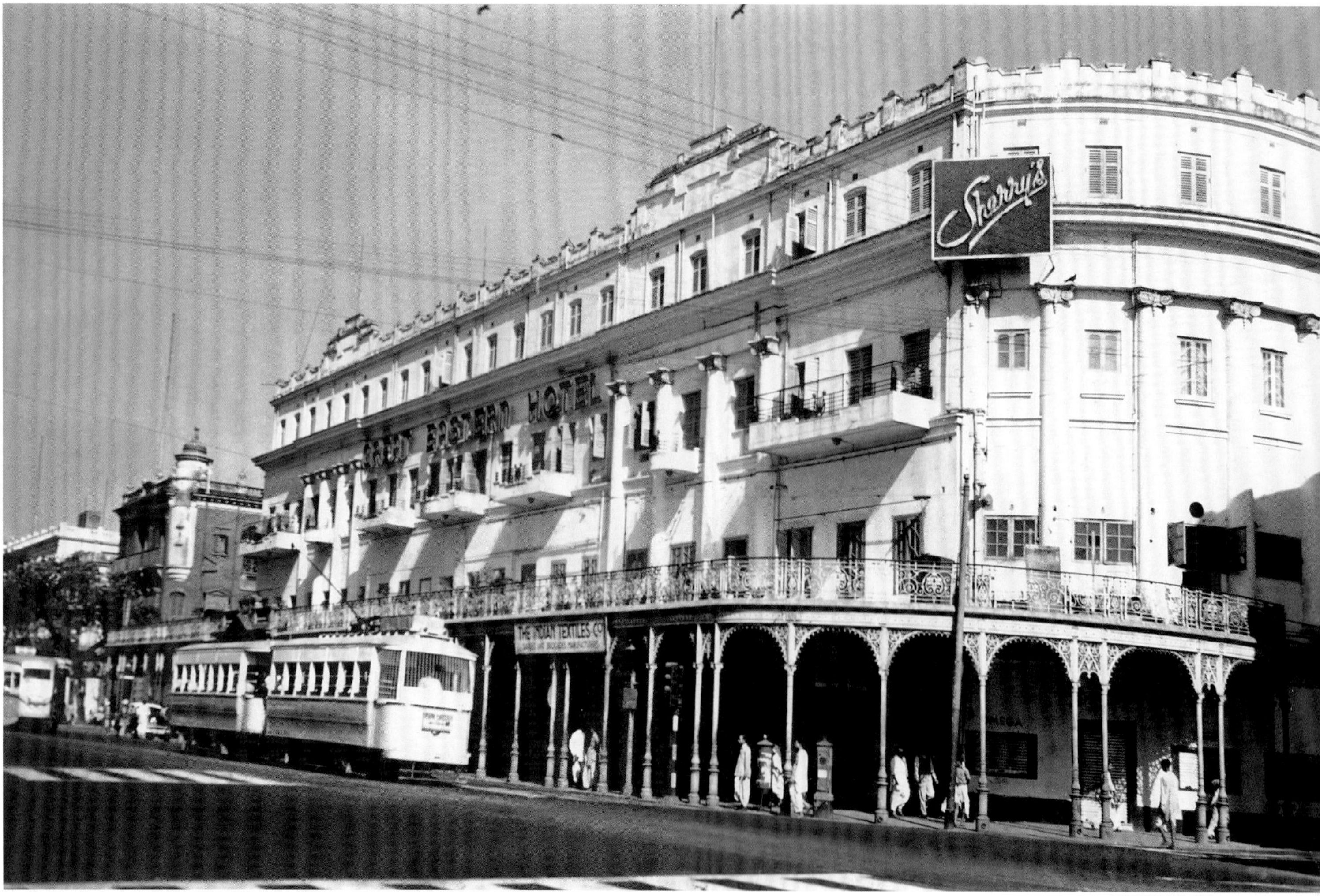

Great Eastern Hotel is one of the oldest colonial hotels established in 1840 or 1841 by David Wilson and named Auckland Hotel after the Governor-General, Earl of Auckland. It was renamed Great Eastern Hotel in 1915. It has been remodelled and goes by the name Lalit Great Eastern, today

c. 1948

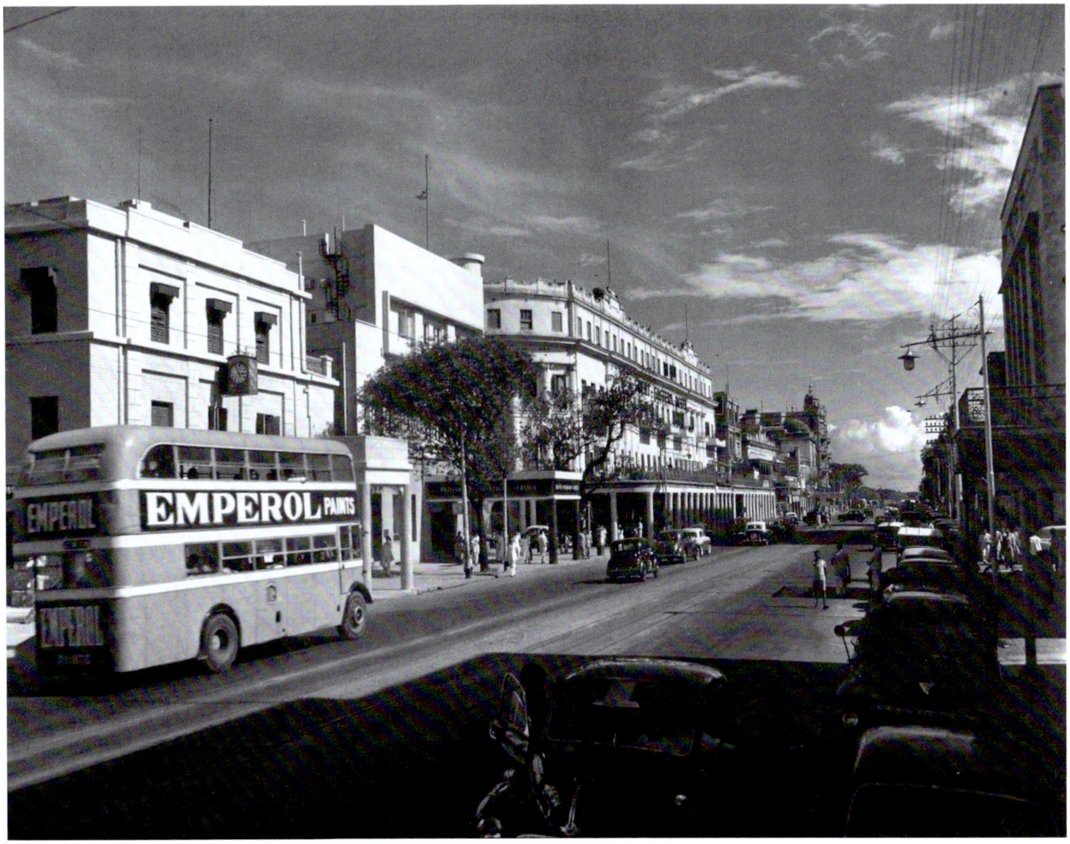

Old Court House Street with the dome of the Esplanade Mansion visible at its extreme end

c. 1954

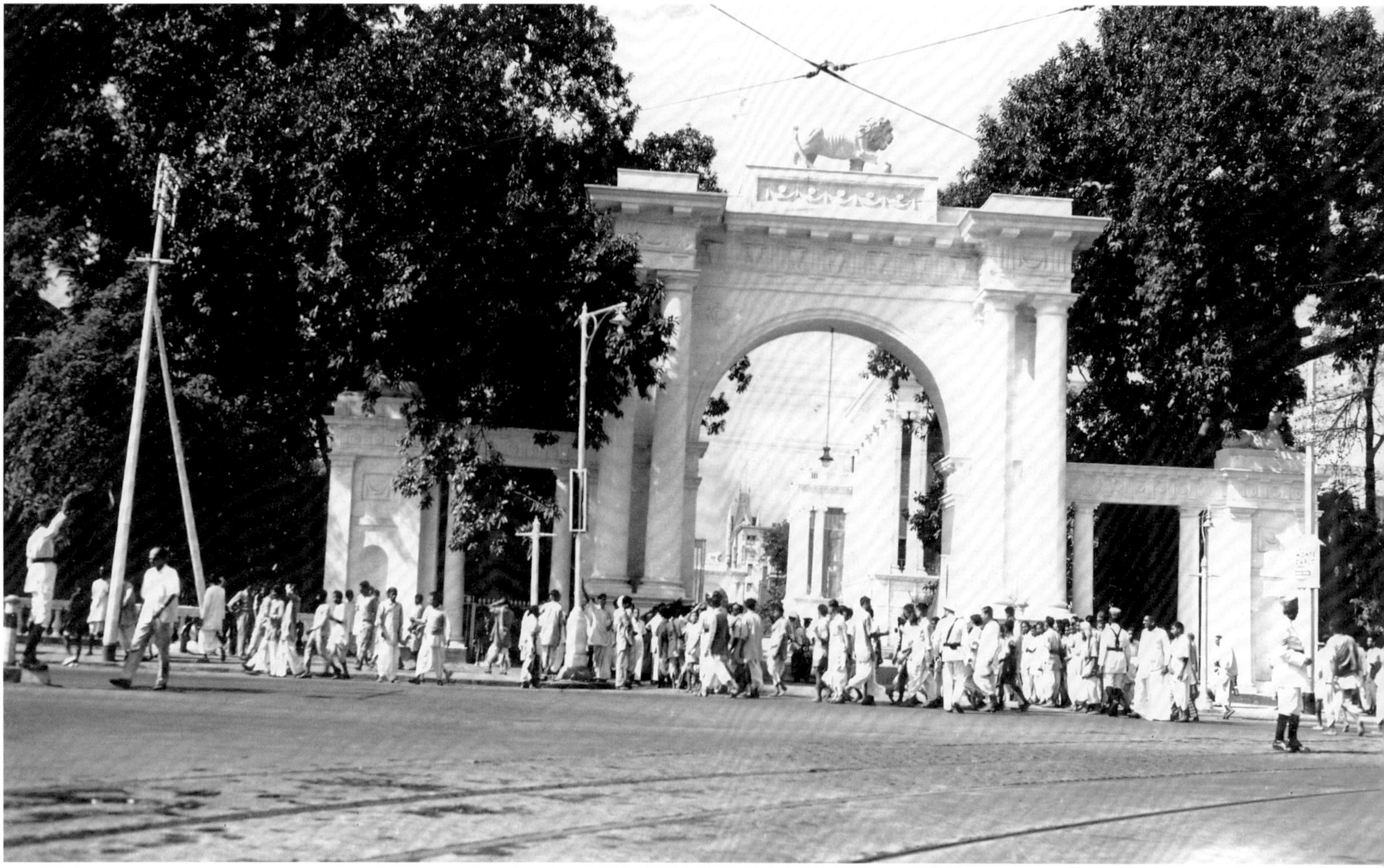

Crowds outside the east gate of the Government House. The tower of the Calcutta High Court building is visible through the arch

c. 1947

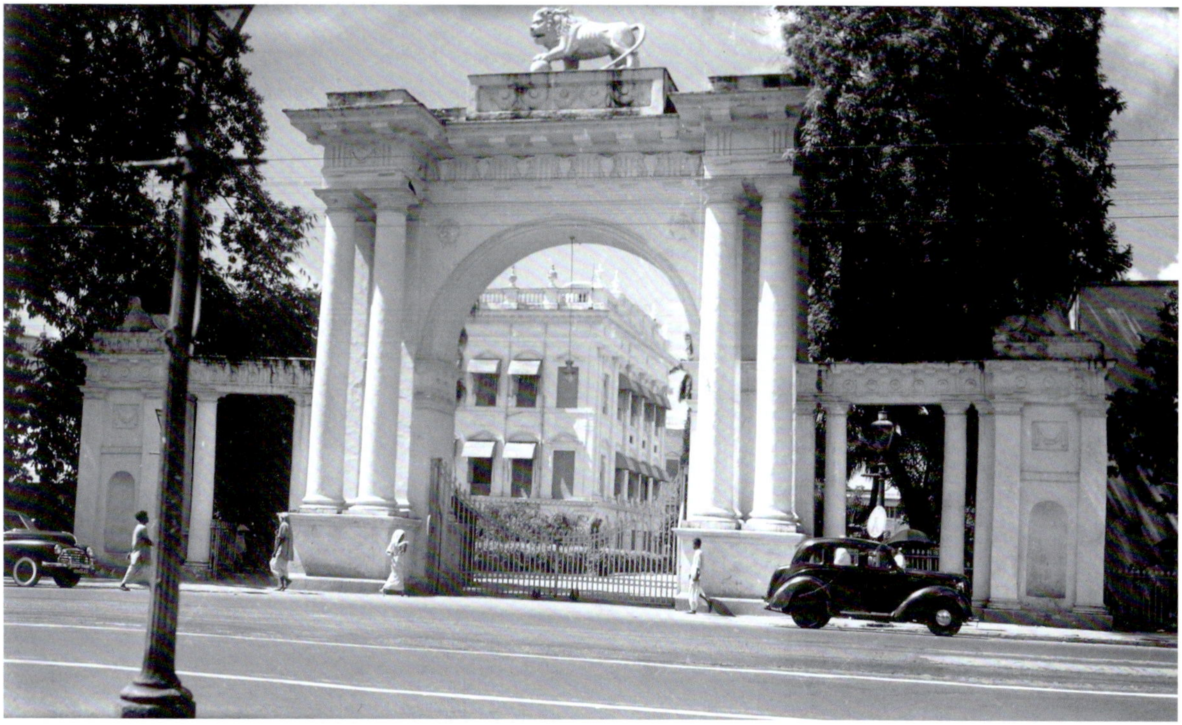

The north-eastern gate of the Government House

c. 1950

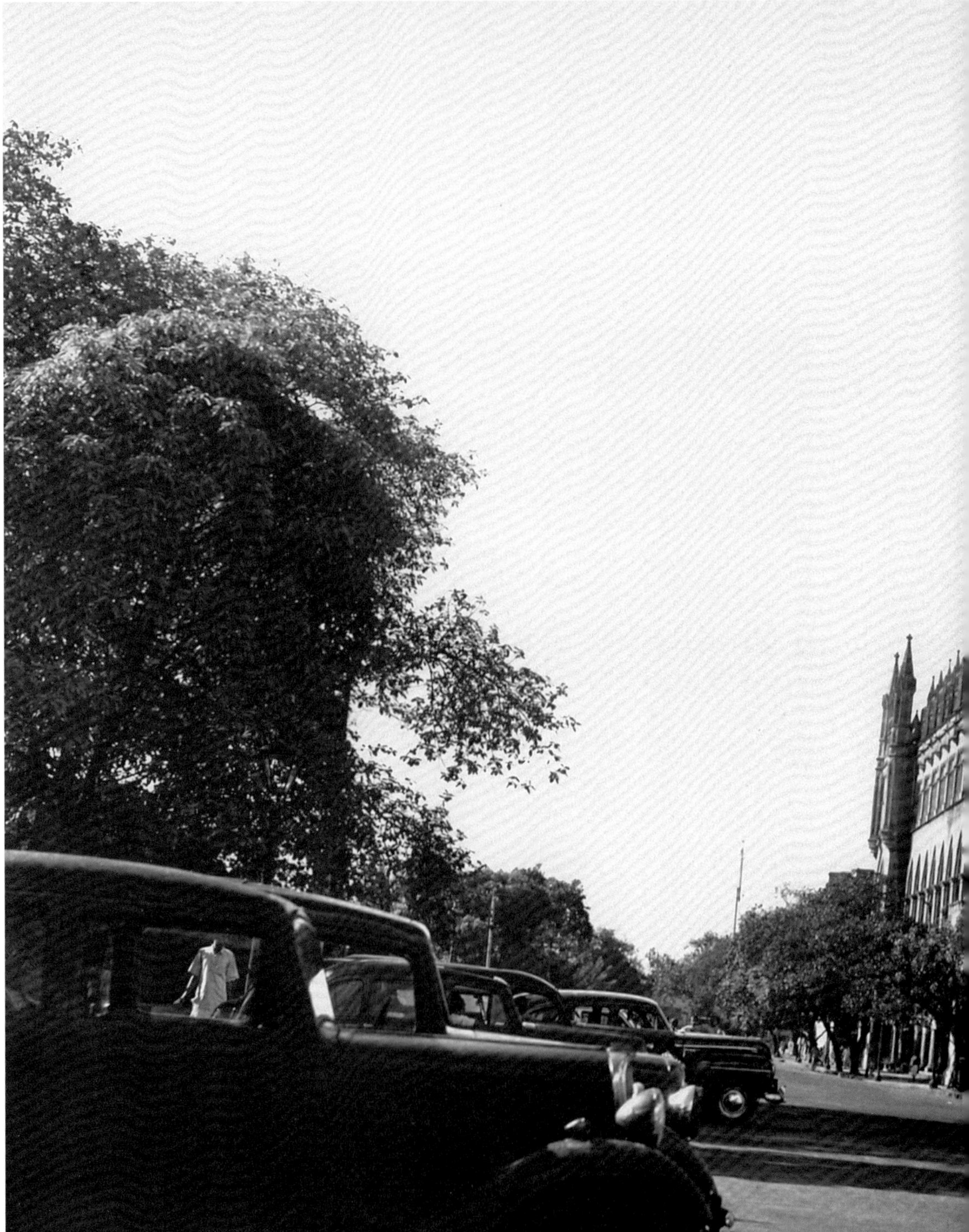

Calcutta High Court, the oldest High Court in India, established on 1 July 1862

c. 1952

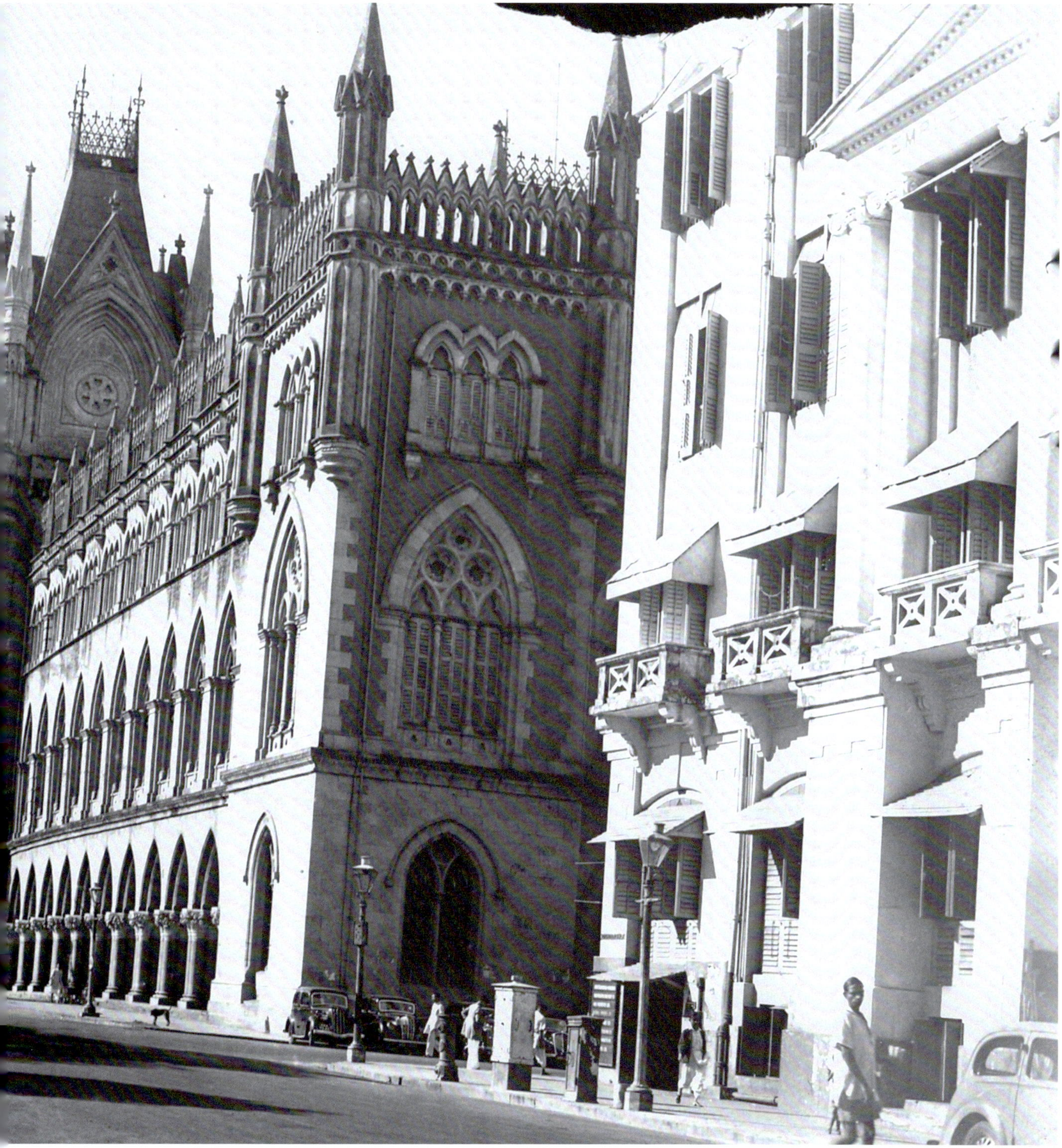

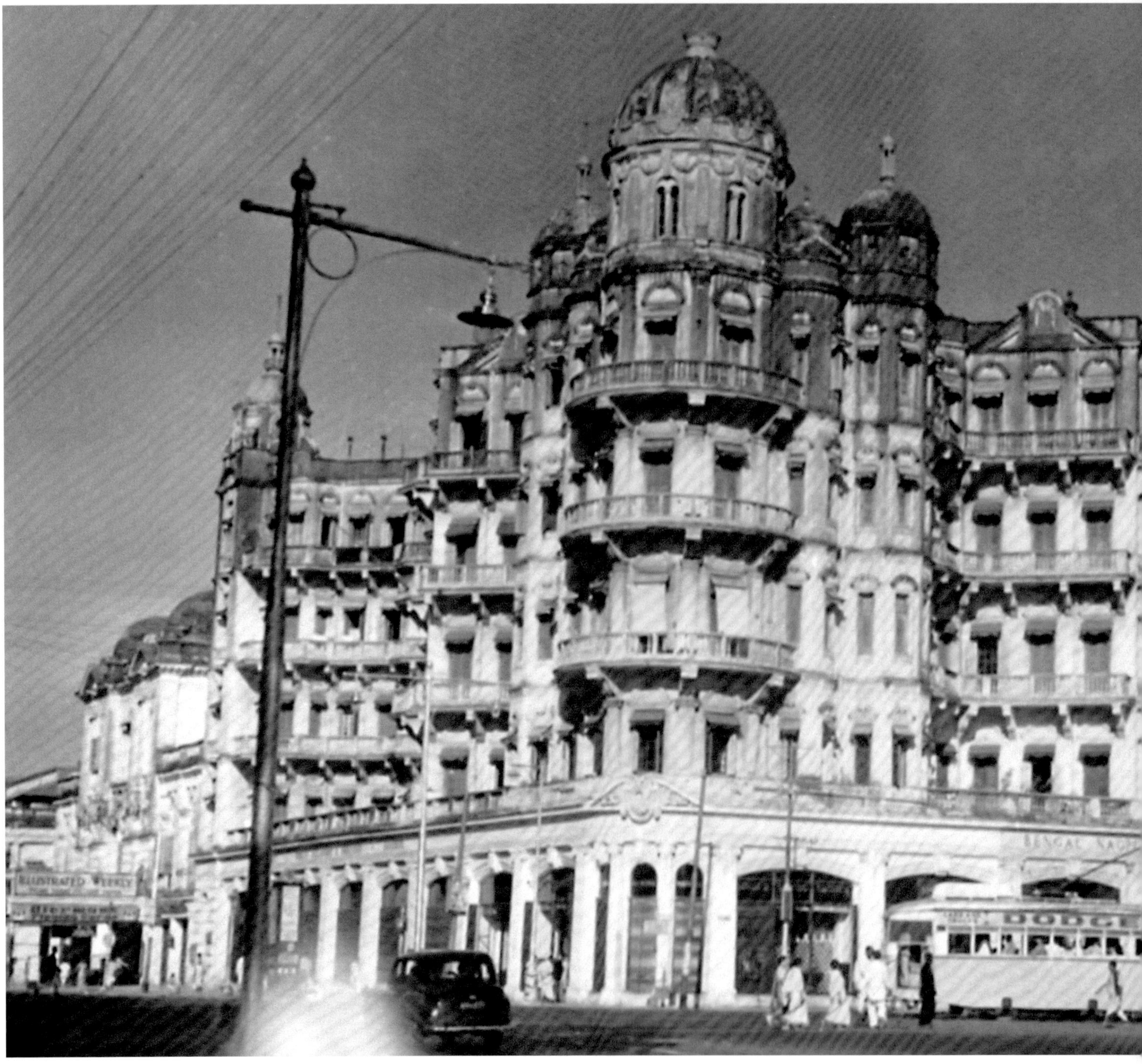
ILLUSTRATED WEEKLY

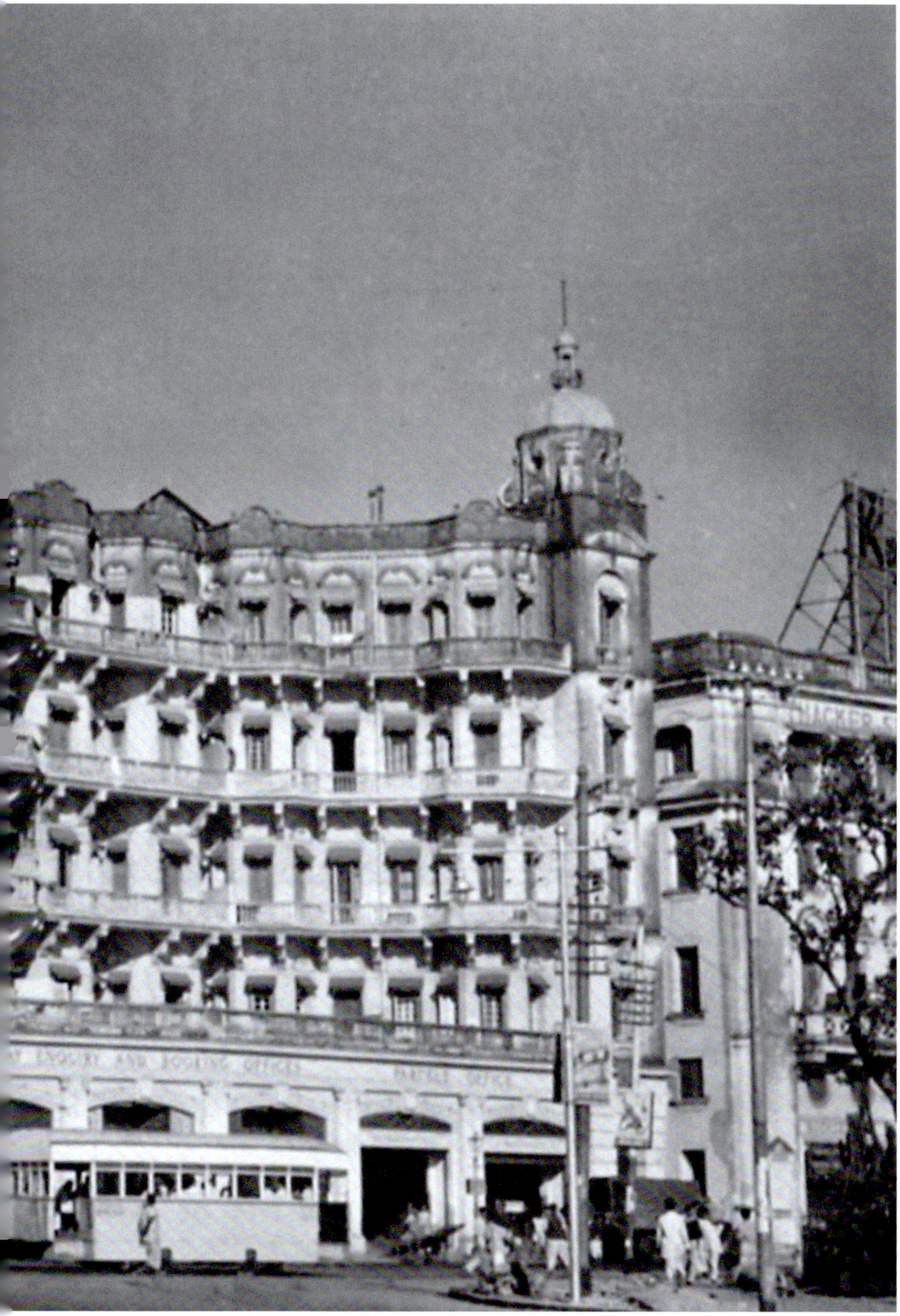

Esplanade Mansion is a magnificent art nouveau apartment block, constructed in 1910 by the Jewish millionaire David Joseph Ezra. It overlooks the garden of the Government House

c. 1945

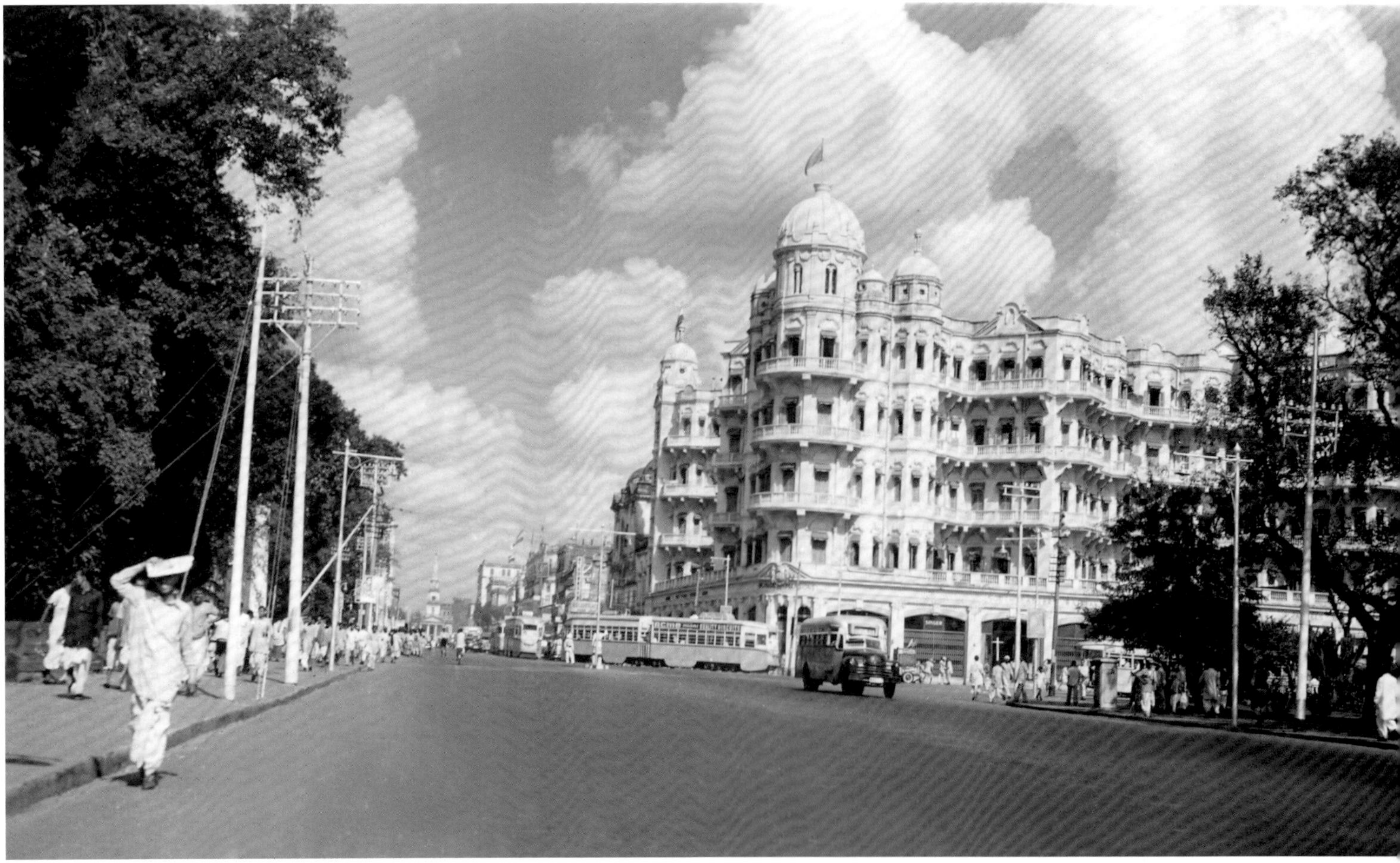

A view of Old Court House Street with Esplanade Mansion in the foreground. St Andrew's Church is visible at the far end

c. 1951

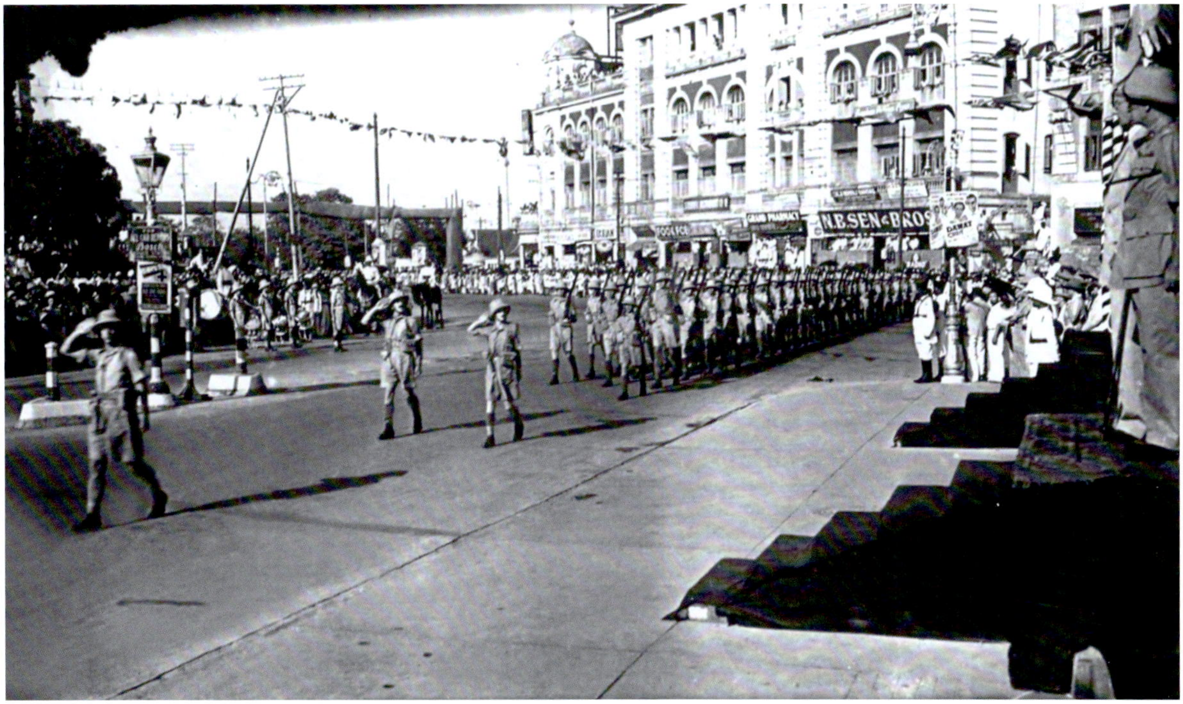

The Calcutta and Presidency Battalion, Auxiliary Force of the British Indian Army, on its way to the Cenotaph for a Remembrance Day parade, during World War II

c. 1944

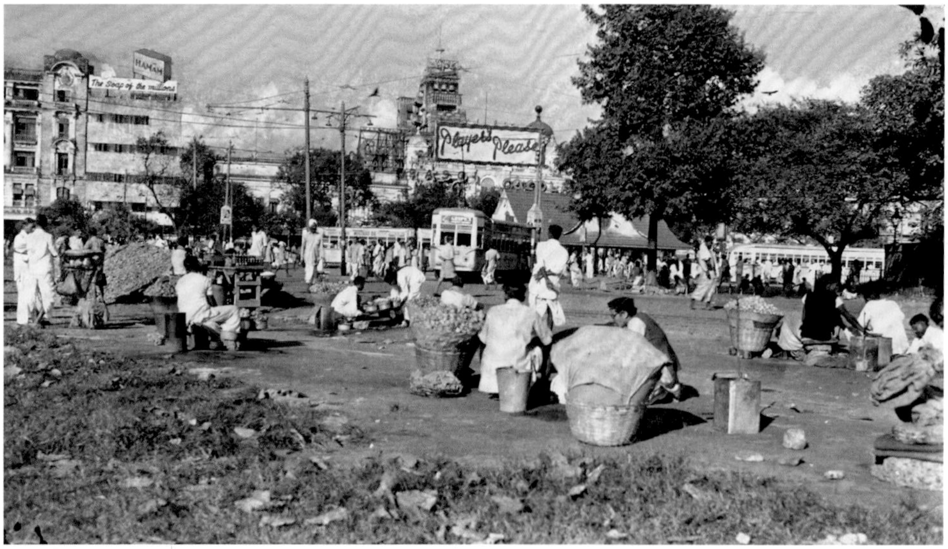

Esplanade Tram Depot. Calcutta is one of few cities in the world where trams are still used for public transport

c. 1948

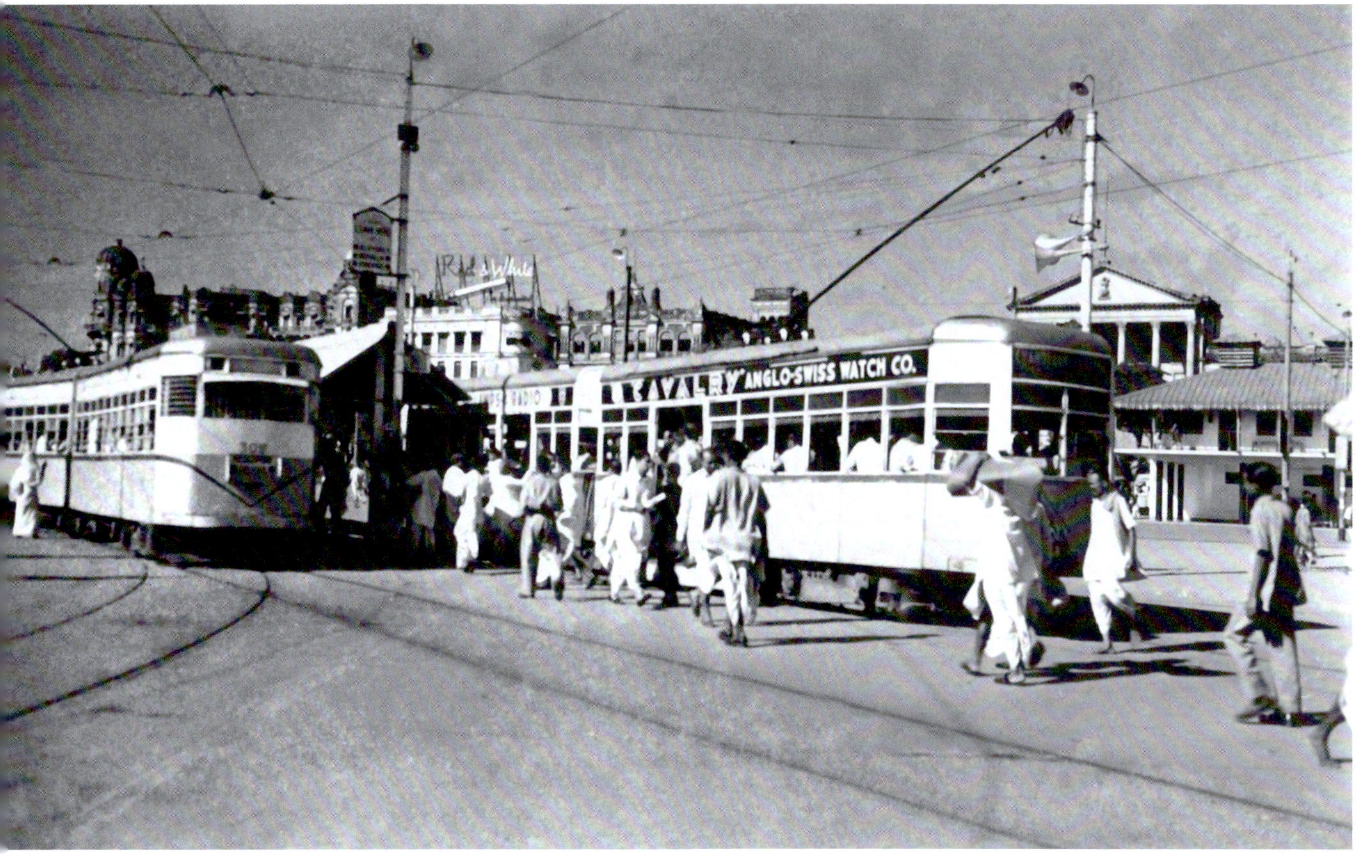

Tram terminus, with the oldest operating electric trams in the world

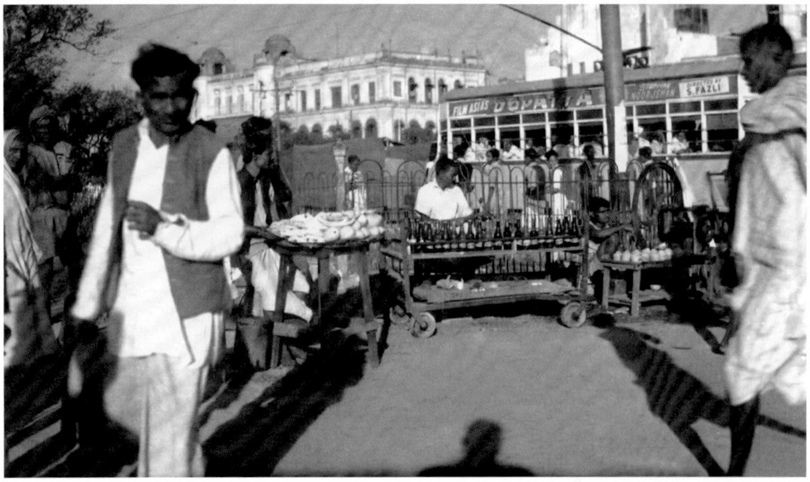

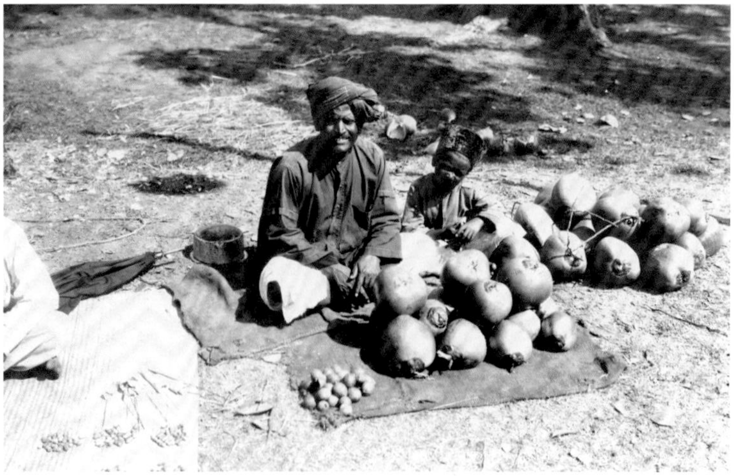

Esplanade, opposite Metro Cinema. Vendors selling fruit salad and sugarcane juice

BELOW A vendor sitting with his son on a hot day, selling coconuts

c. 1961

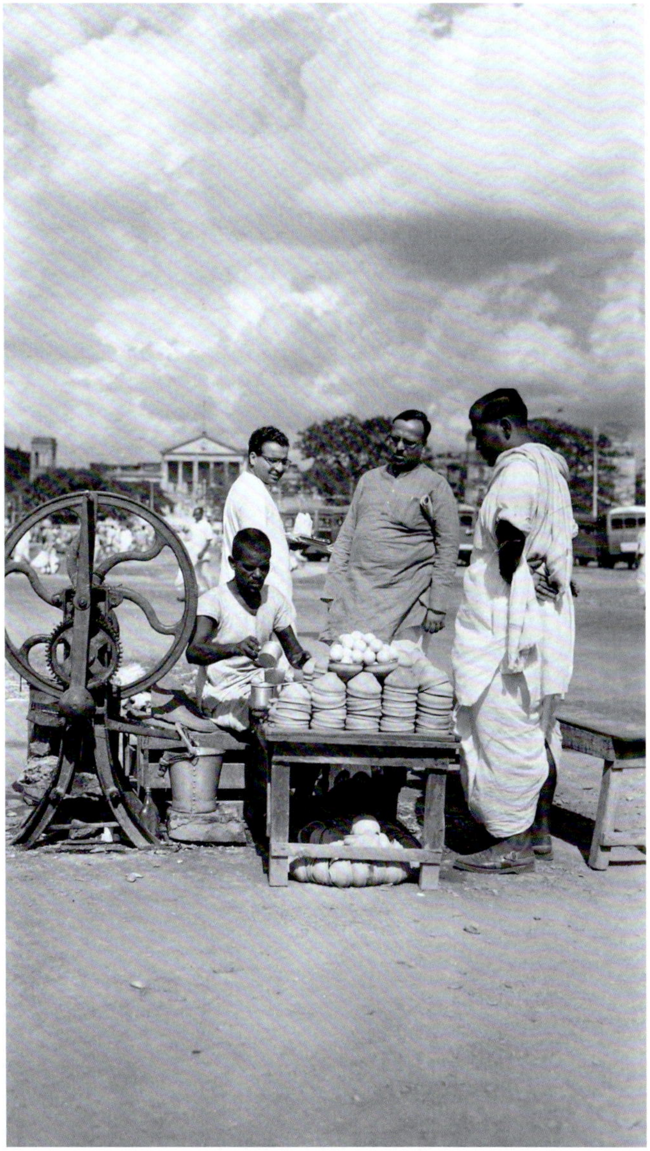

Vendor selling sugarcane juice. Plastic cups have replaced the clay *bhands*

c. 1950

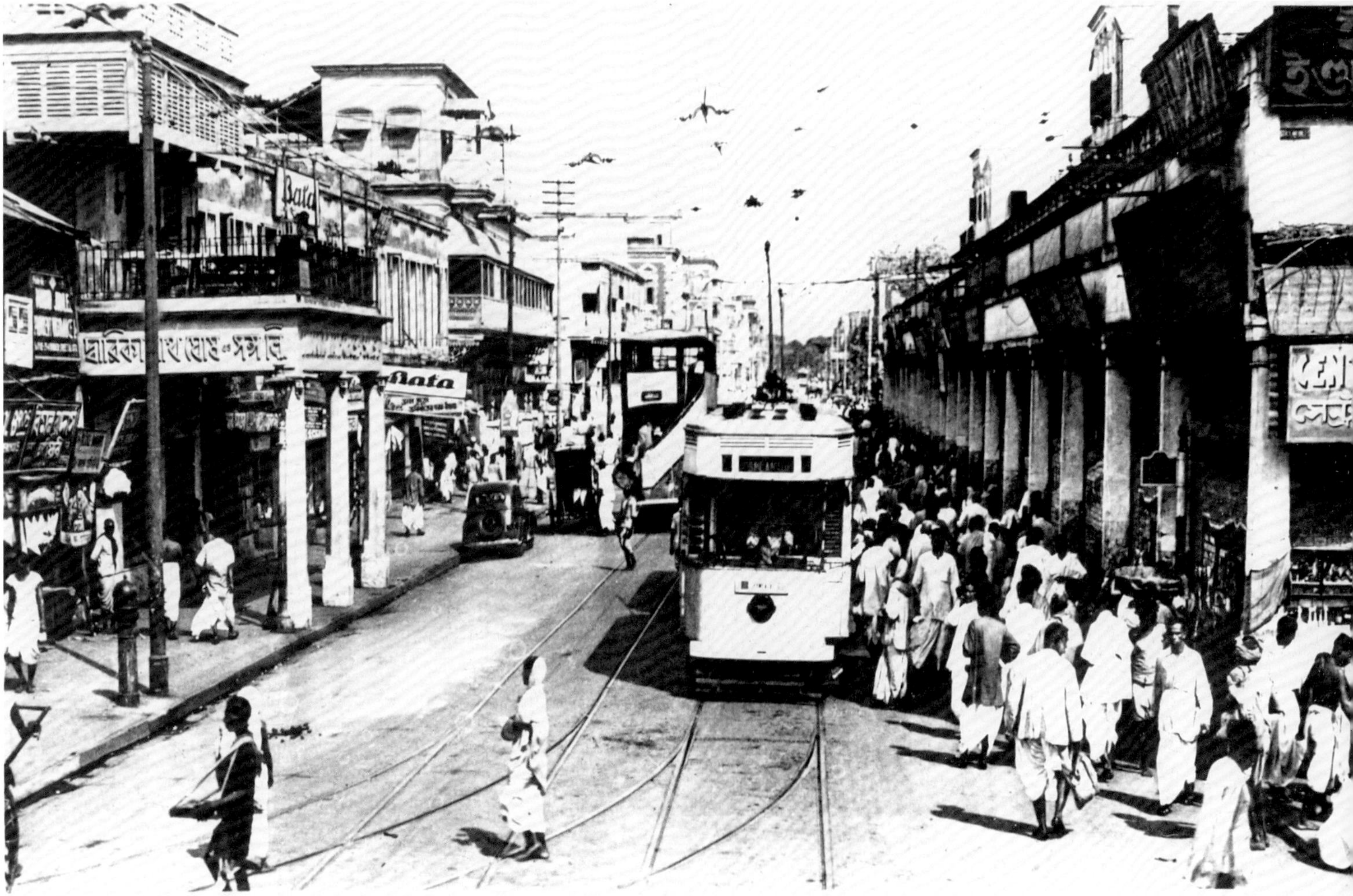

Bustling Hatibagan, close to Shyambazar five-point crossing, has not changed much although most cinemas and theatres have closed down

c. 1948

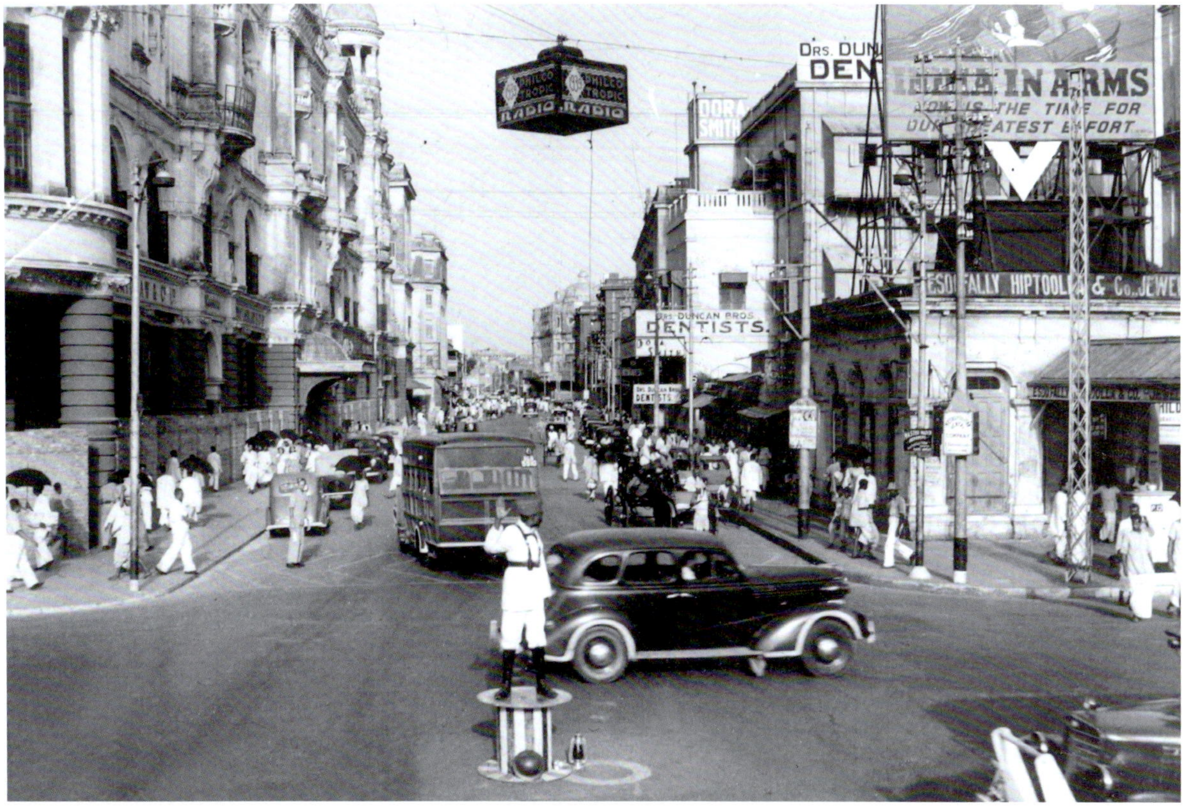

Traffic police on Corporation Street, now S.N. Banerjee Road, and Dharmatala crossing. It was also called the Dorina Crossing after the shop Dora Smith, where fashionable women and actresses did their shopping

c. 1950

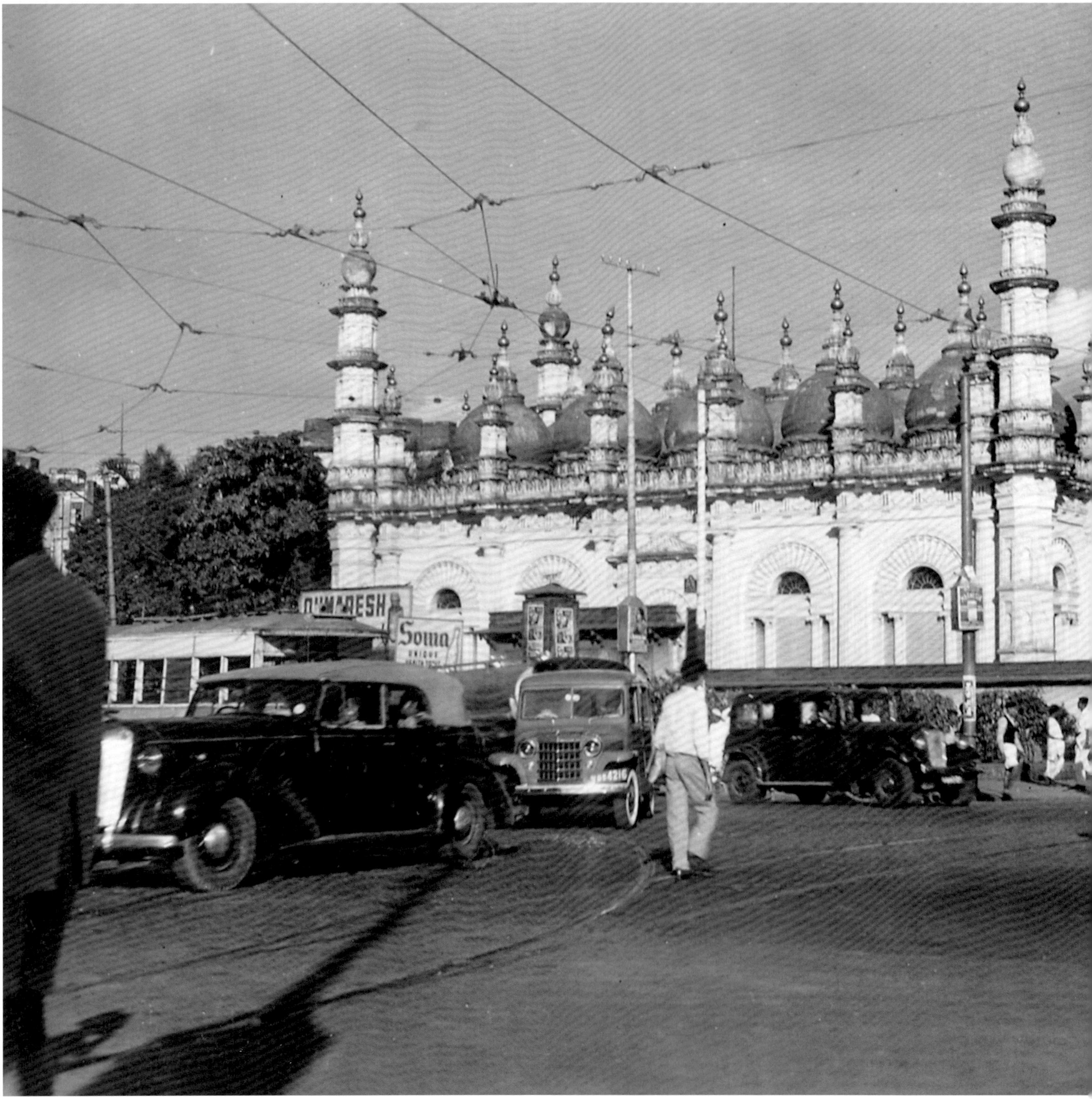
Soma
UNIQUE

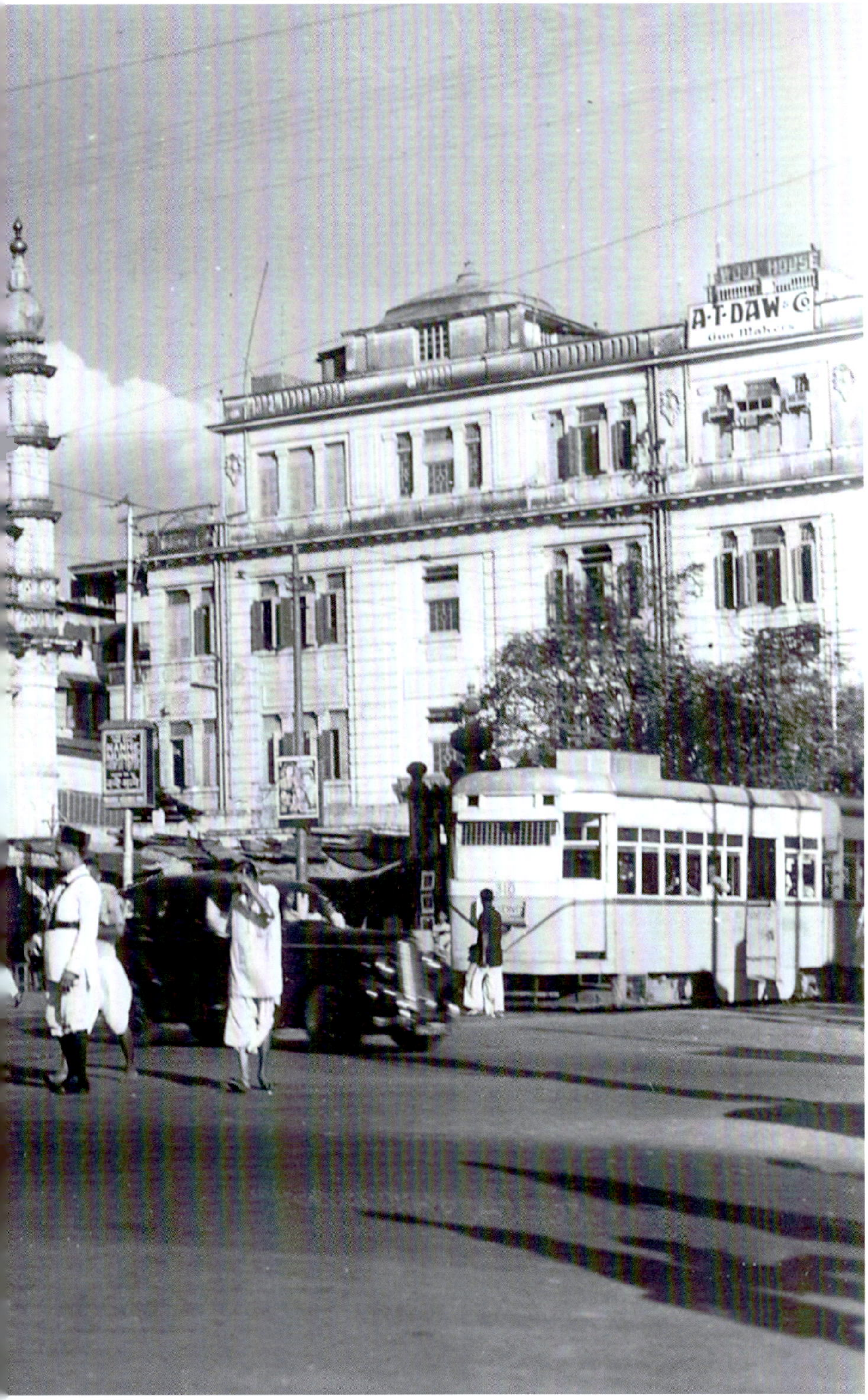

Tipu Sultan Shahi Mosque, located at the Dharmatala Street crossing, was built by Prince Ghulam Mohammed, youngest son of Tipu Sultan, in 1832

c. 1945

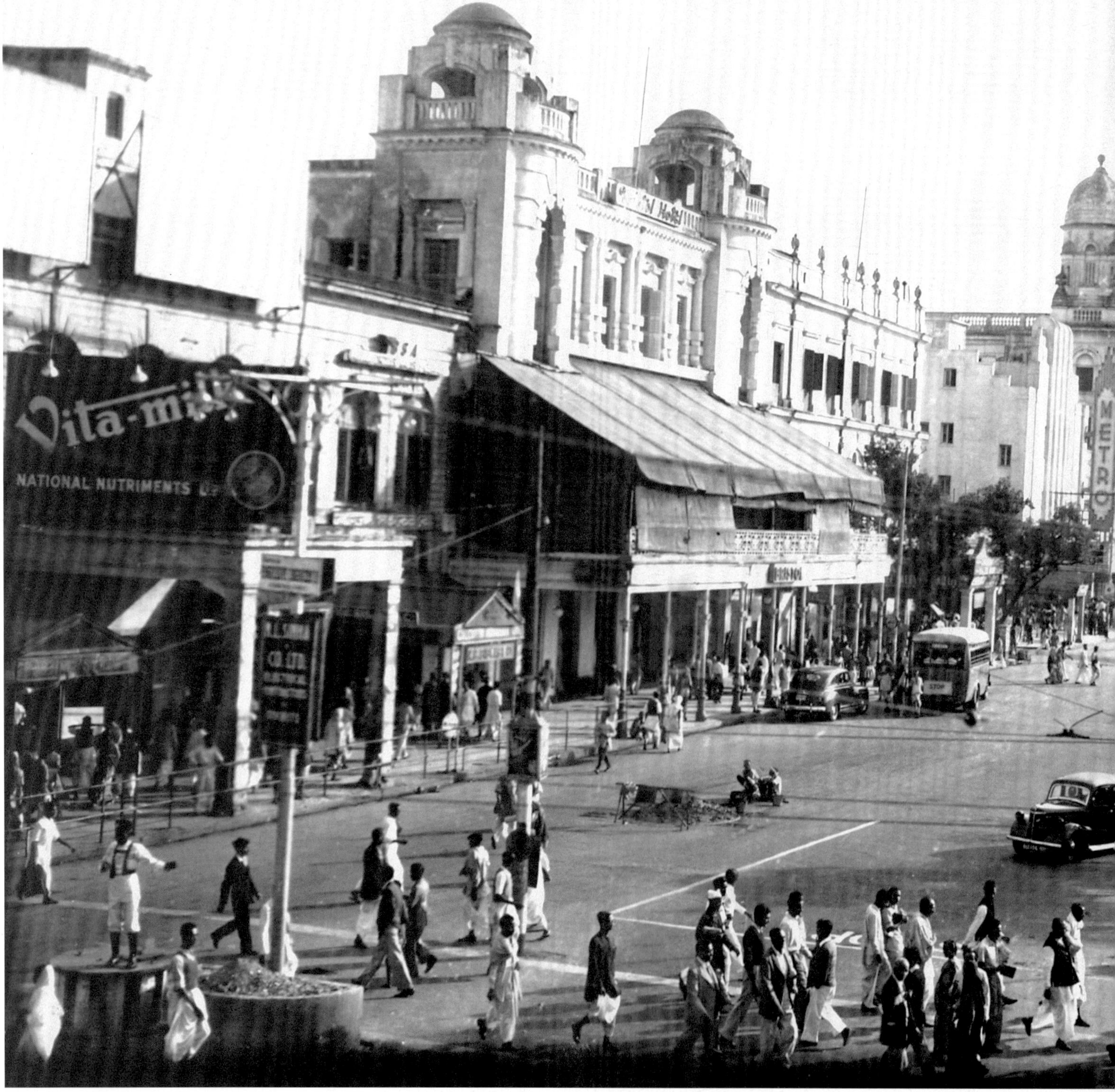
Vita-milk
NATIONAL NUTRIMENTS LTD
METRO
STOP

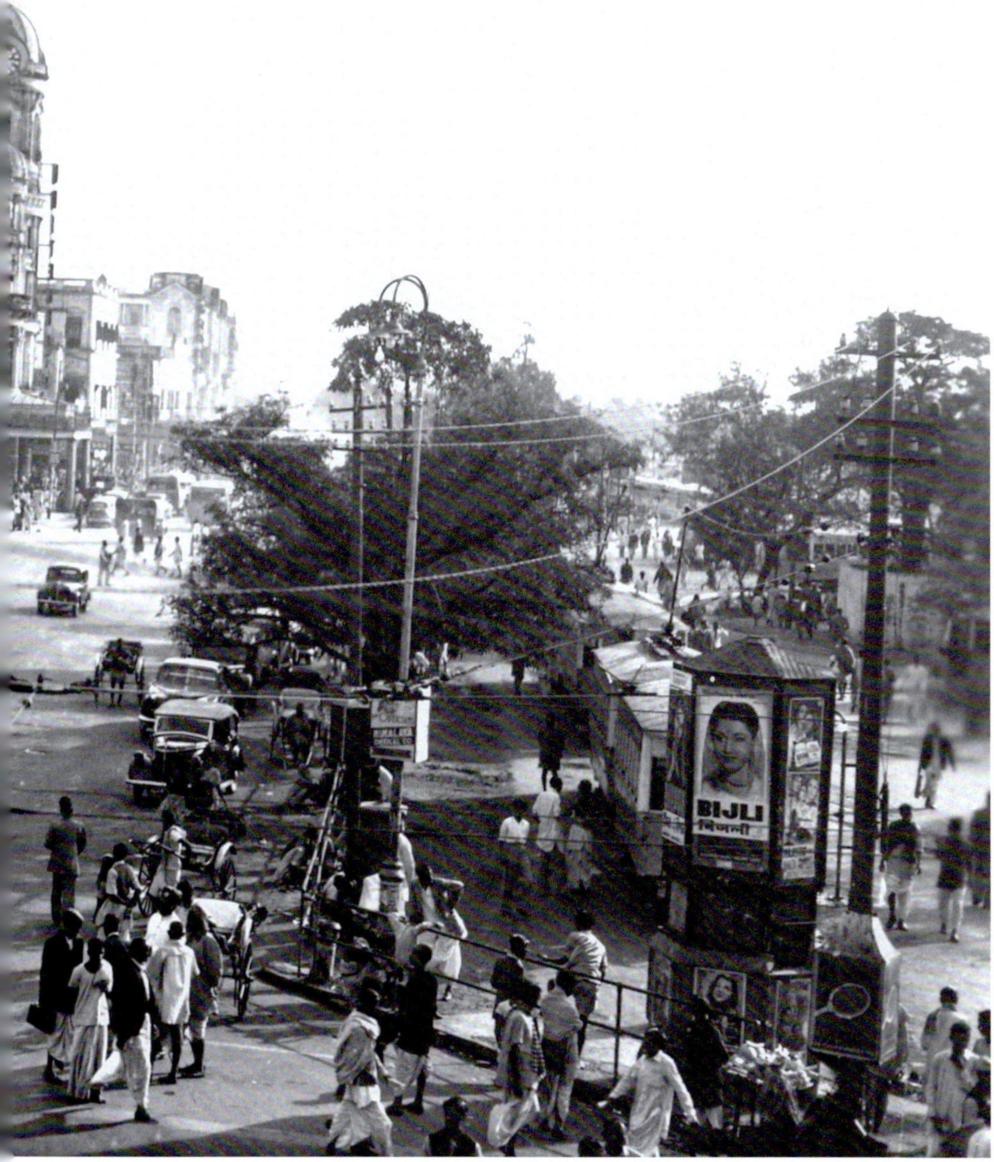

Chowringhee and Dharmatala crossing

c. 1949

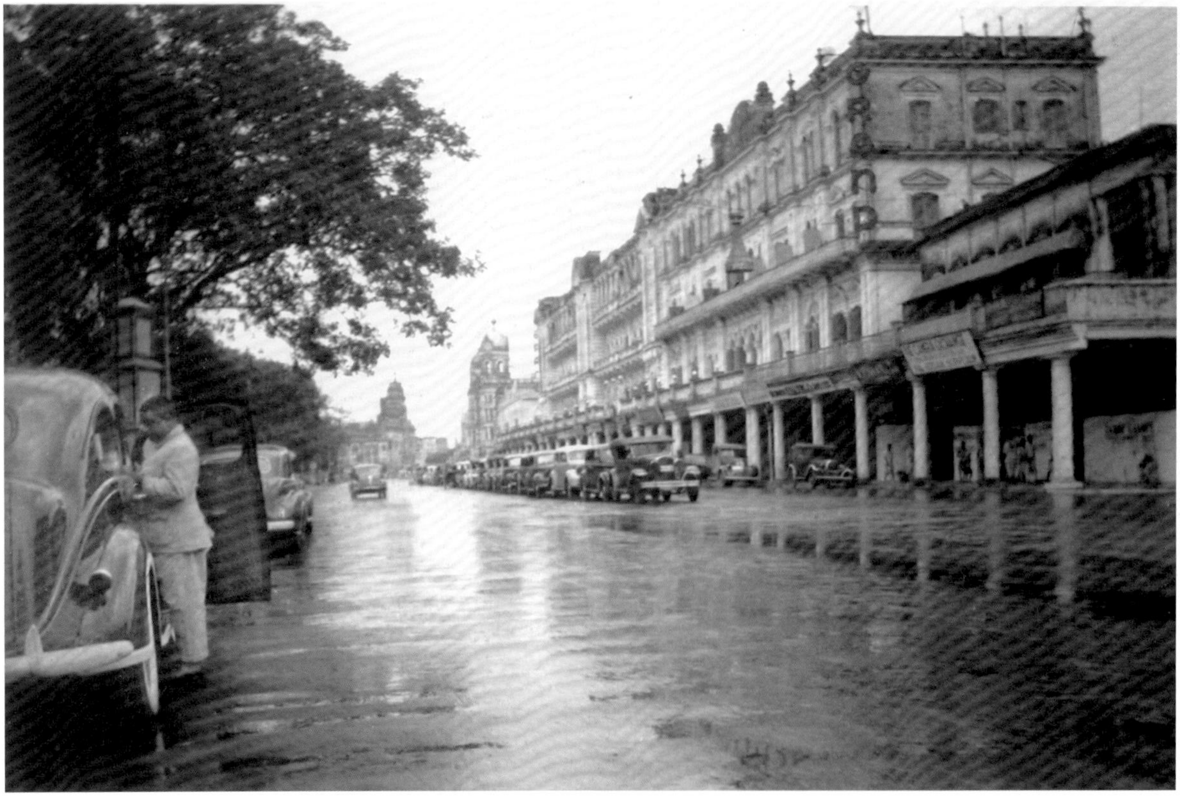

Chowringhee Road on a wet day. Cars used to be parked along the centre of the road in the 1940s

c. 1943

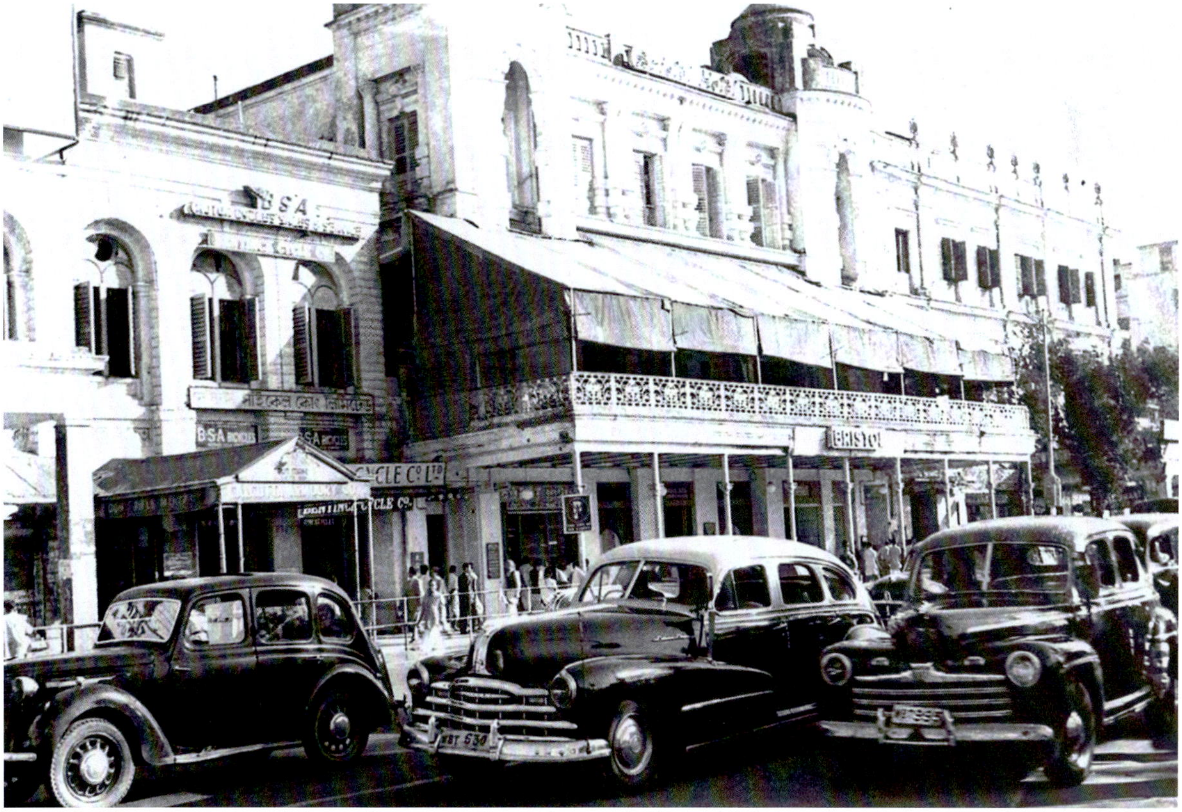

Bristol Hotel on Chowringhee Road

c. 1955

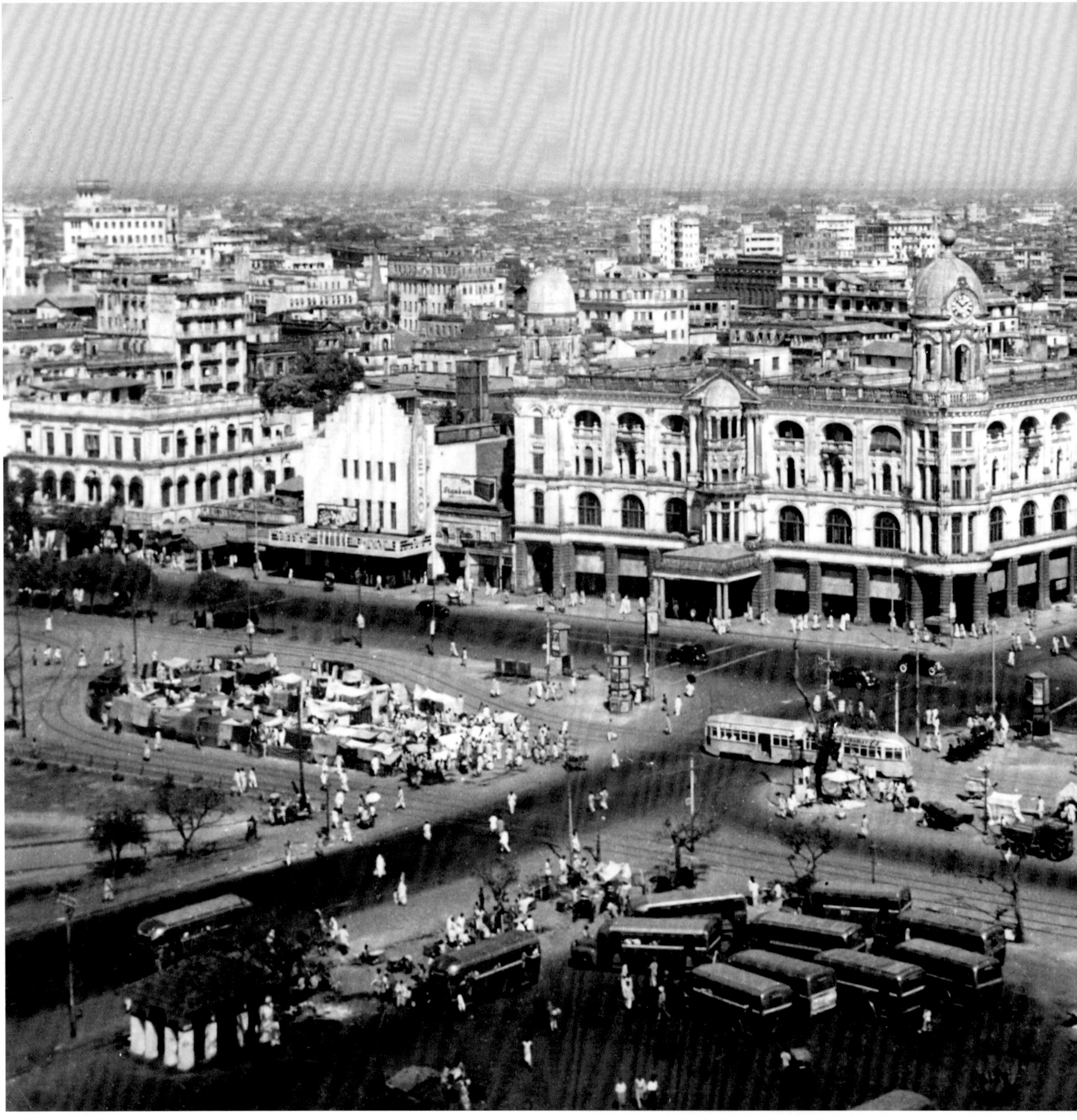

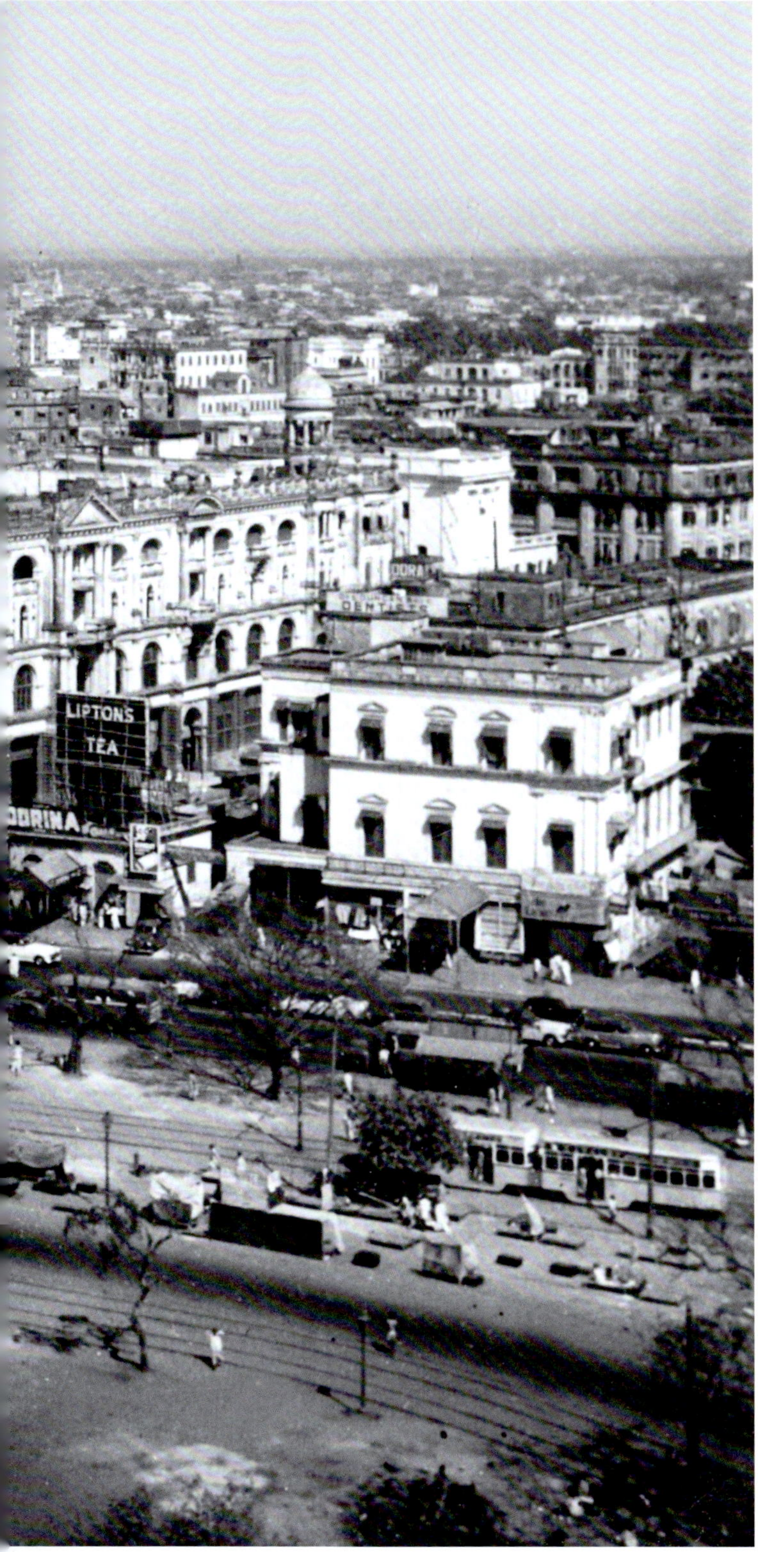

Panoramic view of Chowringhee Road and Corporation Street, now known as S.N. Banerjee Road, with a row of beautiful buildings. It was taken from Ochterlony Monument, later renamed Shahid Minar. Most of the buildings remain. Metro cinema is being made over

c. 1948

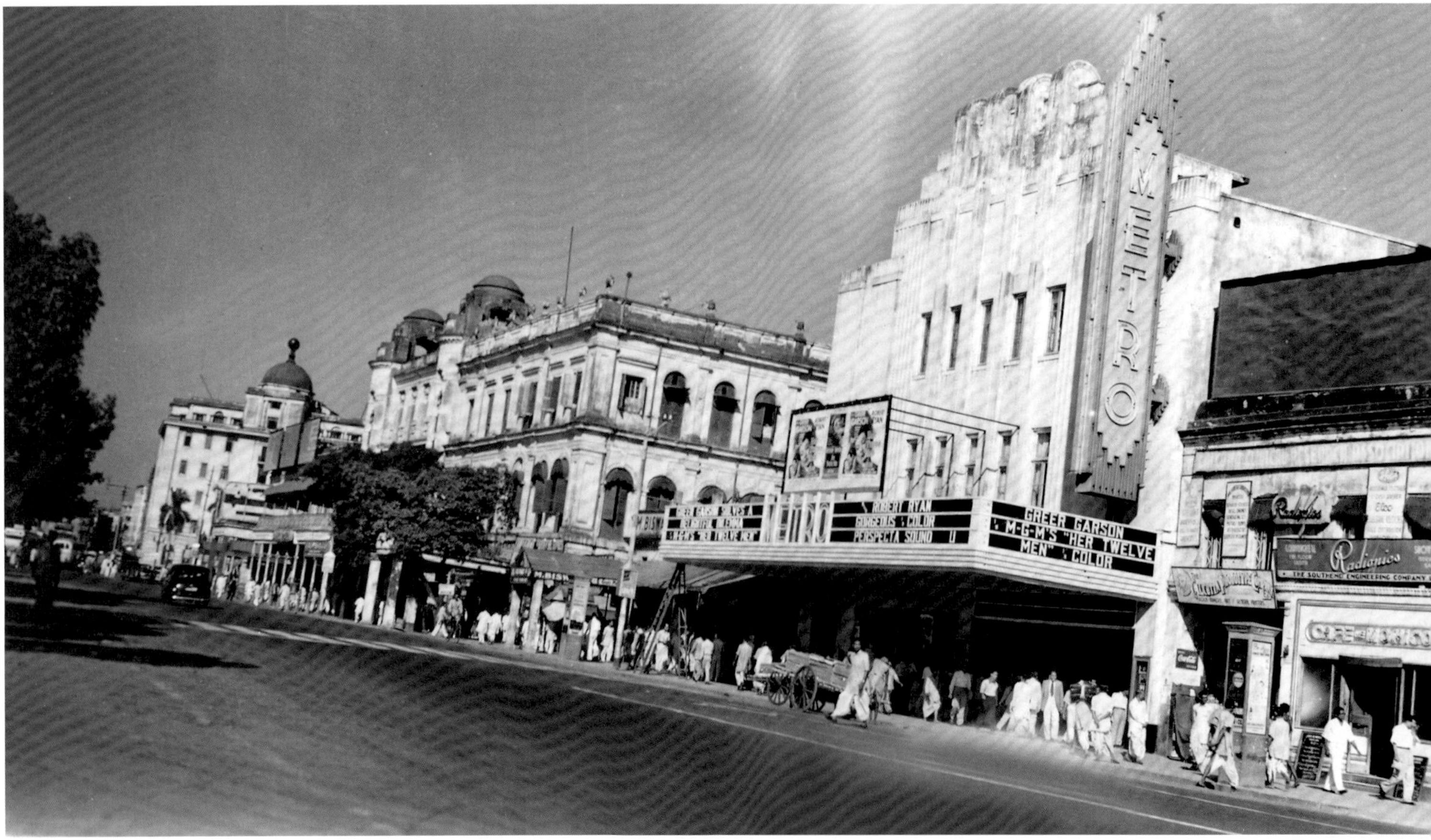

Metro cinema on Chowringhee Road with the dome of Victoria House seen in the distance

c. 1955

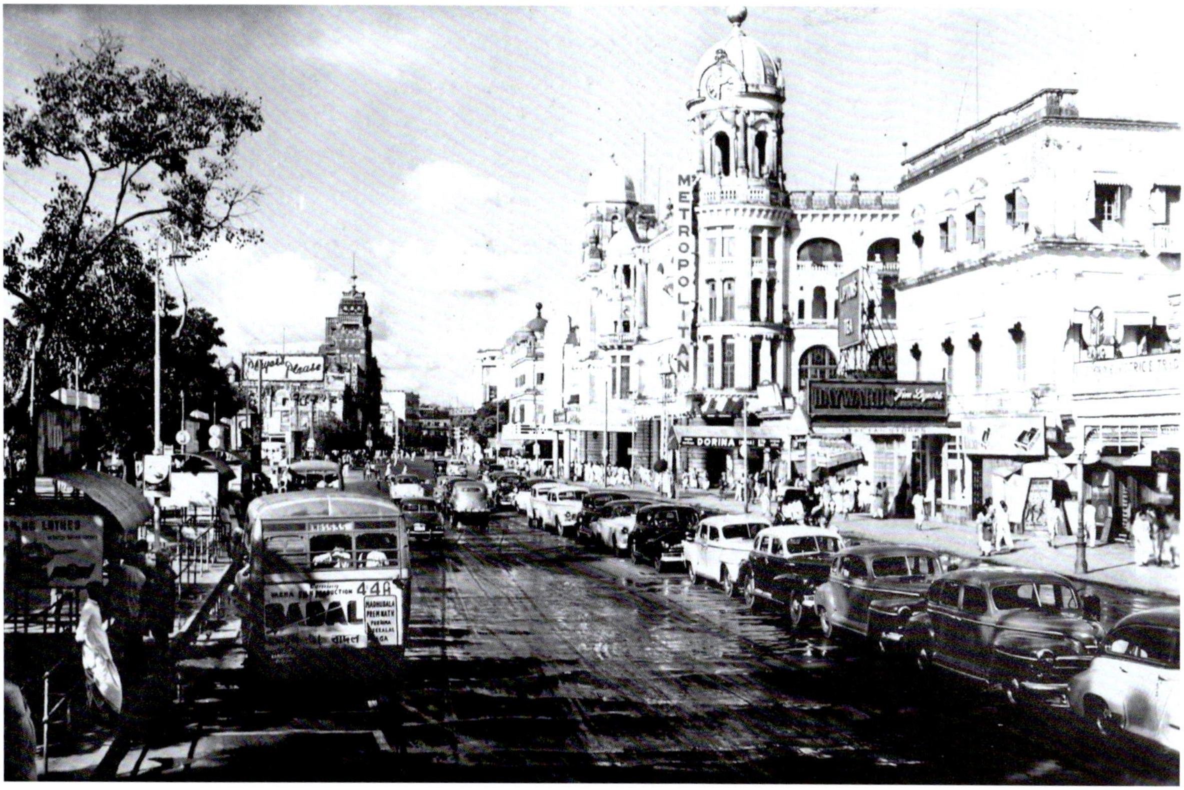

Metropolitan Building on Chowringhee with cars parked along the centre of the road

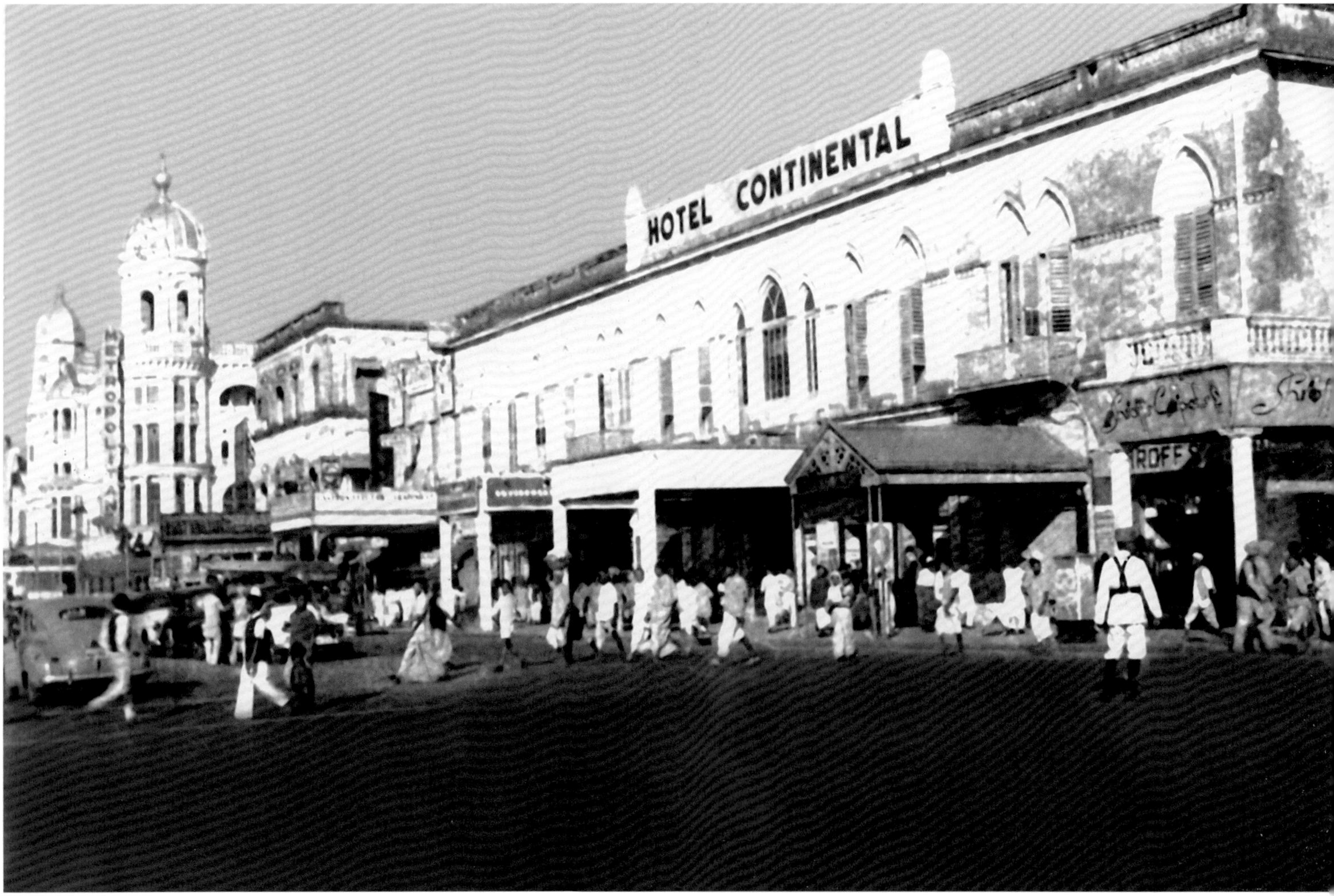

Hotel Continental and Metropolitan building on Chowringhee Road. The hotel was demolished. Today the Peerless Inn stands in its place

c. 1950

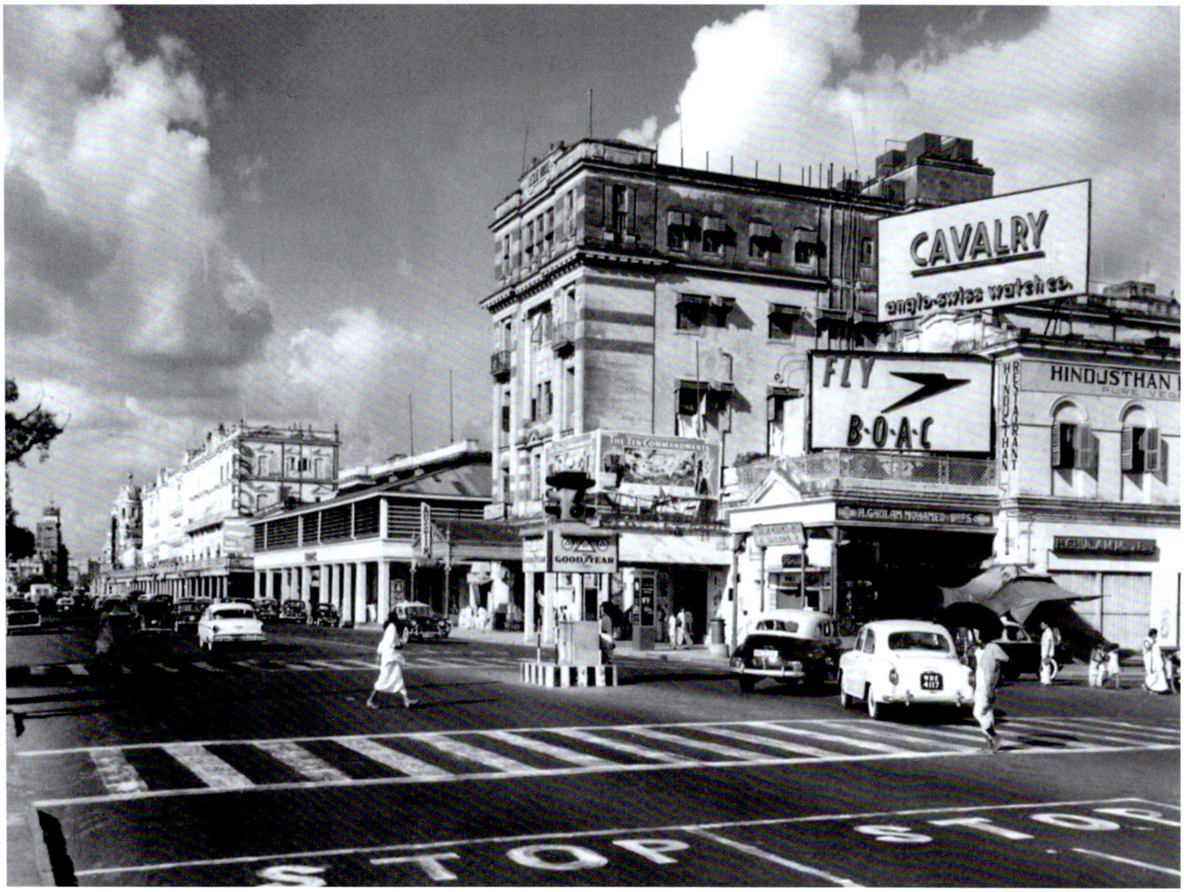

Chowringhee Road, showing Grand Hotel, the night club Firpo's, and the tiny Tiger cinema, now a garment store

c. 1960

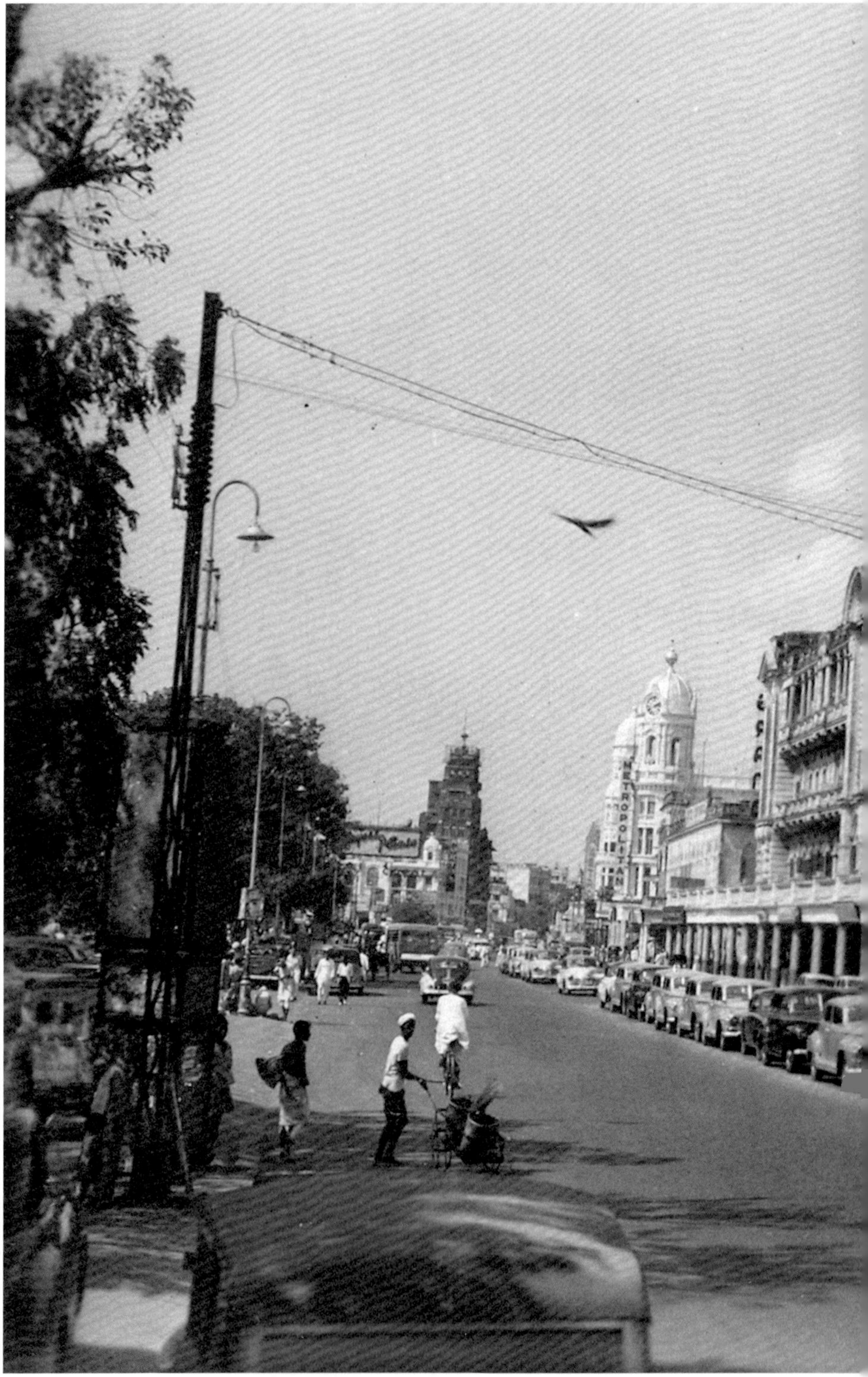

A broad view of Chowringhee, close to the Lindsay Street crossing. The dark profile of Tower House, once Calcutta's tallest building, at the Bentinck Street crossing, is visible at the far end

c. 1952

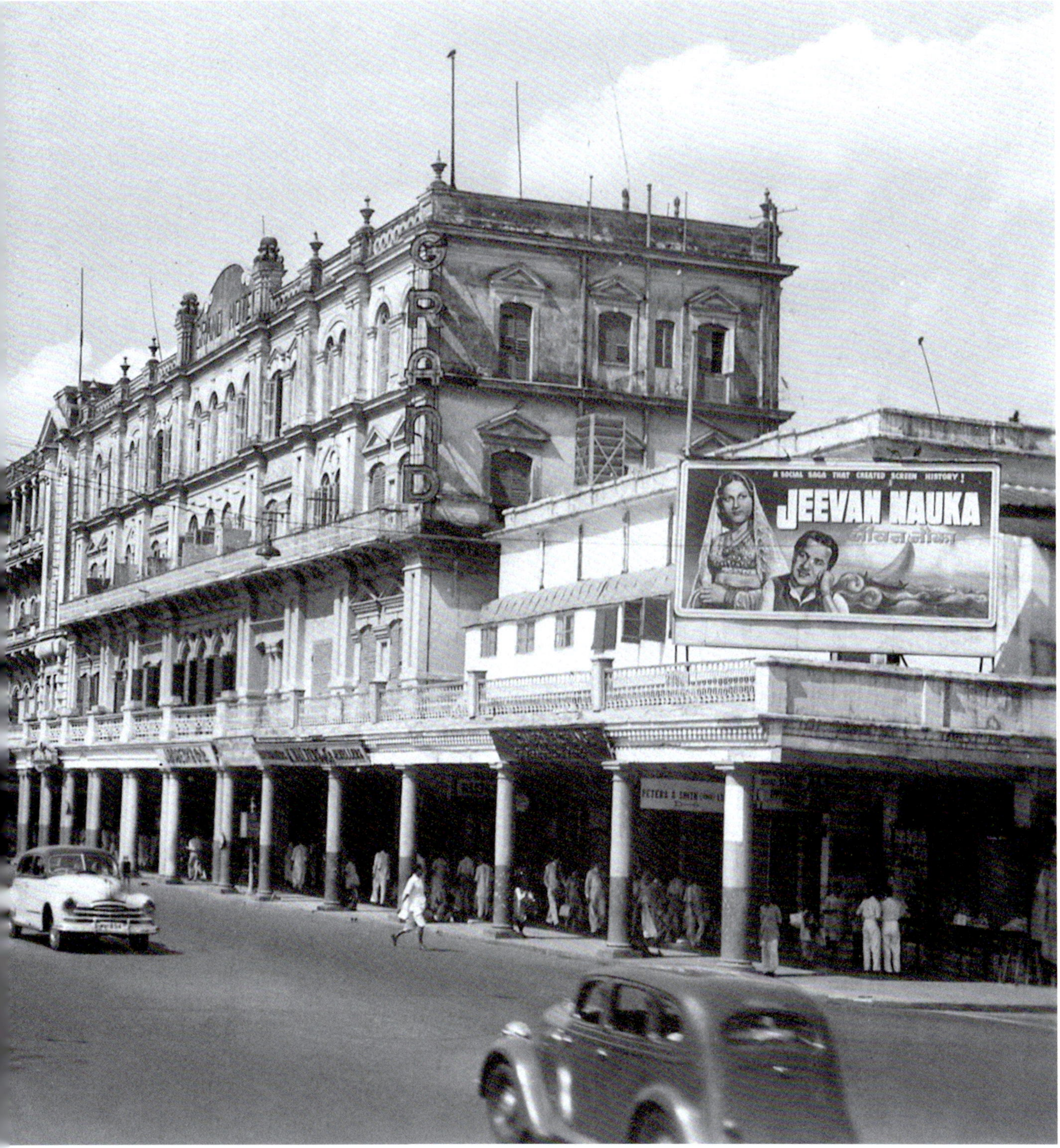
GRAND
A SOCIAL SAGA THAT CREATED SCREEN HISTORY !
JEEVAN NAUKA

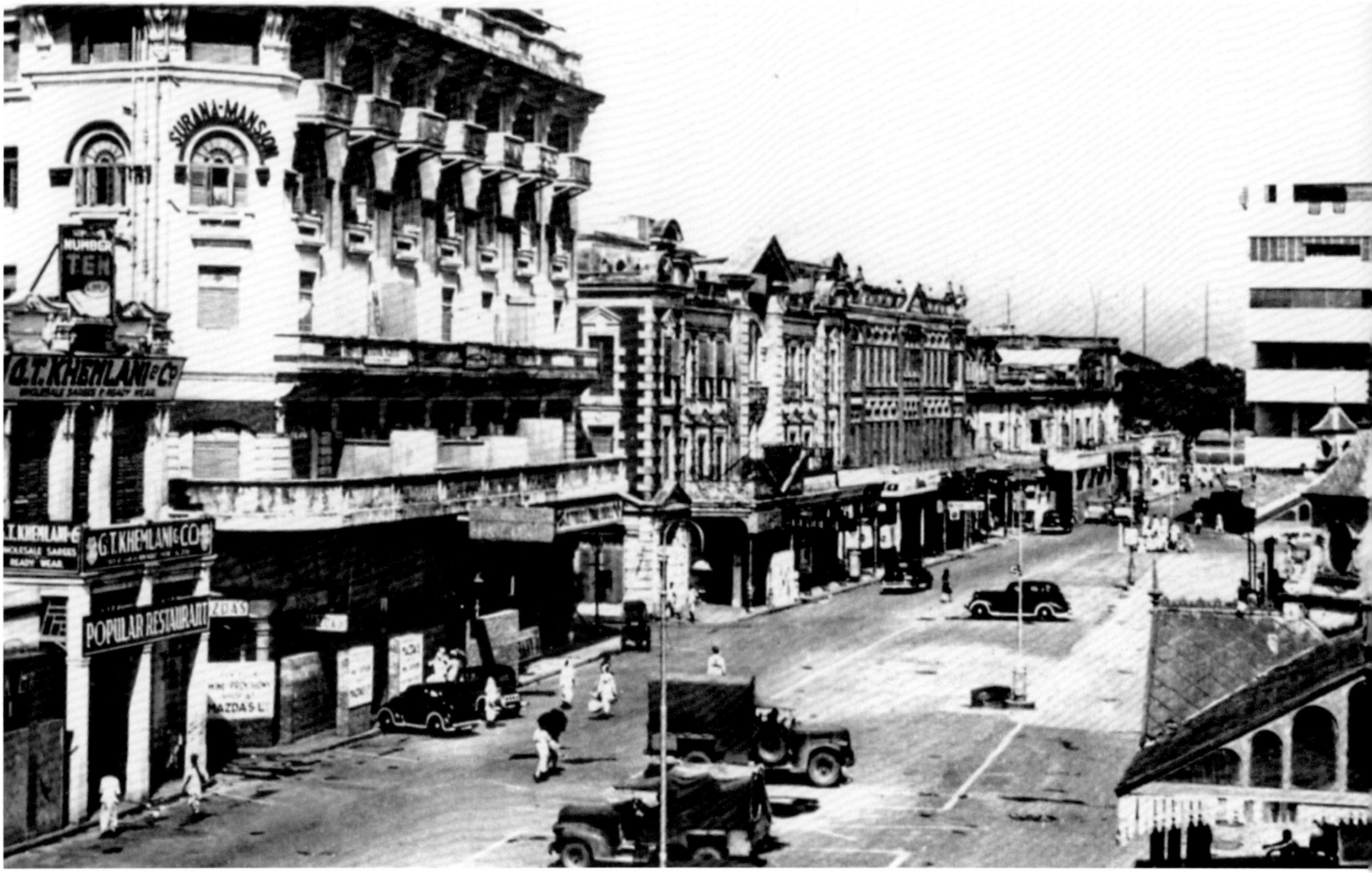

Lindsay Street, connecting Chowringhee Road and Free School Street, today known as Mirza Ghalib Street, has popular landmarks like New Market and what was once Globe Cinema

c. 1945

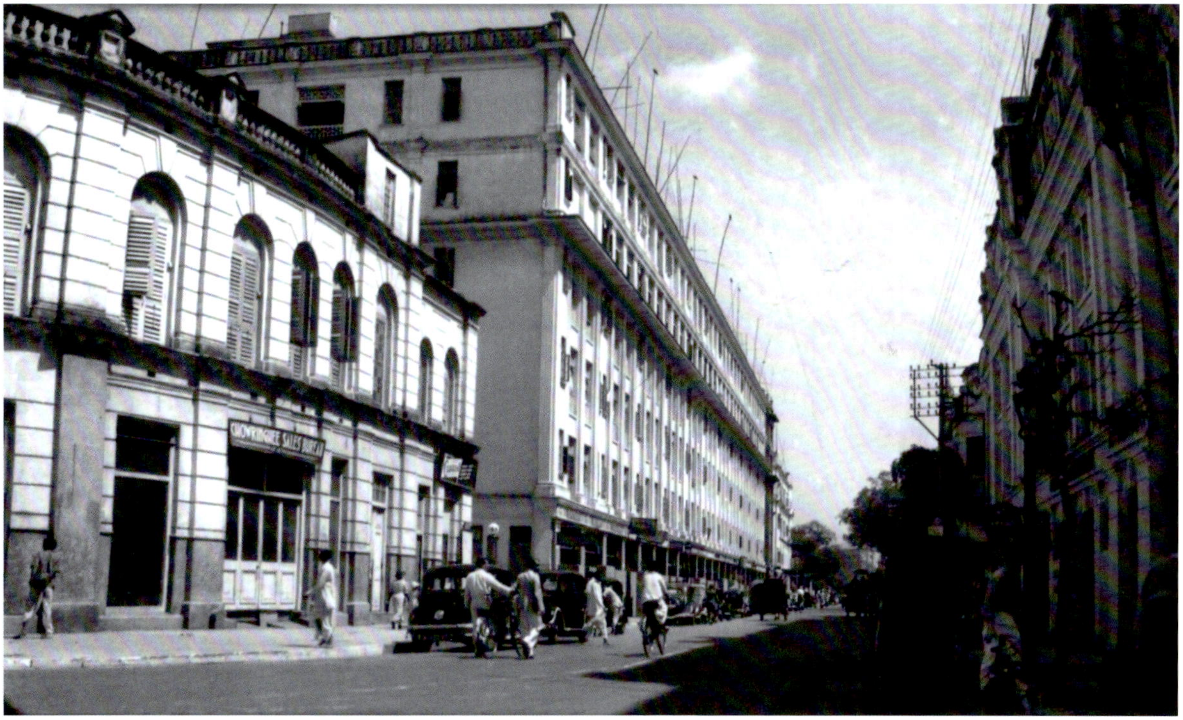

Karnani Mansion (left) at the crossing of Park Street and Free School Street, now known as Mirza Ghalib Street. Opposite it is Park Mansion

c. 1948

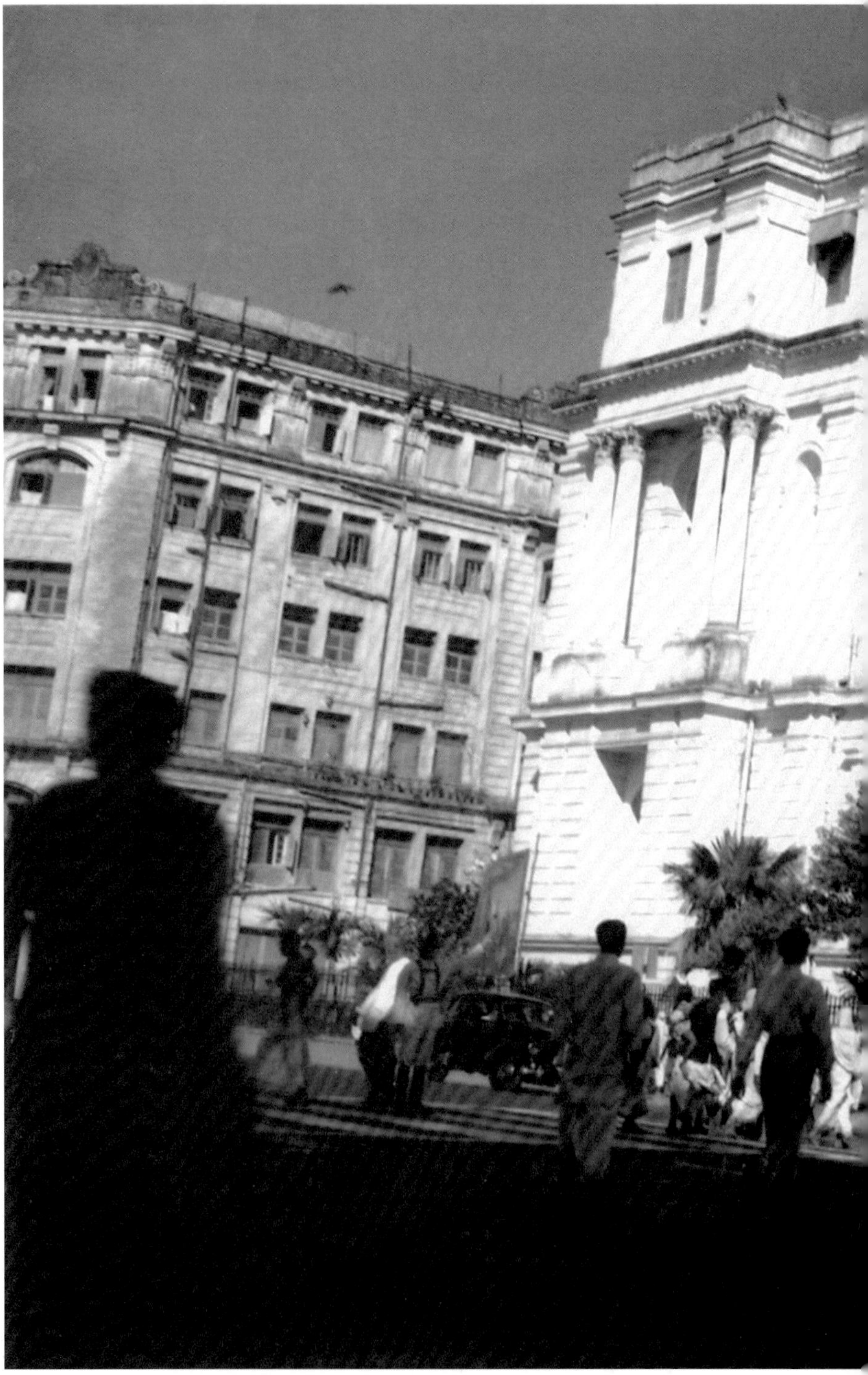

The Indian Museum is one of the largest and oldest museums in the world, dating back to 1814. It has a vast collection of rare artifacts of archeology, art, anthropology, zoology, and geology

c. 1950

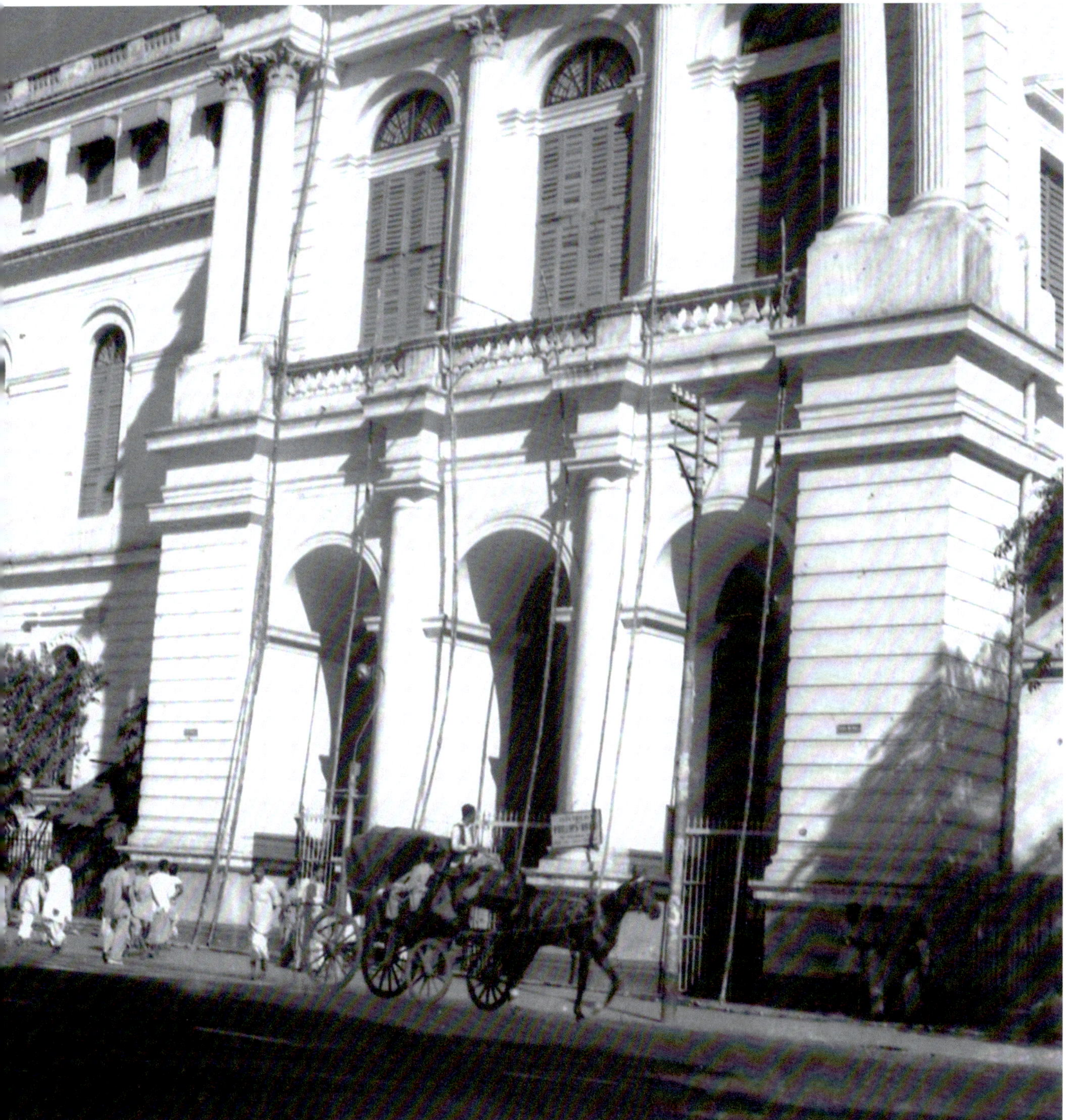

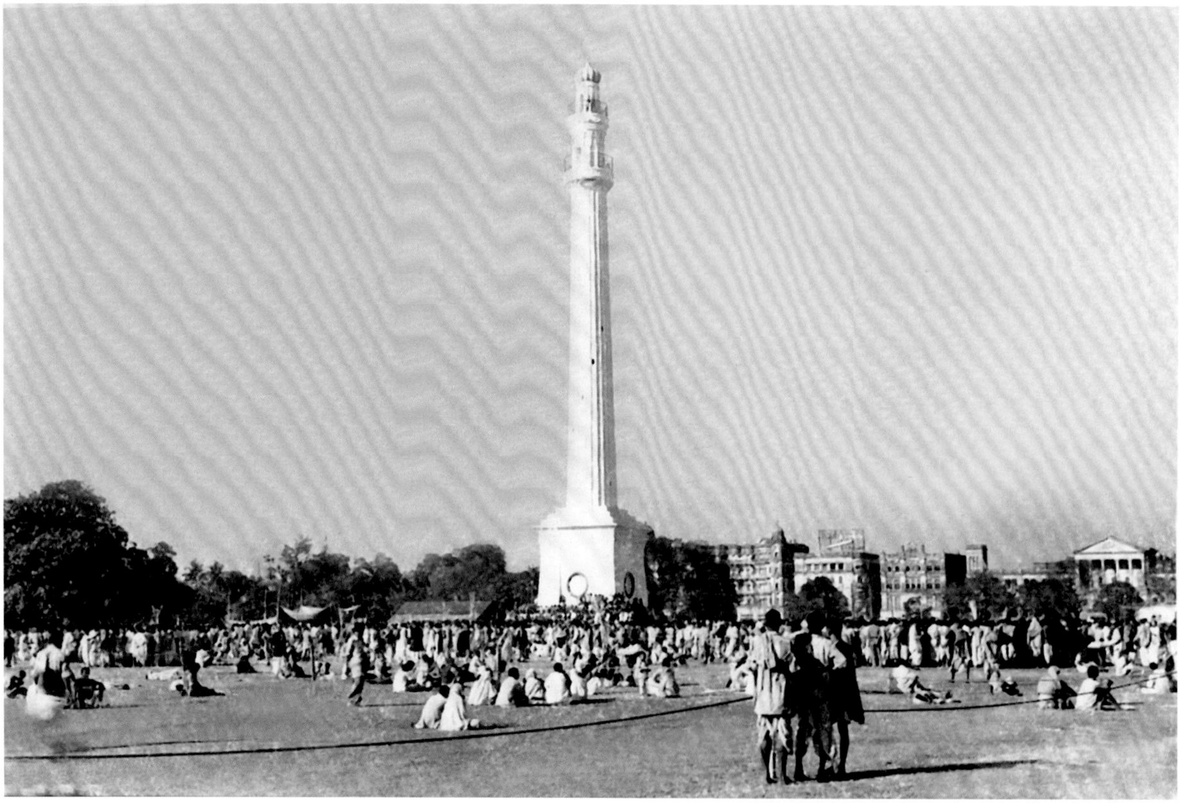

Shahid Minar, formerly known as Ochterlony Monument, erected in 1838 in memory of Major General Sir Ochterlony, commander of the British East-India Company. In August 1969, it was rededicated to the martyrs of the Indian Freedom Movement and renamed Shahid Minar, which means Martyrs' Monument

c. 1954

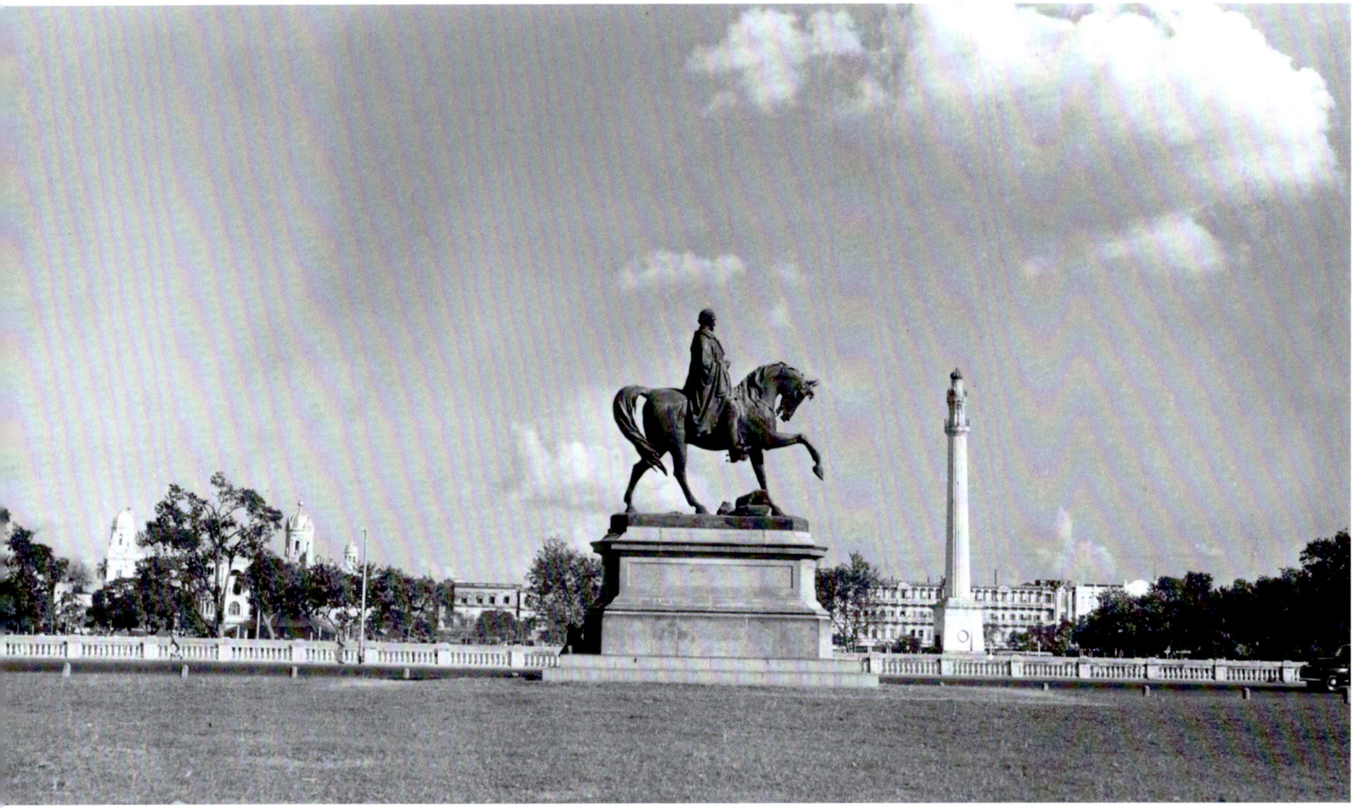

The 19th century equestrian statue of Lord Hardinge on Red Road with the Maidan and Ochterloney Monument behind it

c. 1948

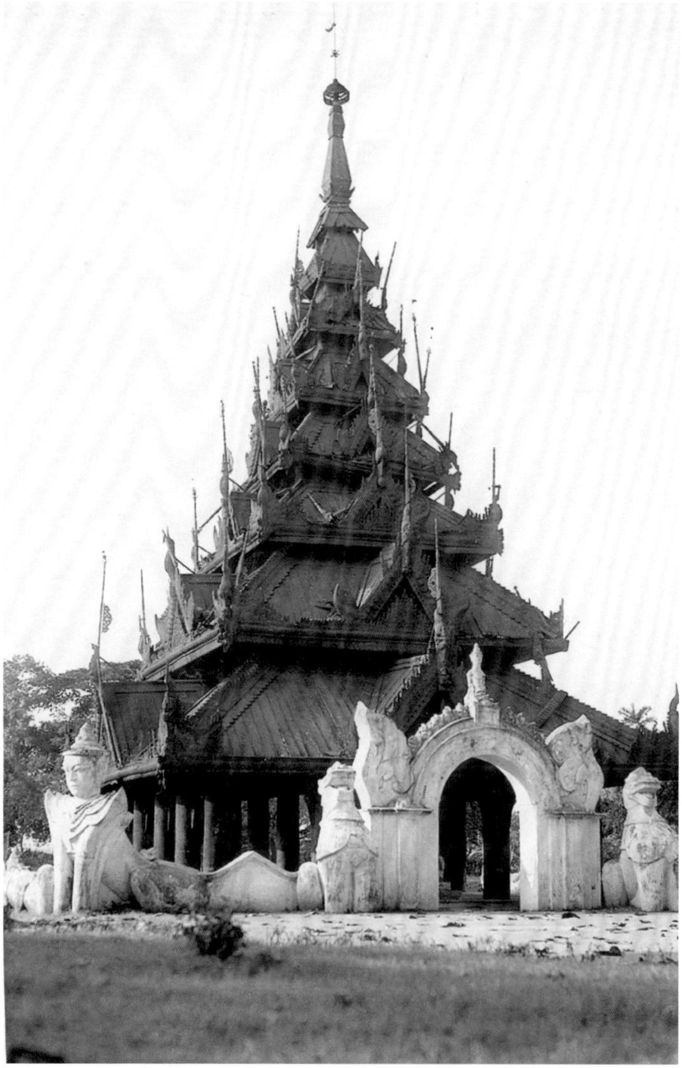

The Burmese Pagoda in Eden Gardens, situated at the northern end of the Calcutta Maidan. The Pagoda was brought from Prome in Burma by Lord Dalhousie and erected in the gardens in 1854

c. 1948

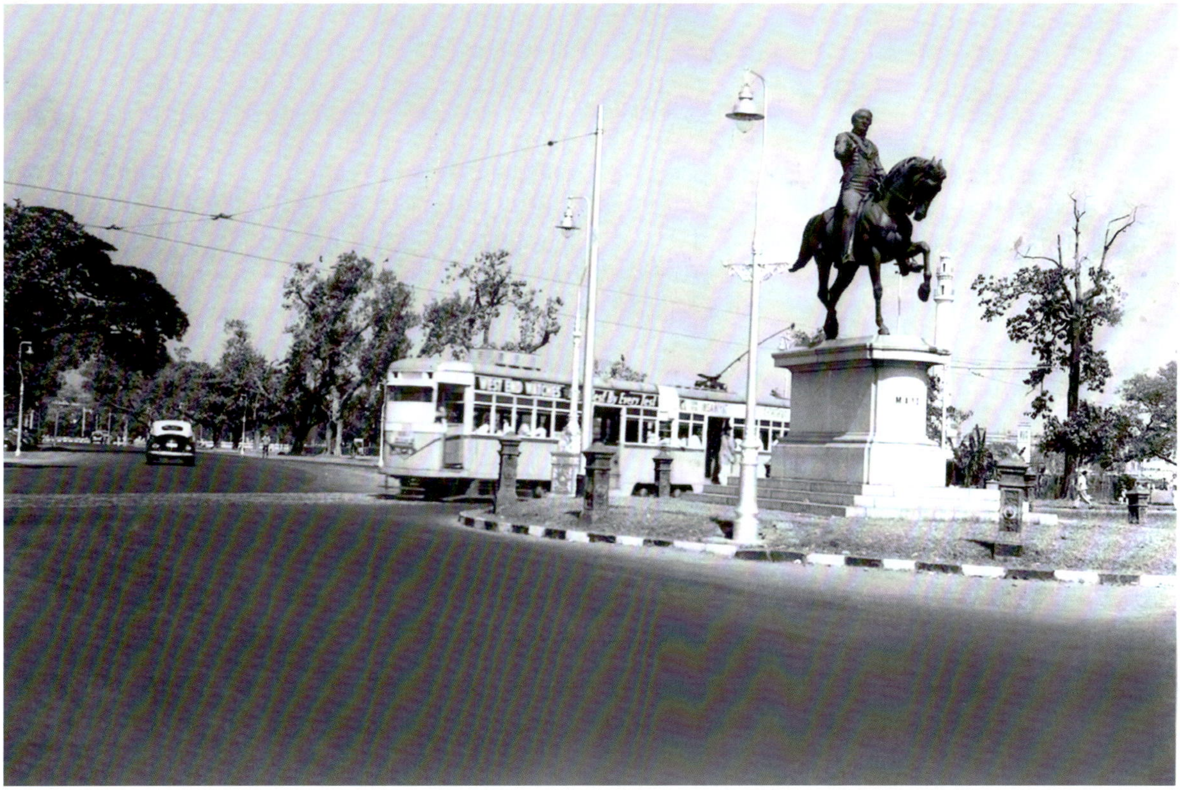

Lord Mayo's equestrian statue on Red Road

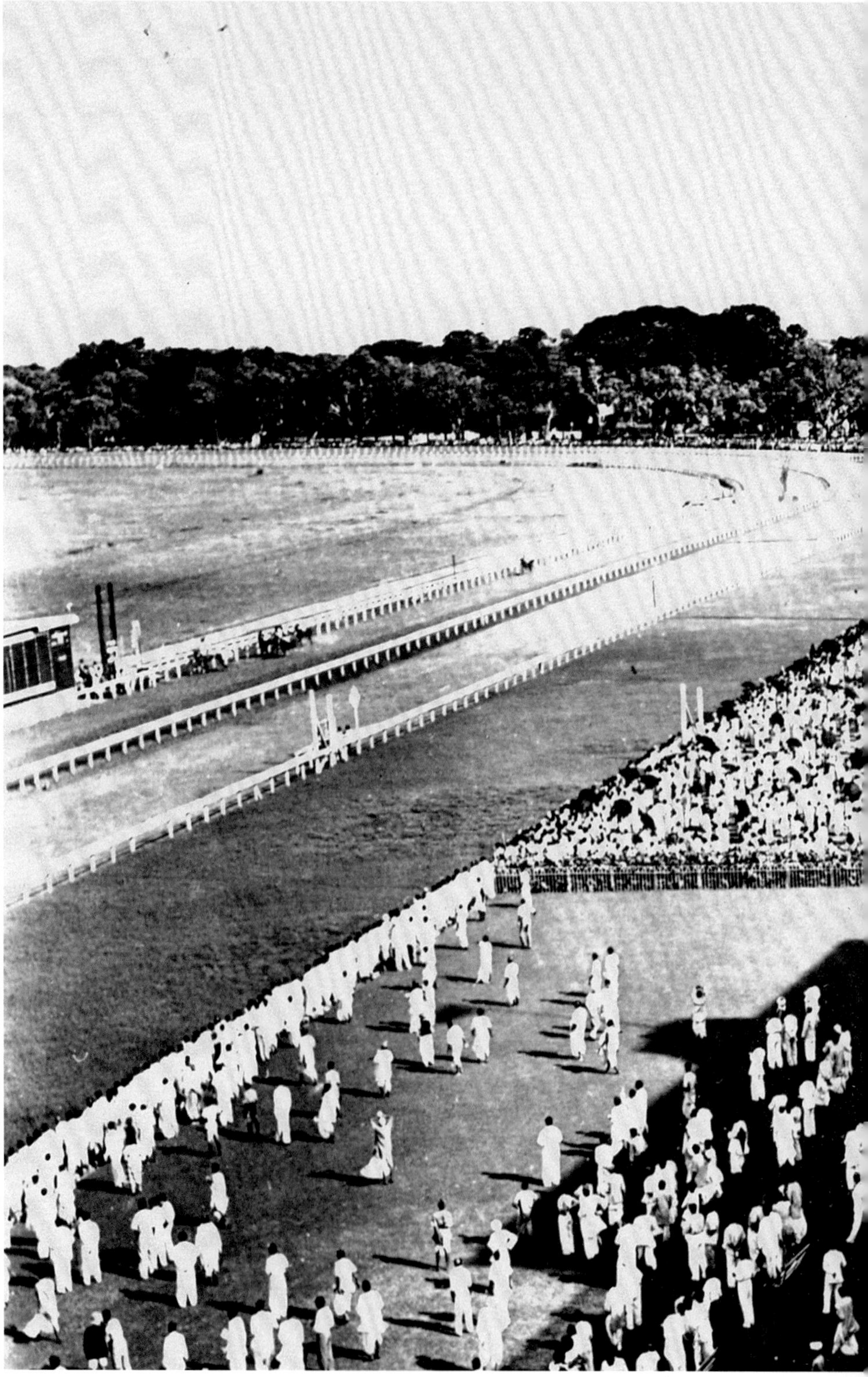

The Independence Cup is being run in 1953 at Calutta Race Course, one of the oldest horse race courses in India, built in 1820. The Royal Calcutta Turf Club was founded in 1847

c. 1953

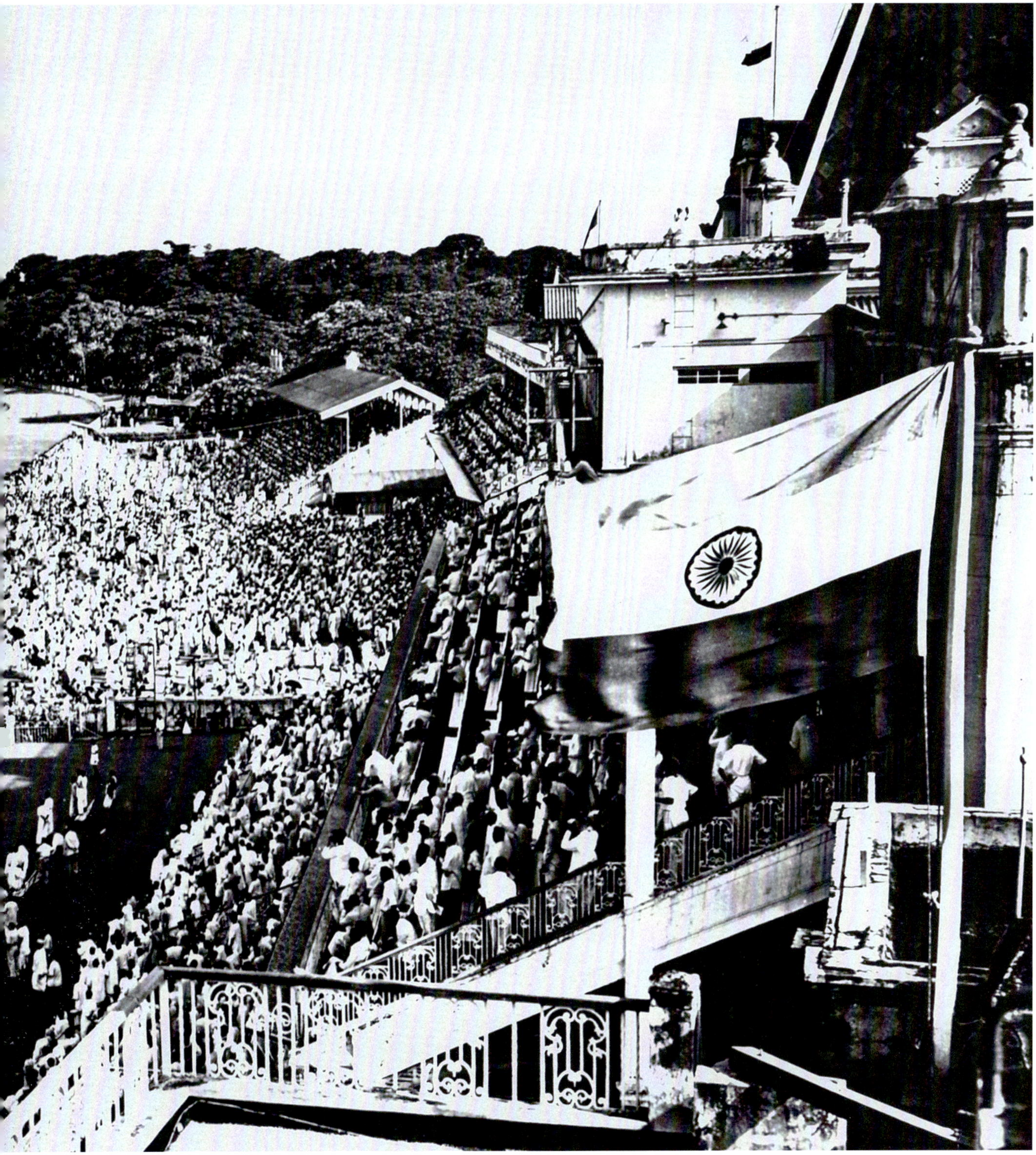

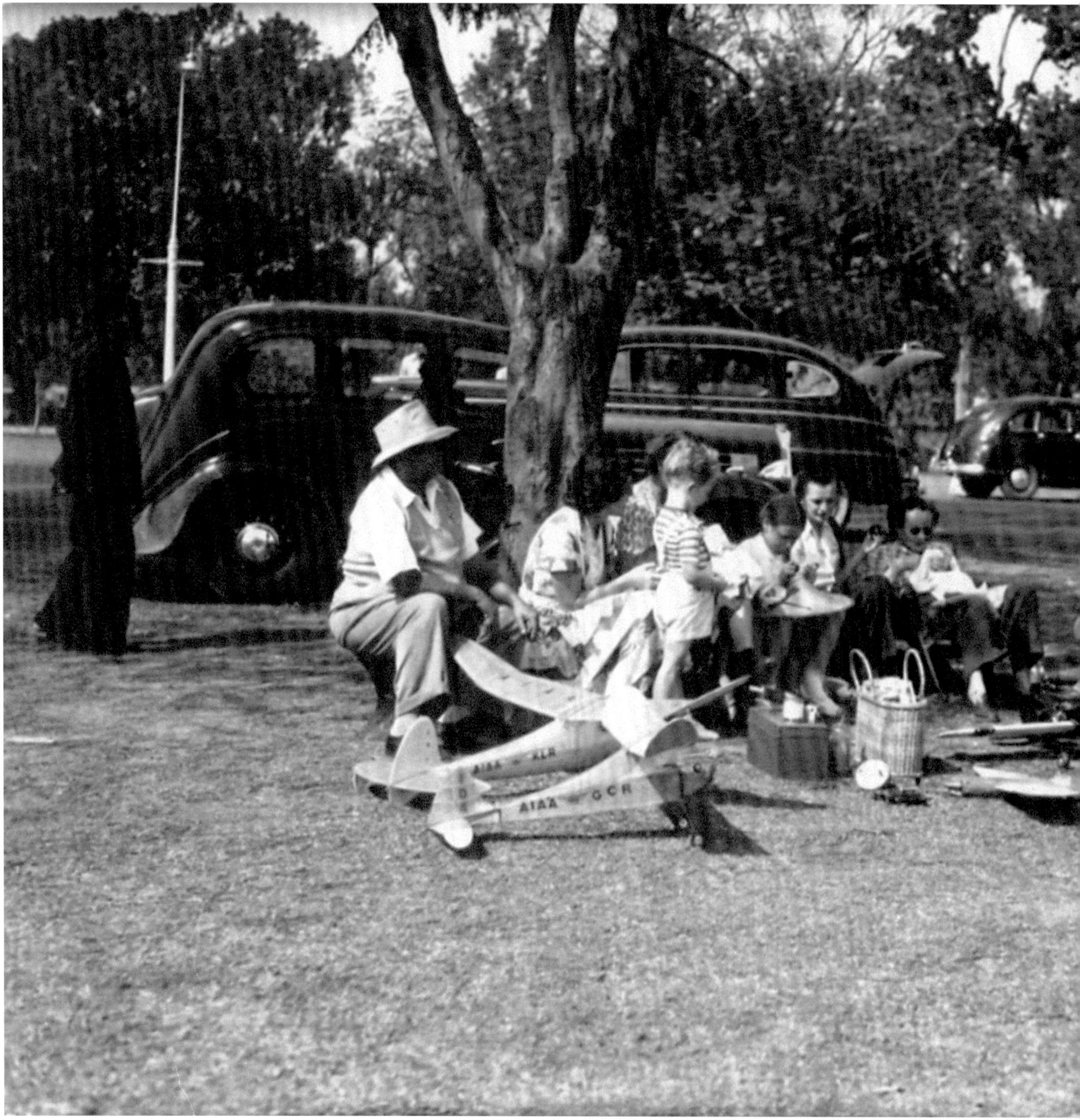
AIAA ALR
AIAA GCR

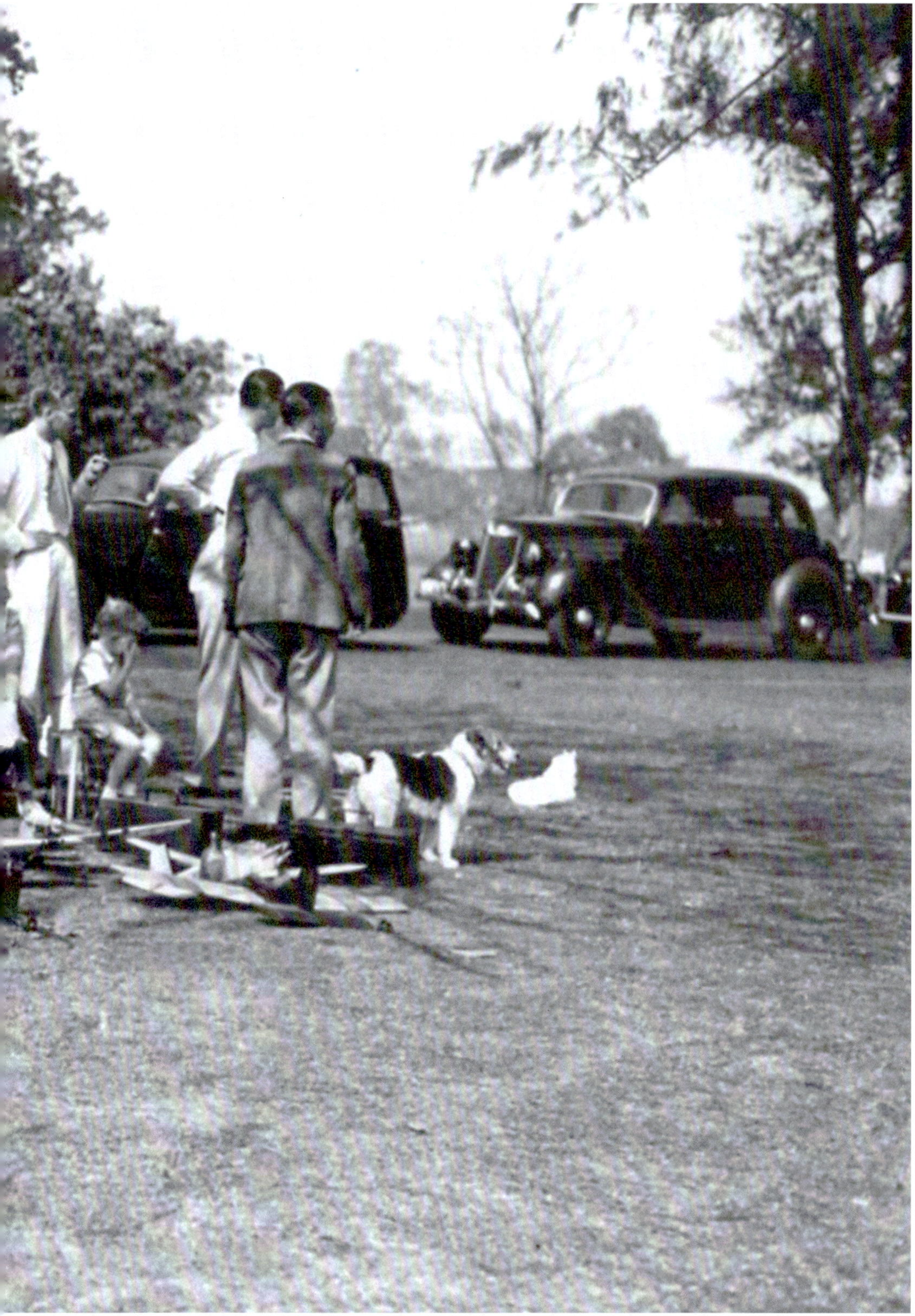

European family enjoying aero-modeling in the Maidan

c. 1945

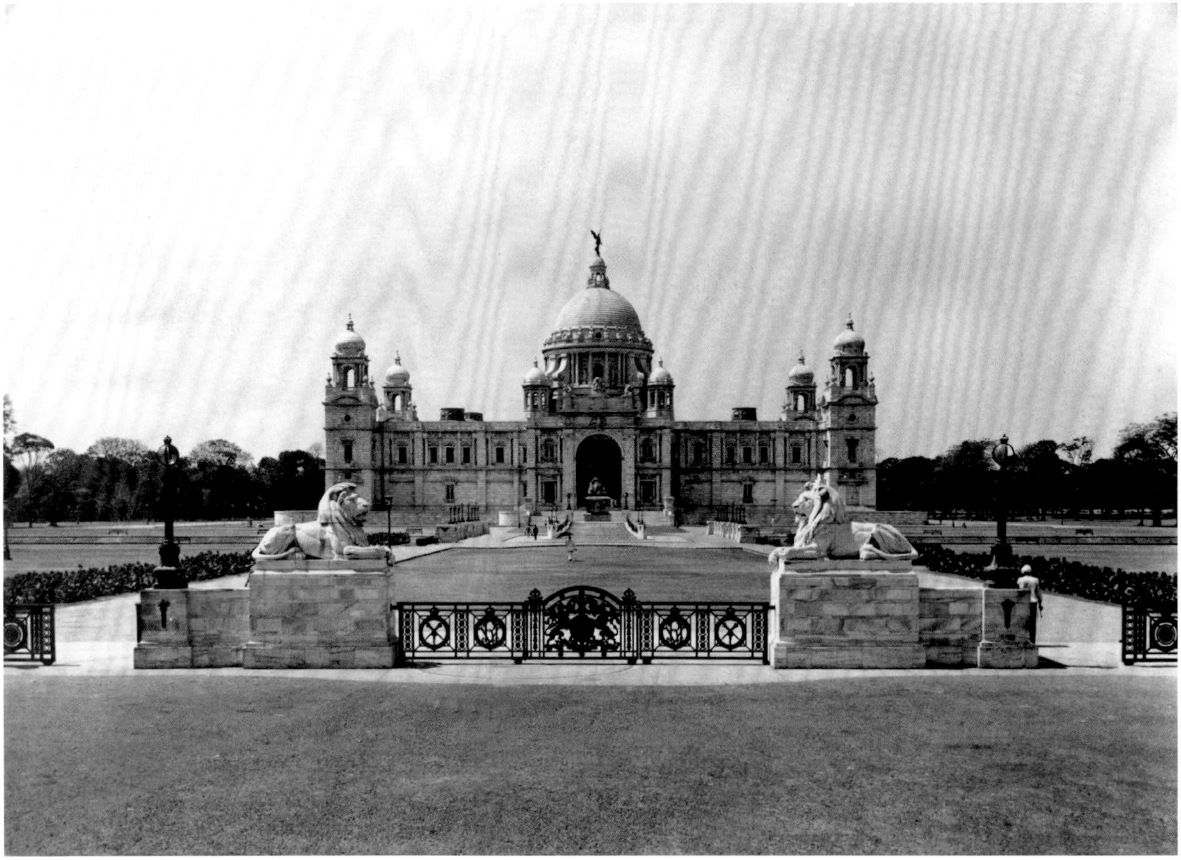

Victoria Memorial Hall north view, displaying lions on either side of the entrance. It was built with Makrana marble and although its form and massing are wholly European in conception, the detailing is Saracenic

c. 1944

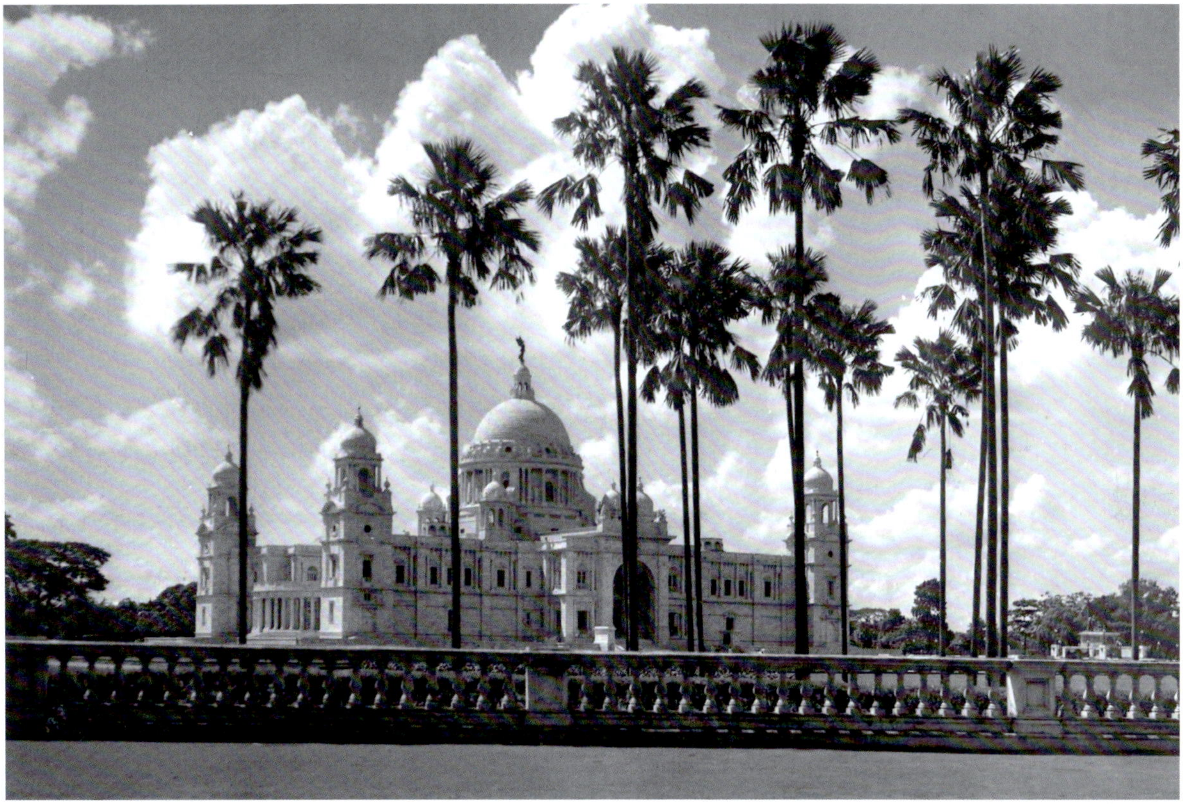

Victoria Memorial Hall was opened in 1921 and is visited by hundreds of tourists every day. It has a huge, invaluable collection of oil paintings, photographs, and artwork collected from all over the country. Some statues of British rulers are displayed in its grounds

c. 1960

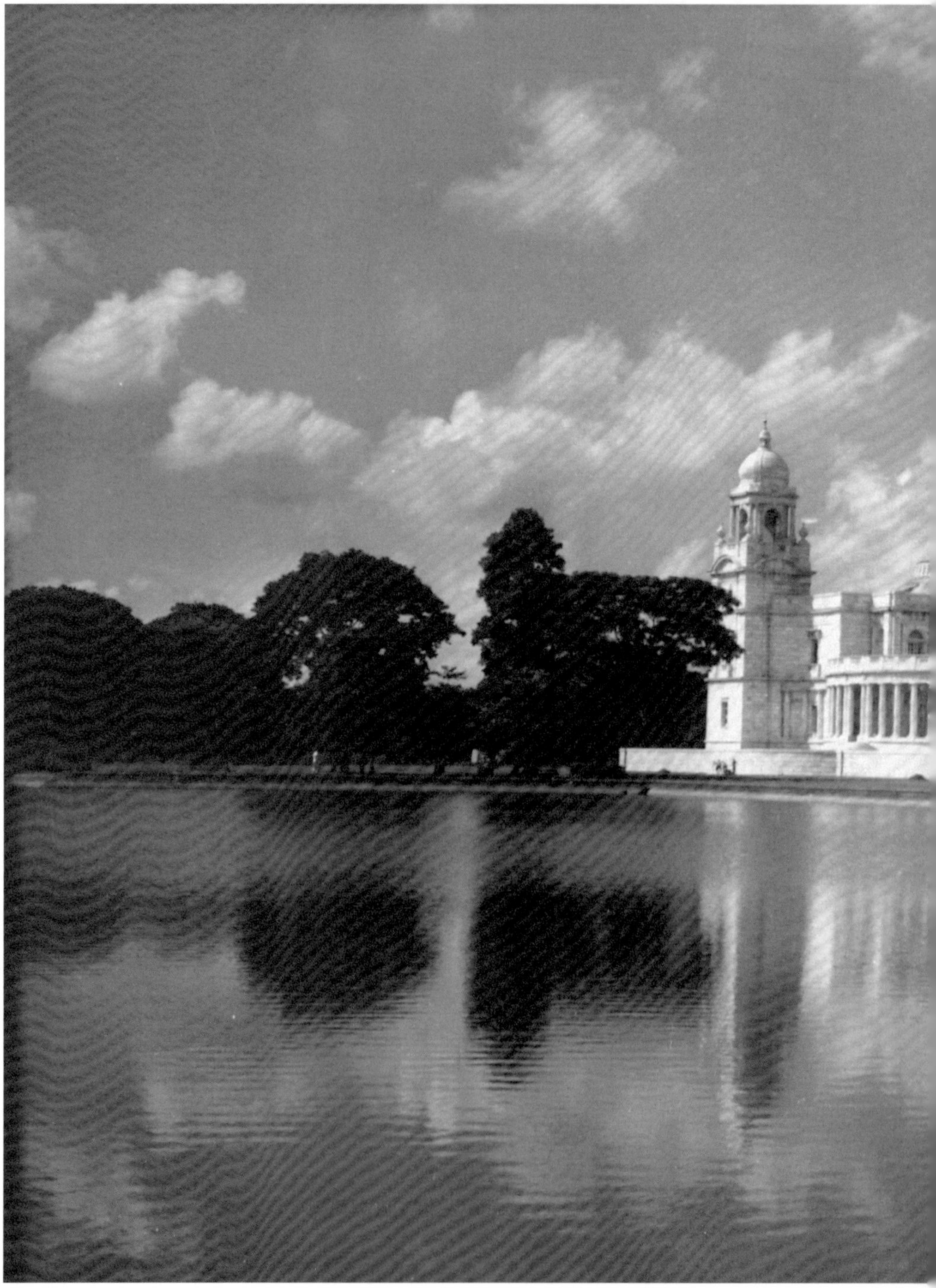

Victoria Memorial Hall, a marble mausoleum built in 1906–1921 in memory of Queen Victoria

c. 1946

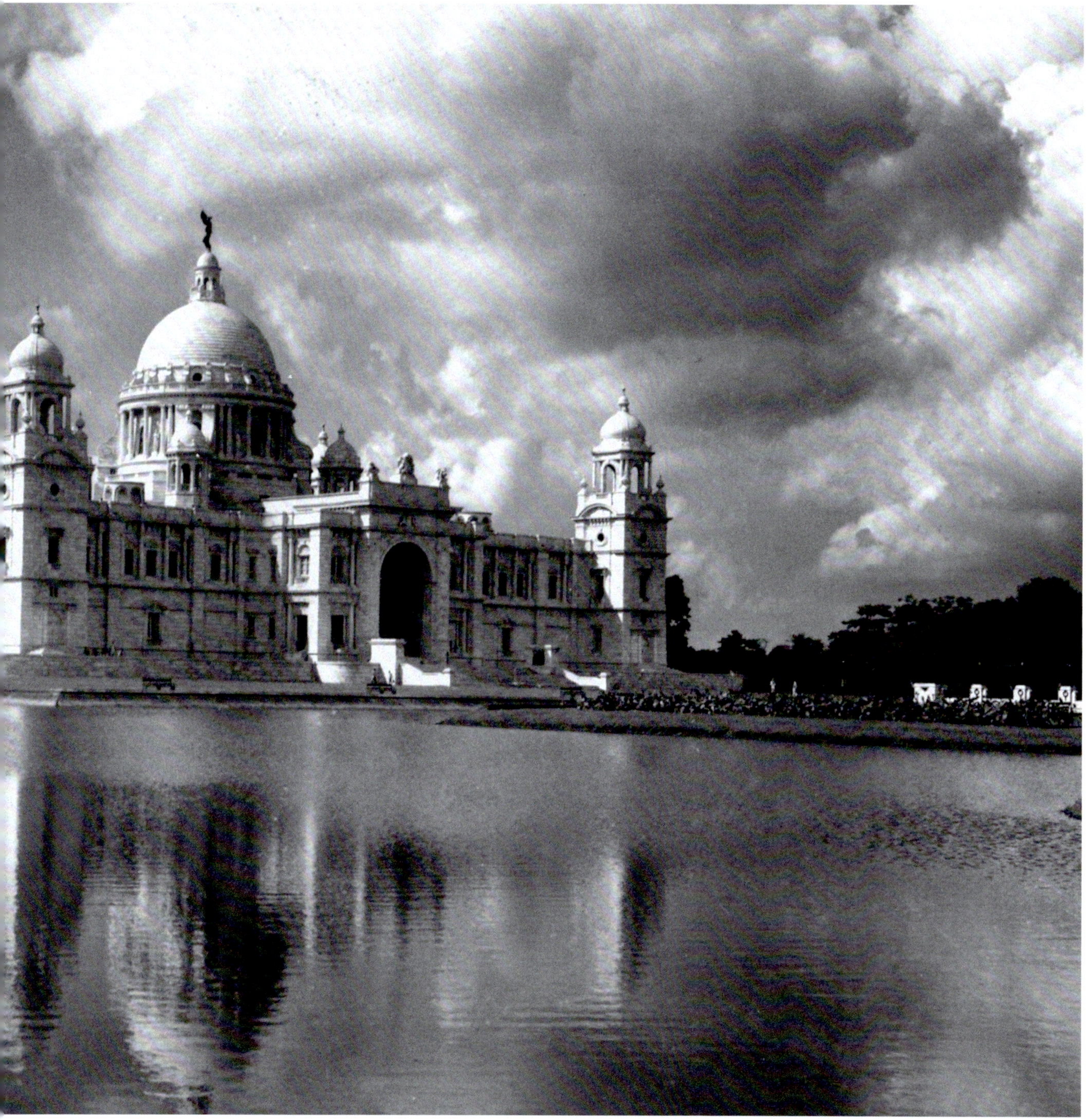

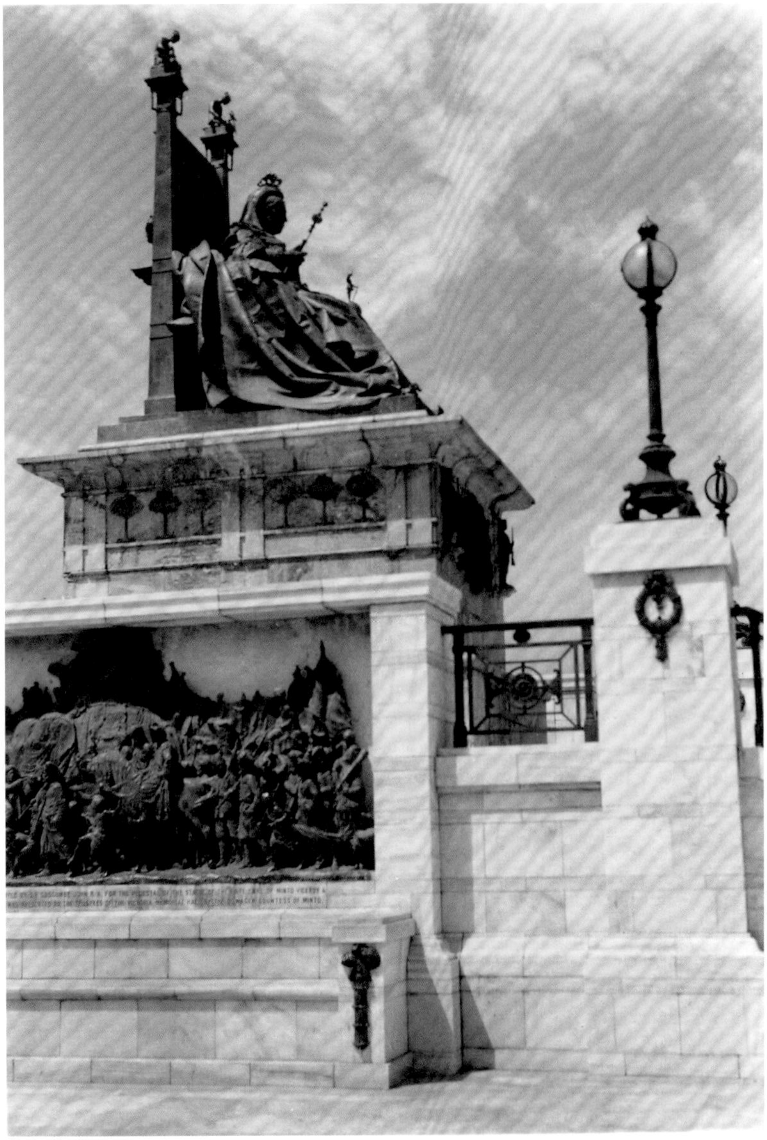

A bronze statue of Victoria Regina on a marble pedestal, installed outside the main entrance of the Victoria Memorial Hall

c. 1955

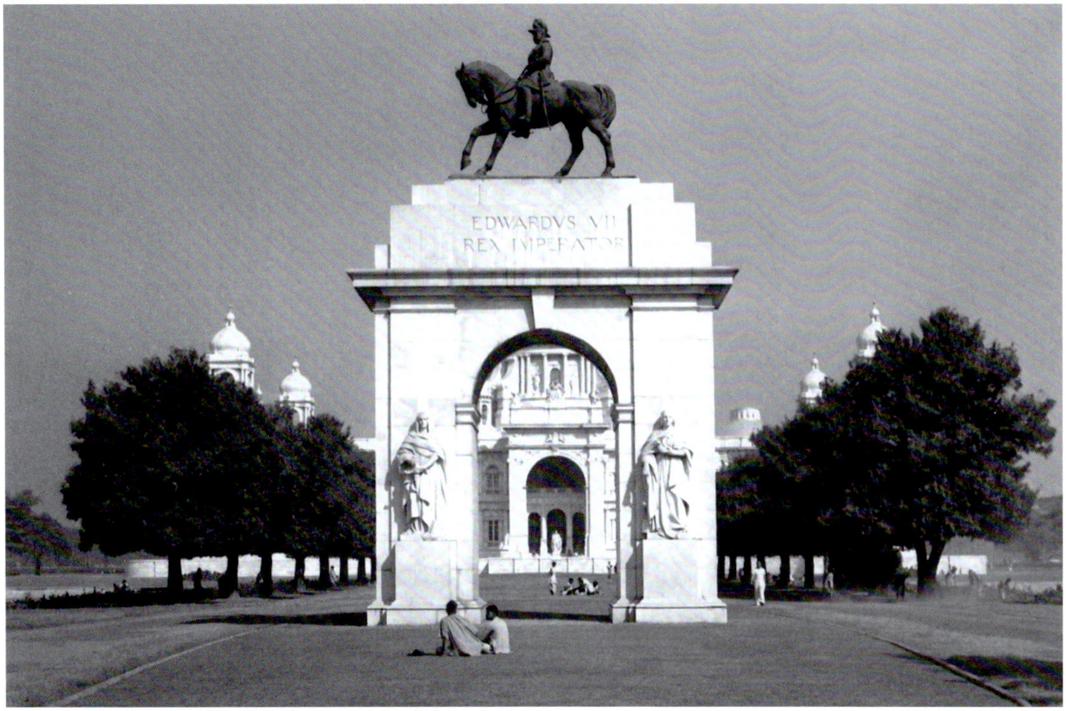

King Edward VII's Memorial Arch with an equestrian bronze statue of the monarch.
Victoria Memorial south view

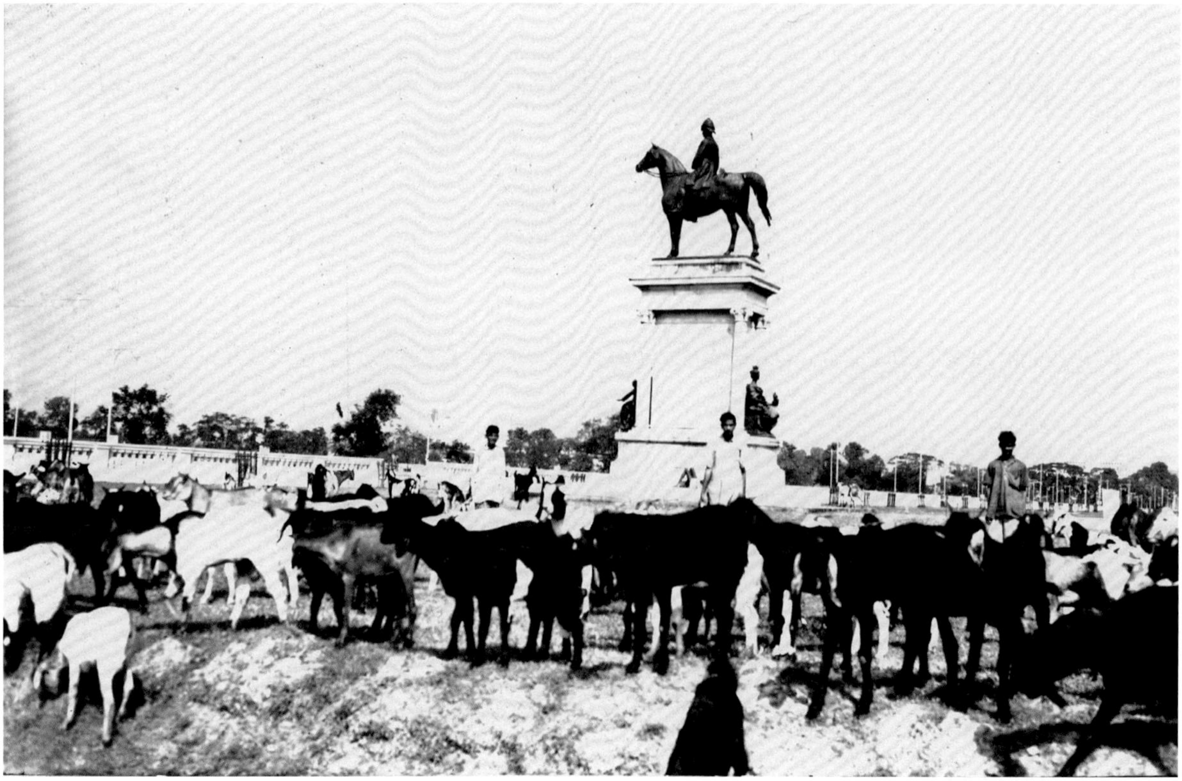

A statue of Lord Lansdowne in the Maidan surrounded by a herd of goats

c. 1955

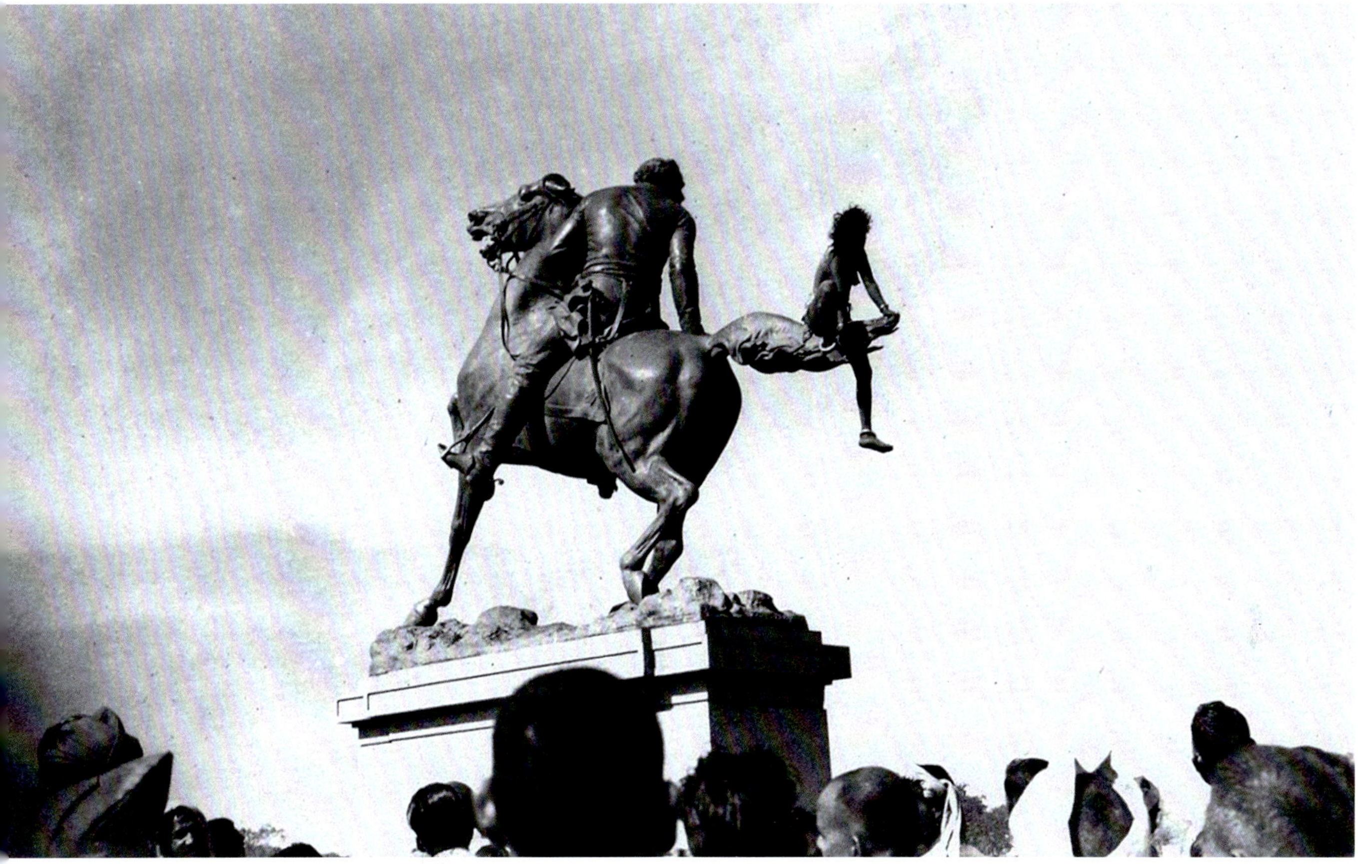

An outstanding statue of Lord Outram on his horse. A mentally unstable man astride the horse's tail has attracted a crowd

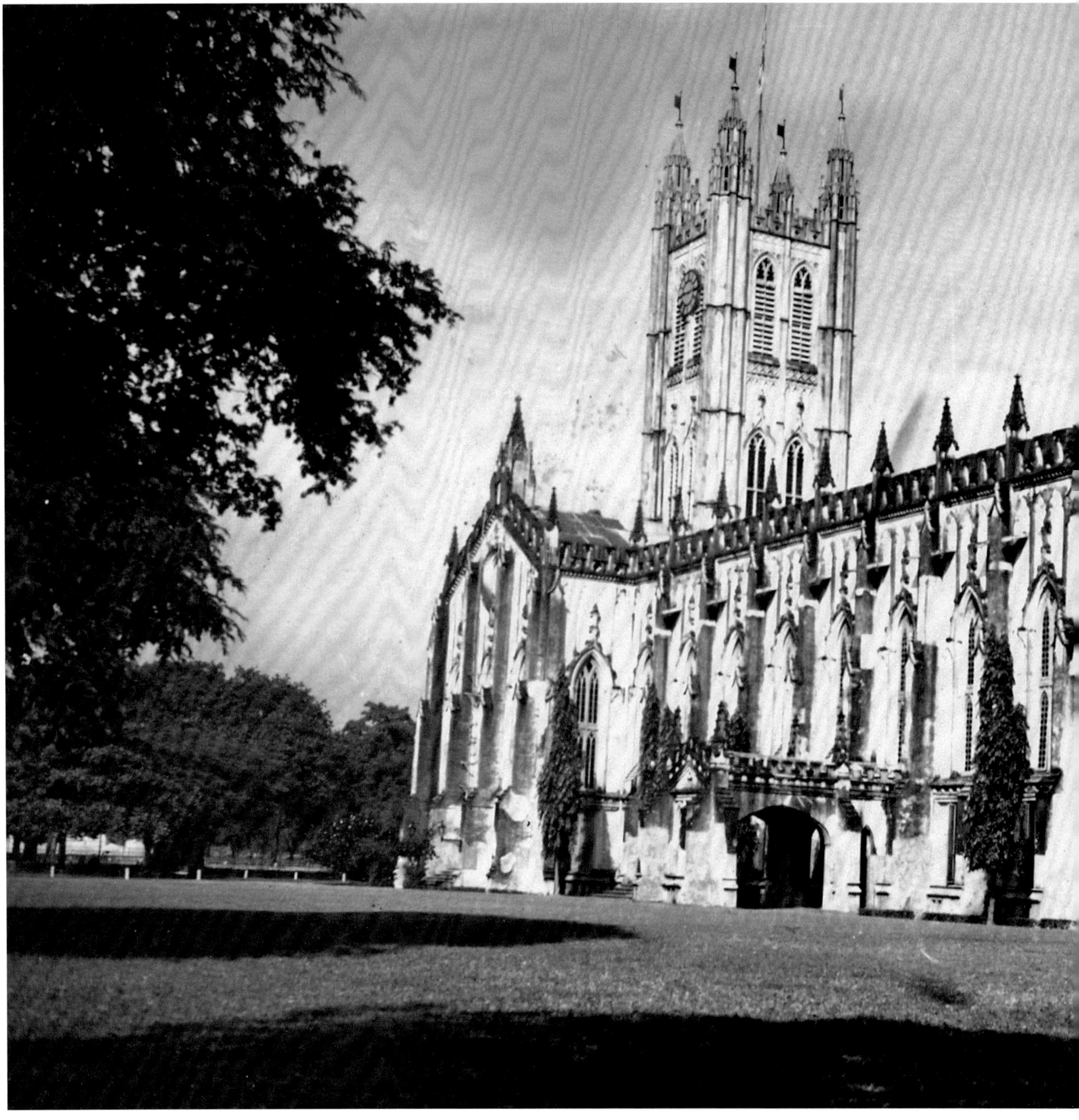

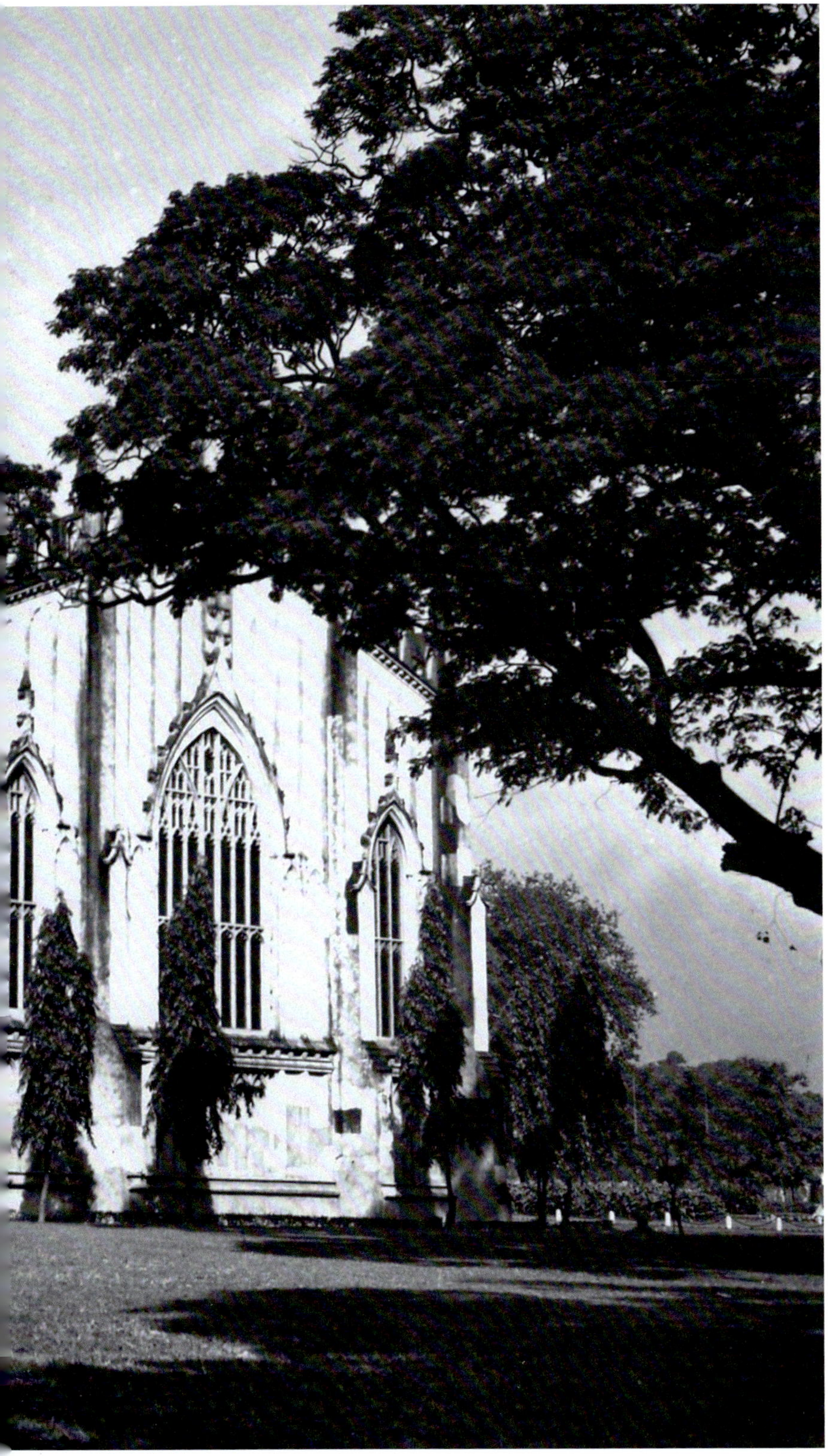

St Paul's Cathedral, built in 1839–1847, is one of India's most important churches. The building stands on Cathedral Road. It has magnificent stained-glass windows designed by Edward Burne-Jones. The original steeple crumbled during a great earthquake in 1897

c. 1948

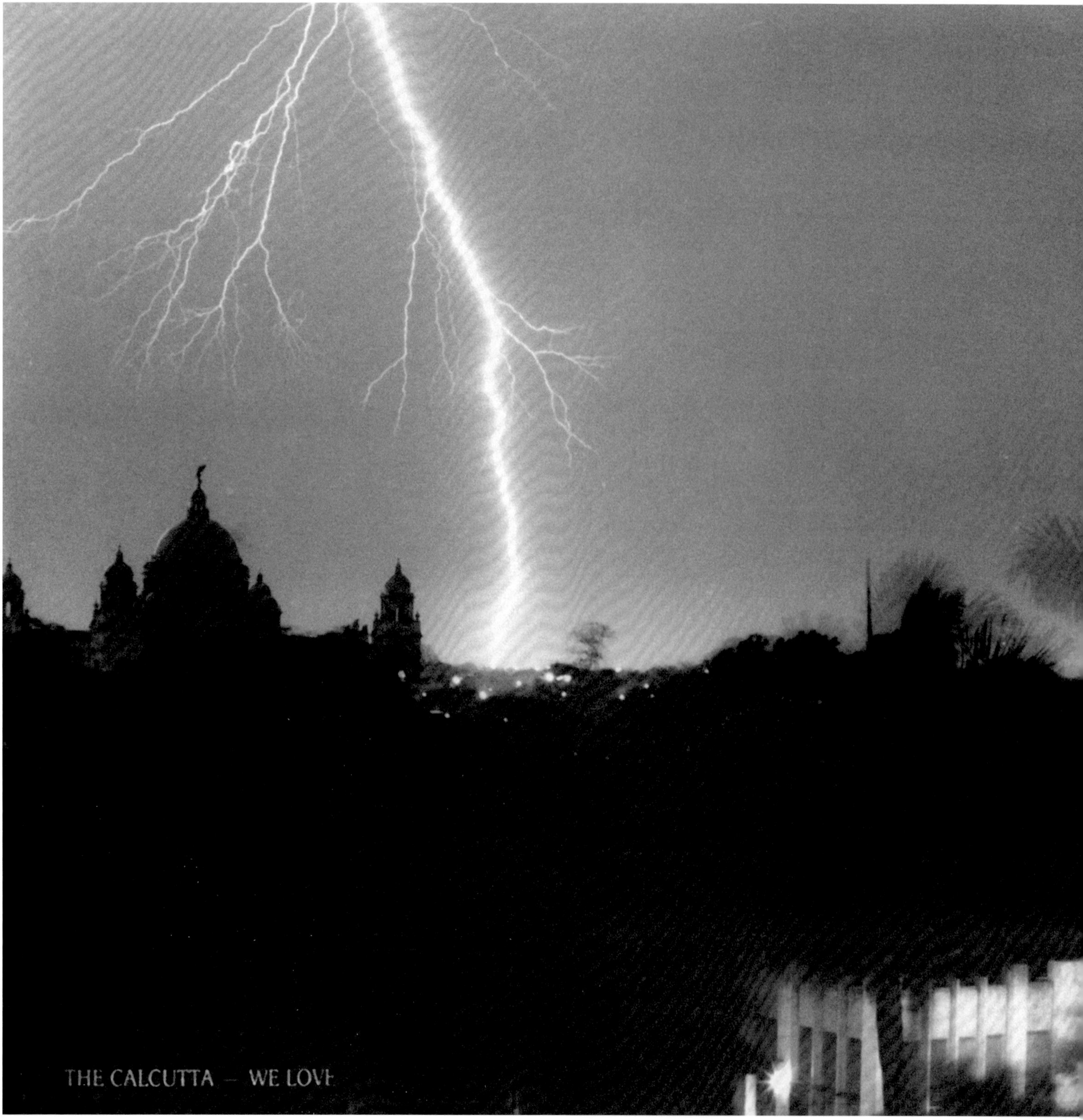
THE CALCUTTA – WE LOVE

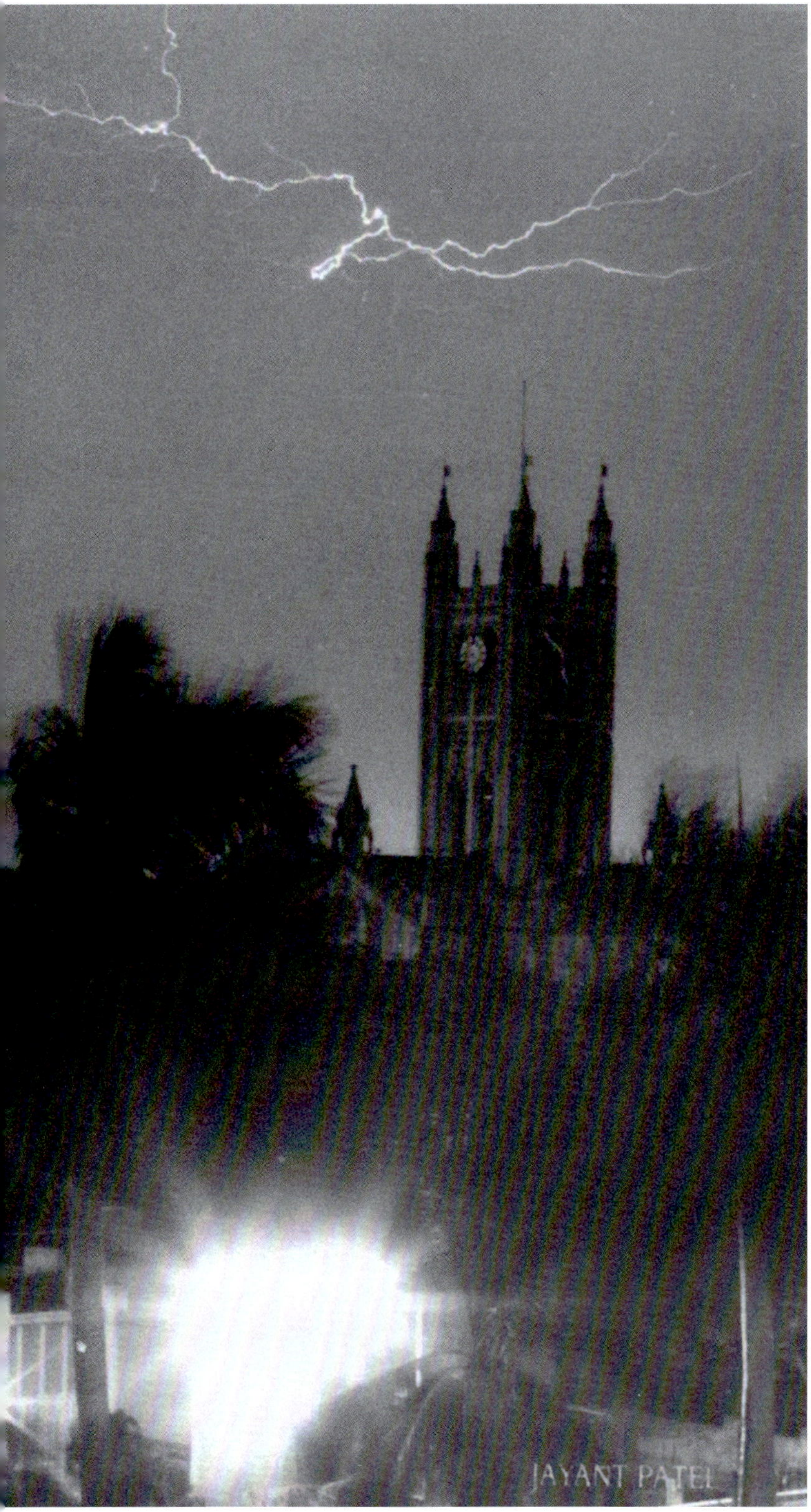

Victoria Memorial opposite St Paul's Cathedral, captured during a thunderstorm

c. 1969

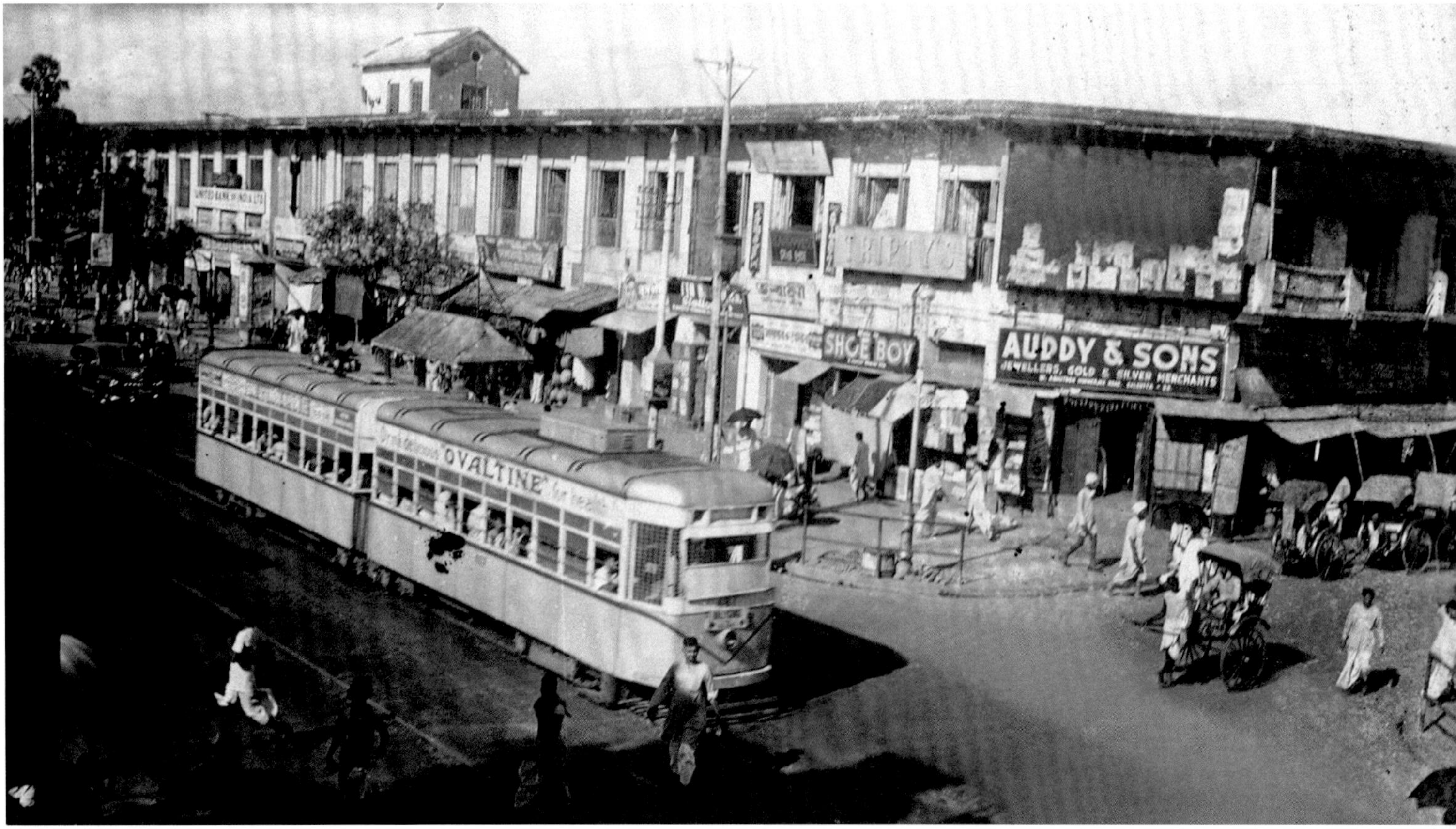

Jadubabur Bazar on Ashutosh Mukherjee Road, Bhowanipore, is a popular market. Many of these shops still exist

c. 1950

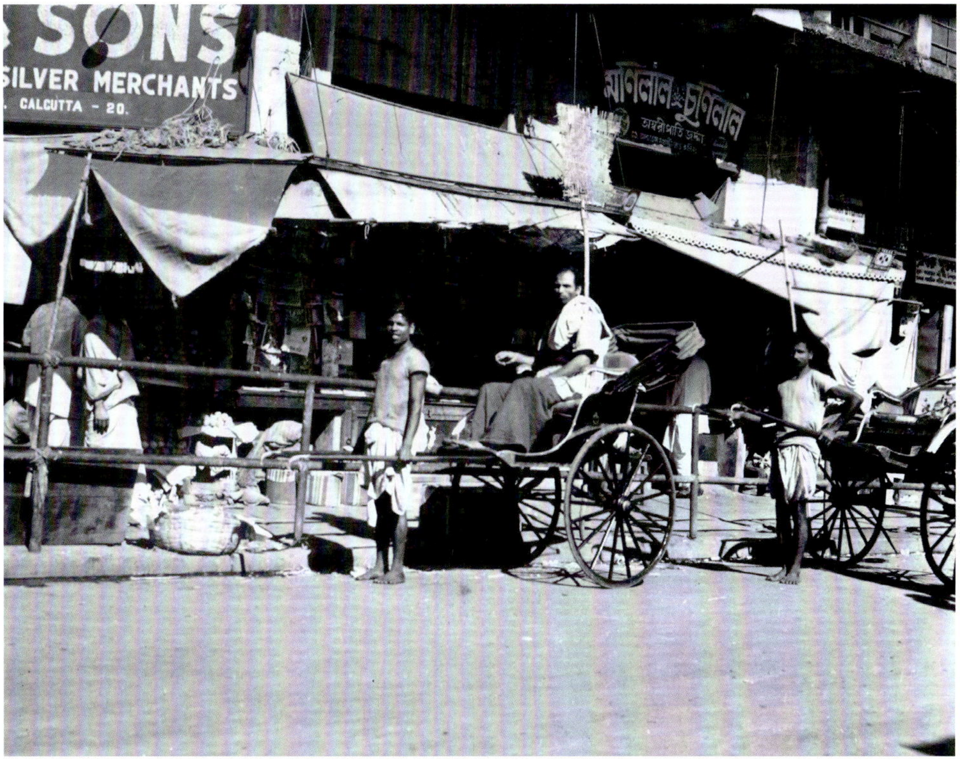

Rickshaws waiting outside Jadubabur Bazar

c. 1950

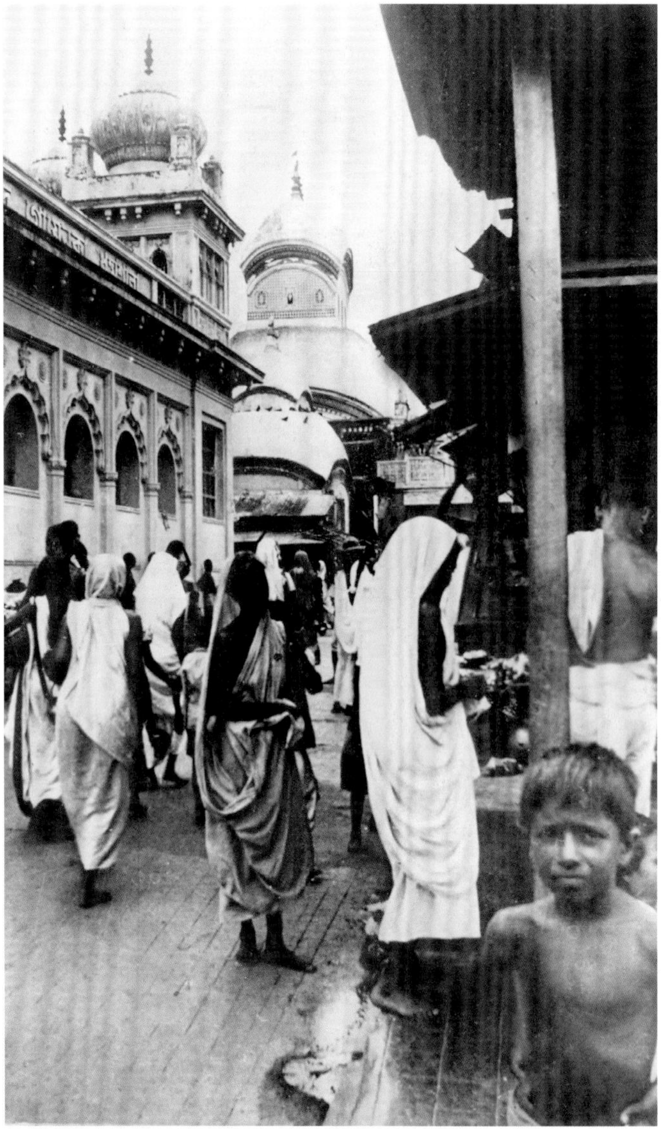

Kalighat temple courtyard

c. 1945

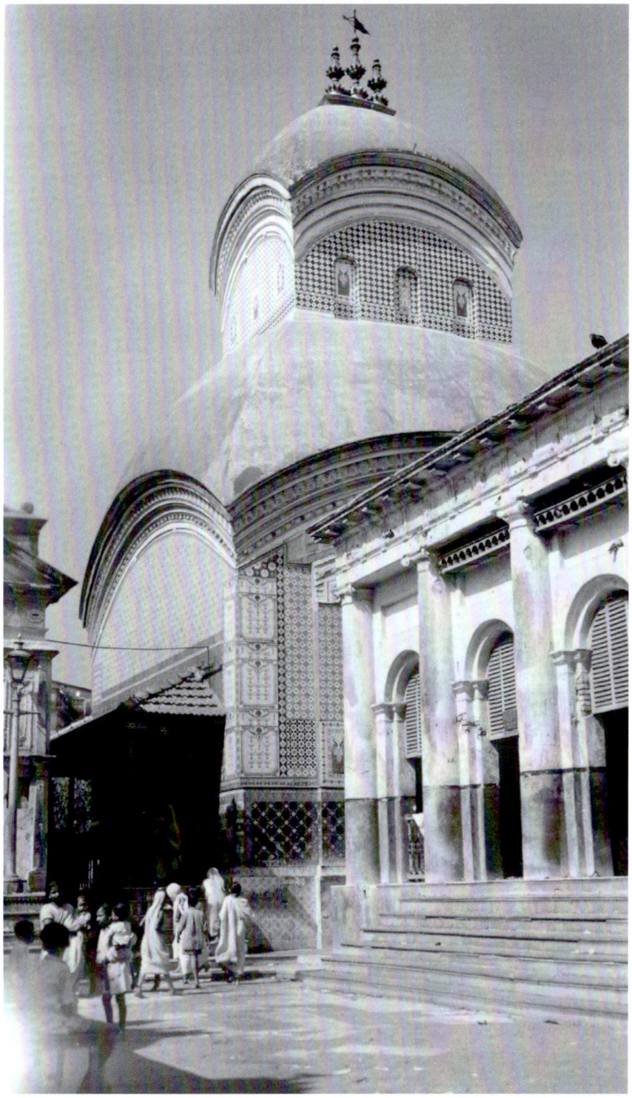

Kali Temple, Kalighat, erected in 1809, dedicated to Goddess Kali, situated on the banks of a canal called Adi Ganga, which connects it to the River Hooghly

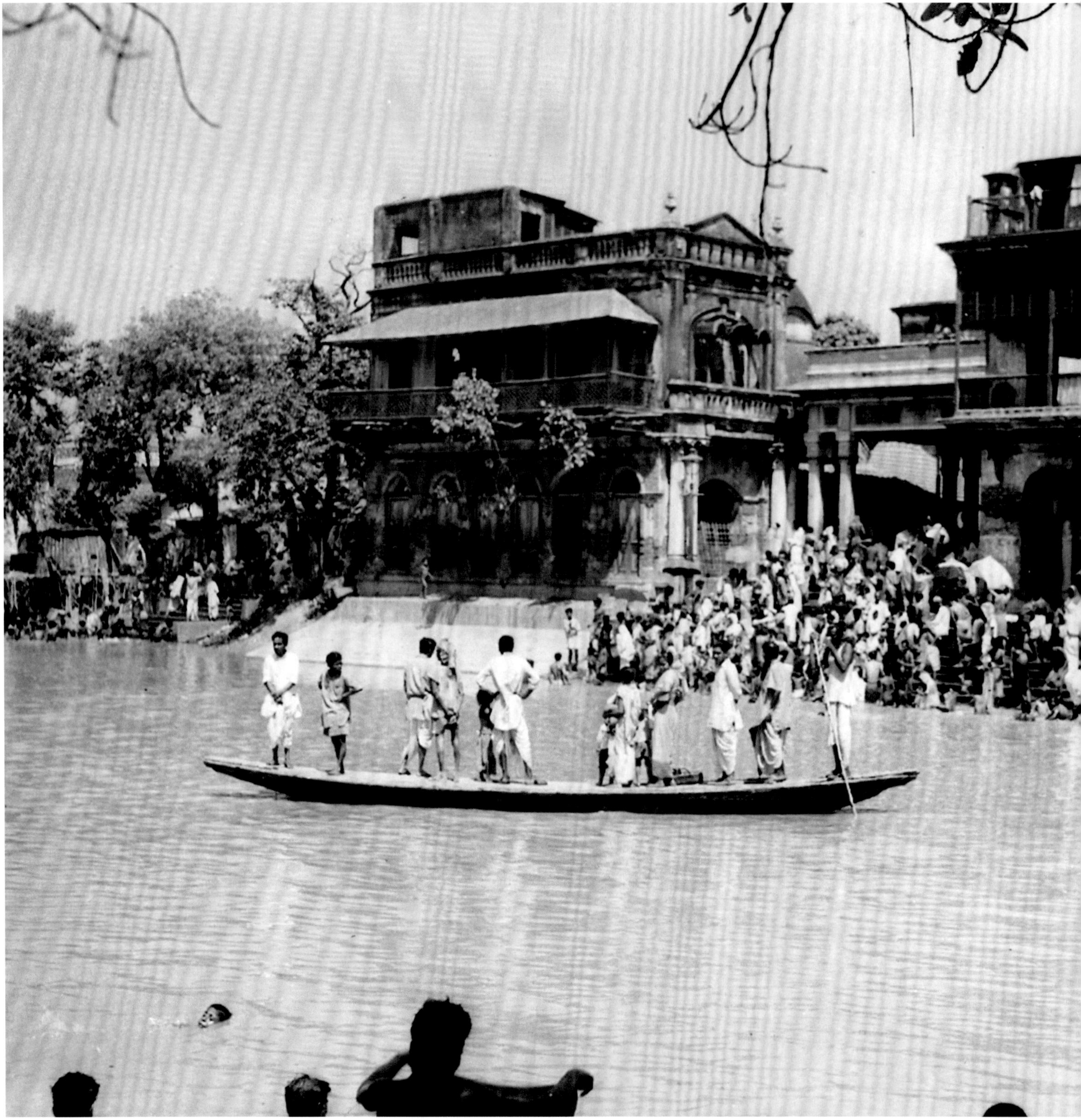

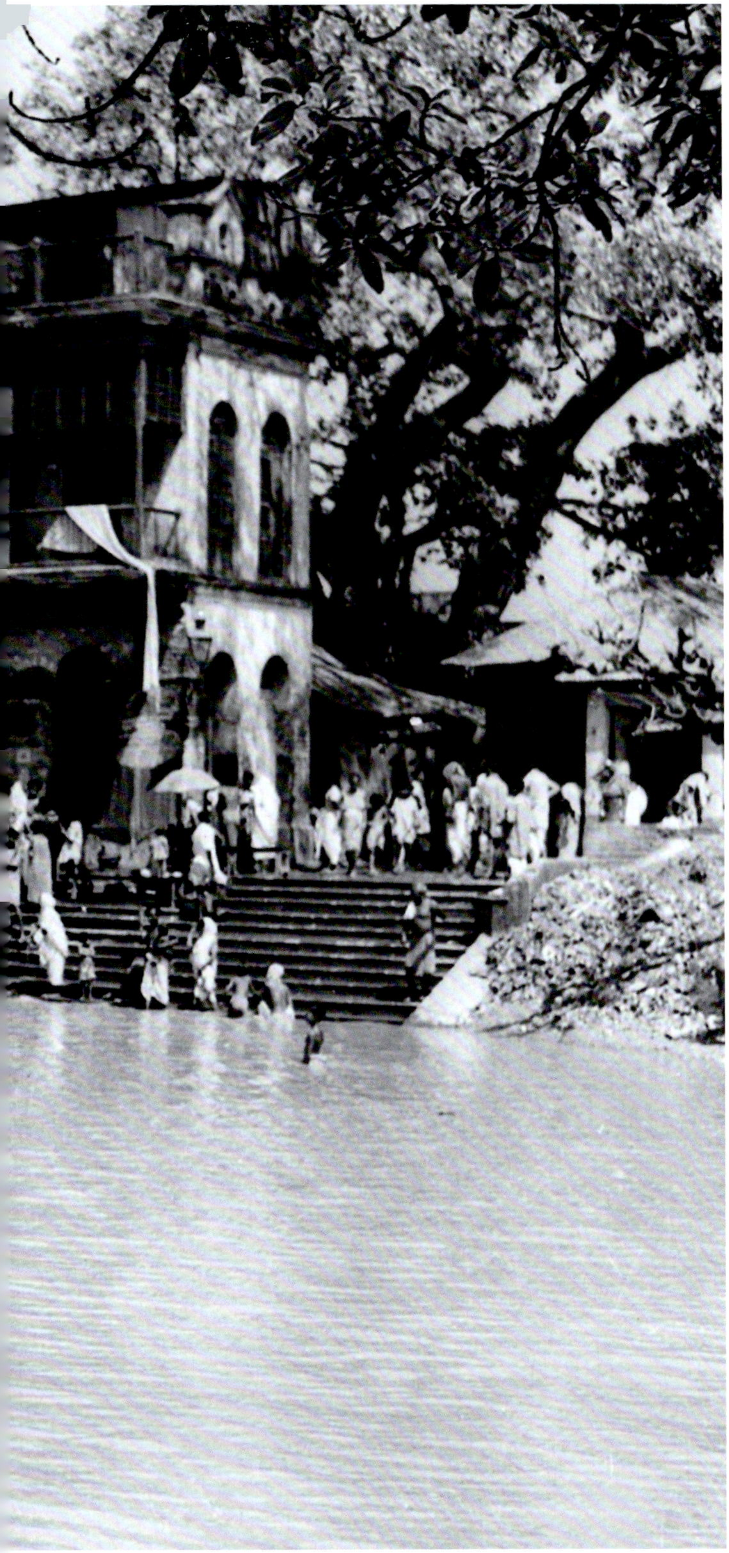

People crossing Adi Ganga in a boat

c. 1945

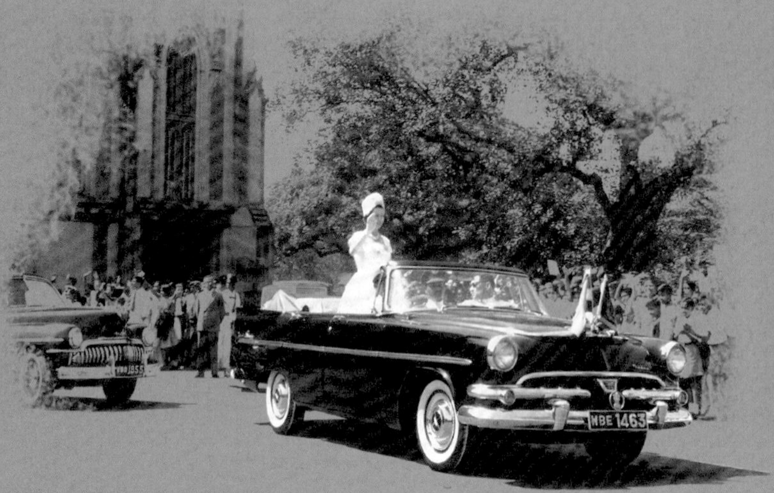

Events

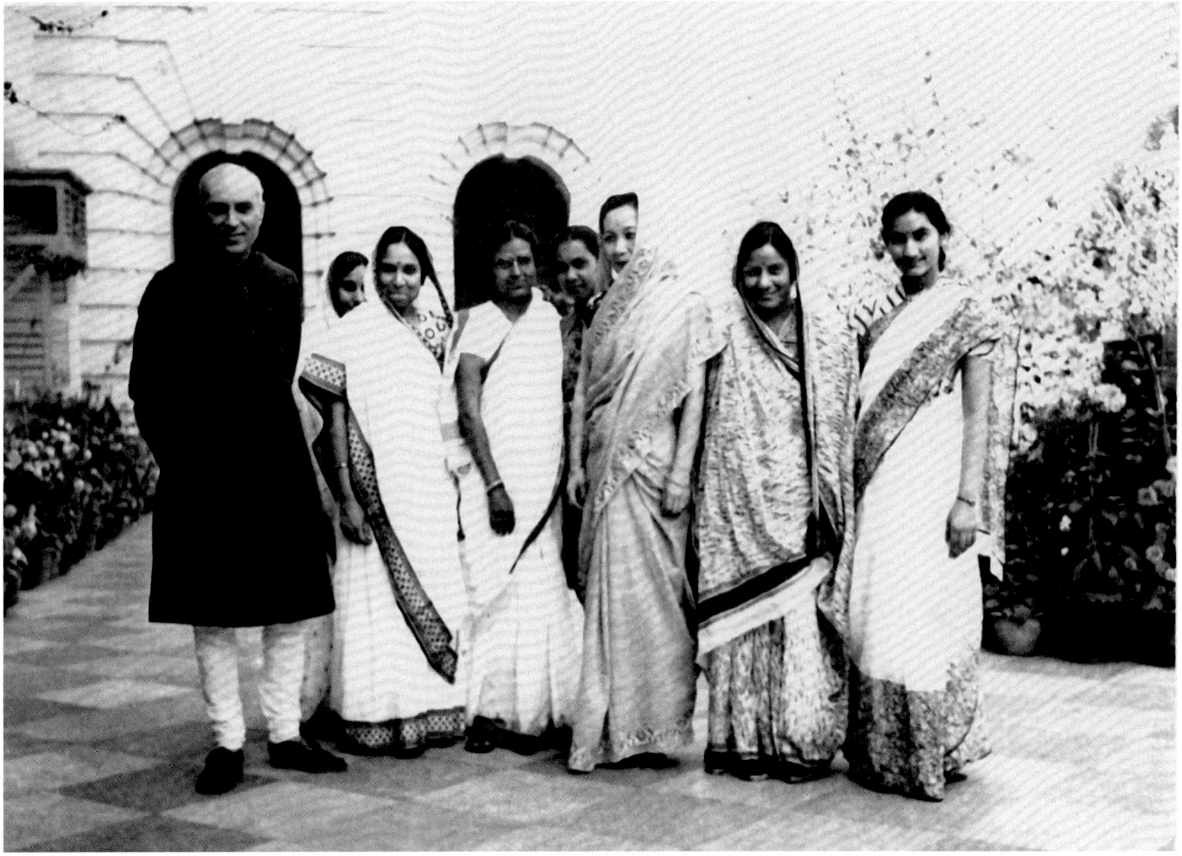

Madam Chiang Kai-shek, dressed in a sari, with Pt Nehru and ladies of the Birla family

1942

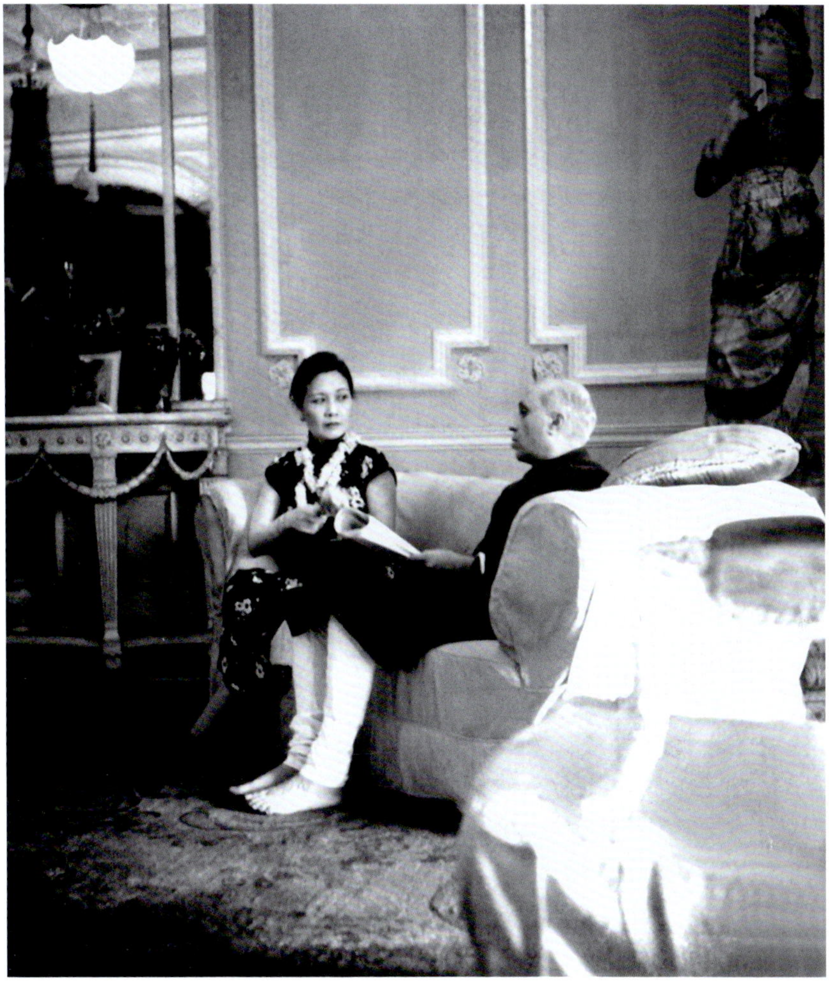

Pt Nehru with Madam Chiang Kai-shek, deep in conversation at Birla House. Their feet are bare in keeping with the Birla family traditions, followed till today

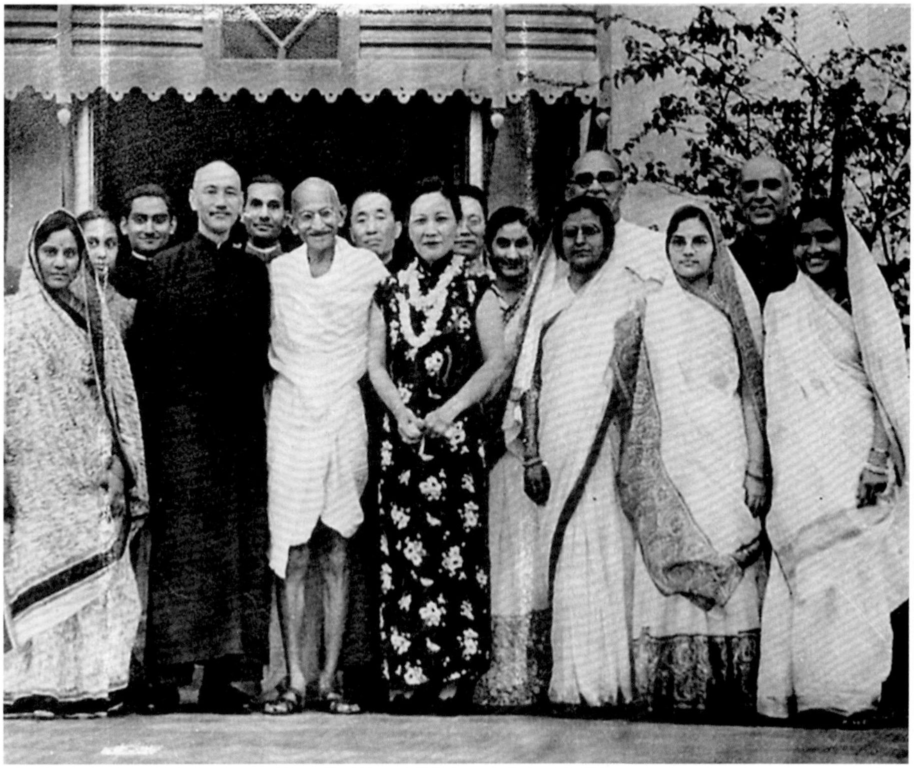

Gandhiji with Madam and General Chiang Kai-shek and members of the Birla family. Behind them to the extreme right stand Mahadev Desai, Gandhiji's personal secretary, and Pt Nehru

1942

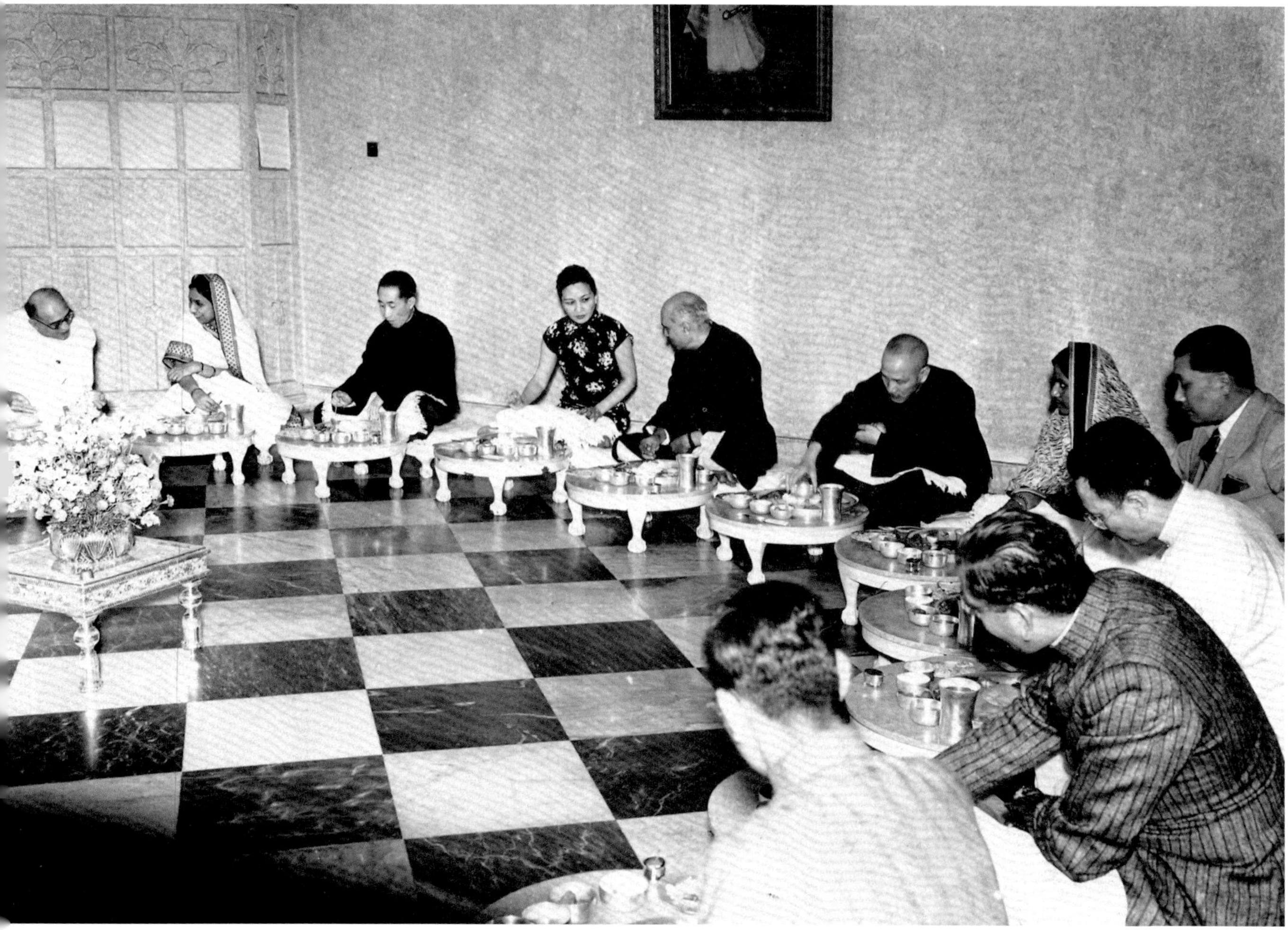

General and Madam Chiang Kai-shek, enjoying a traditional Indian *thali* meal on the floor along with Pt Nehru and other members of the Birla family

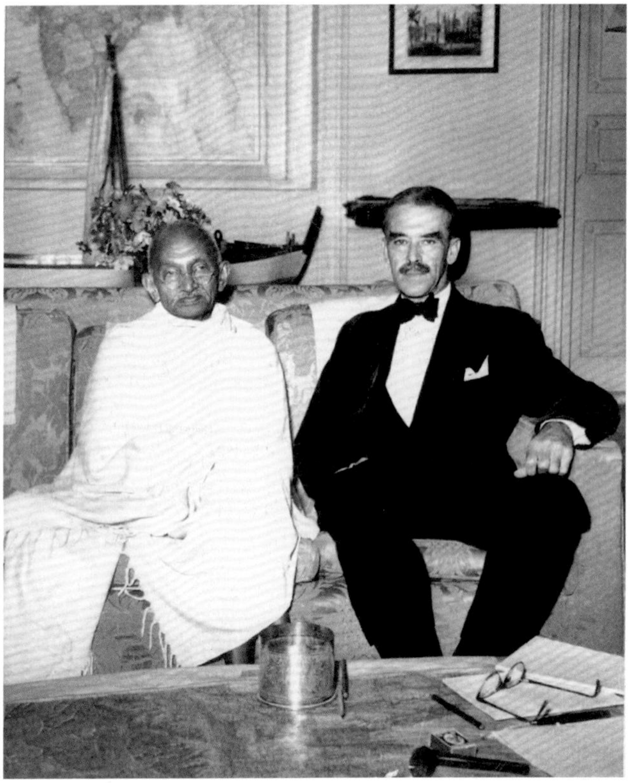

Gandhiji with Governor Casey at Government House

1944

LORD CASEY

TELEGRAMS CORESEARCH MELBOURNE
TELEPHONE 419 1333

C/o CSIRO,
314 ALBERT STREET,
P.O. BOX 89,
EAST MELBOURNE, VIC. 3002

Monday, 6th October 1969.

Dear Mr Patel -

Thank you for your letter of 25th September and for the photographs taken at Government House, Calcutta, of Mahatma Gandhi and myself, which I am most glad to have. It was good of you to think of sending them to me.

I am enclosing one set of the photographs, which I have autographed, for your studio display during the Gandhi Centenary Celebrations.

With my thanks and best wishes - I am

Yours sincerely

Casey.

I am also sending you copy of a book written by my wife "Tides and Eddies", in which some of your photographs appear & for which she acknowledges that they are your photographs, on an early page of the book.

Casey.

Jayant C. Patel, Esq.,
Director,
Bombay Photo Stores Private Ltd.,
33-34 Park Mansions,
Park Street,
CALCUTTA-16. INDIA.

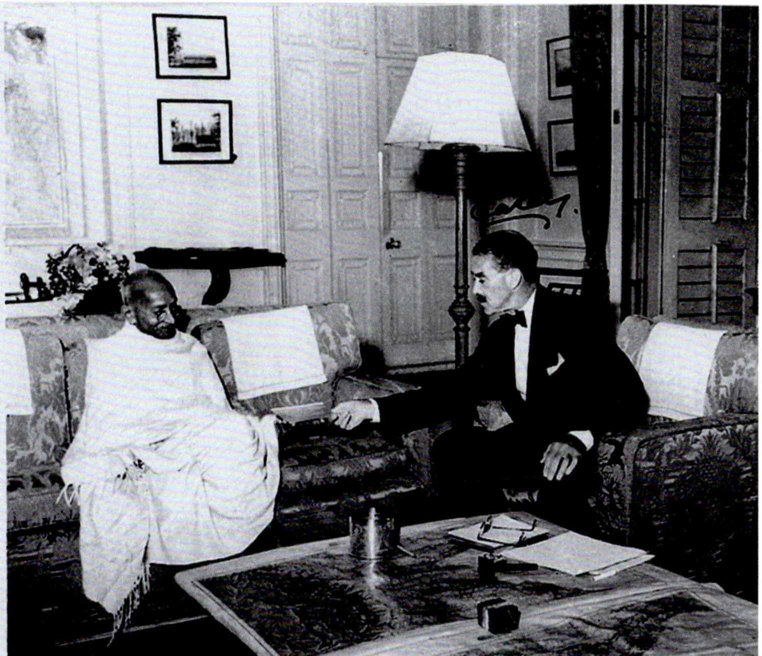

191

Gandhiji on a vow of silence (*maunvrat*). He replies to Governor Casey's question with a hand-written note

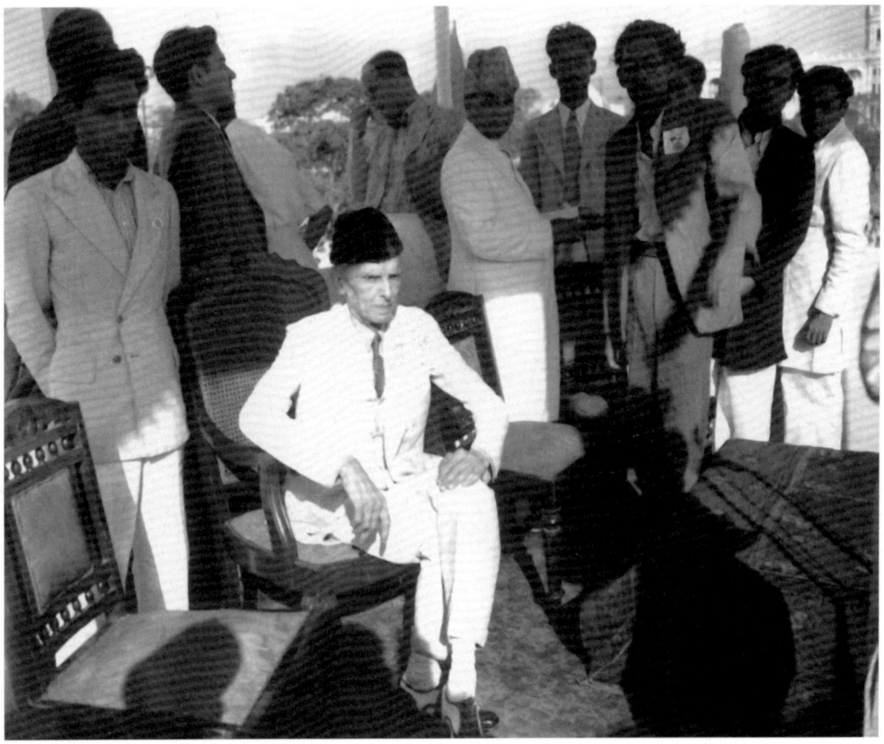

Mohammed Ali Jinnah on a dais in Calcutta Maidan at a meeting, which precipitated the Great Calcutta Killings on 16 August 1946. Members of the Muslim League, along with Suhrawardy, watch him expectantly

1946

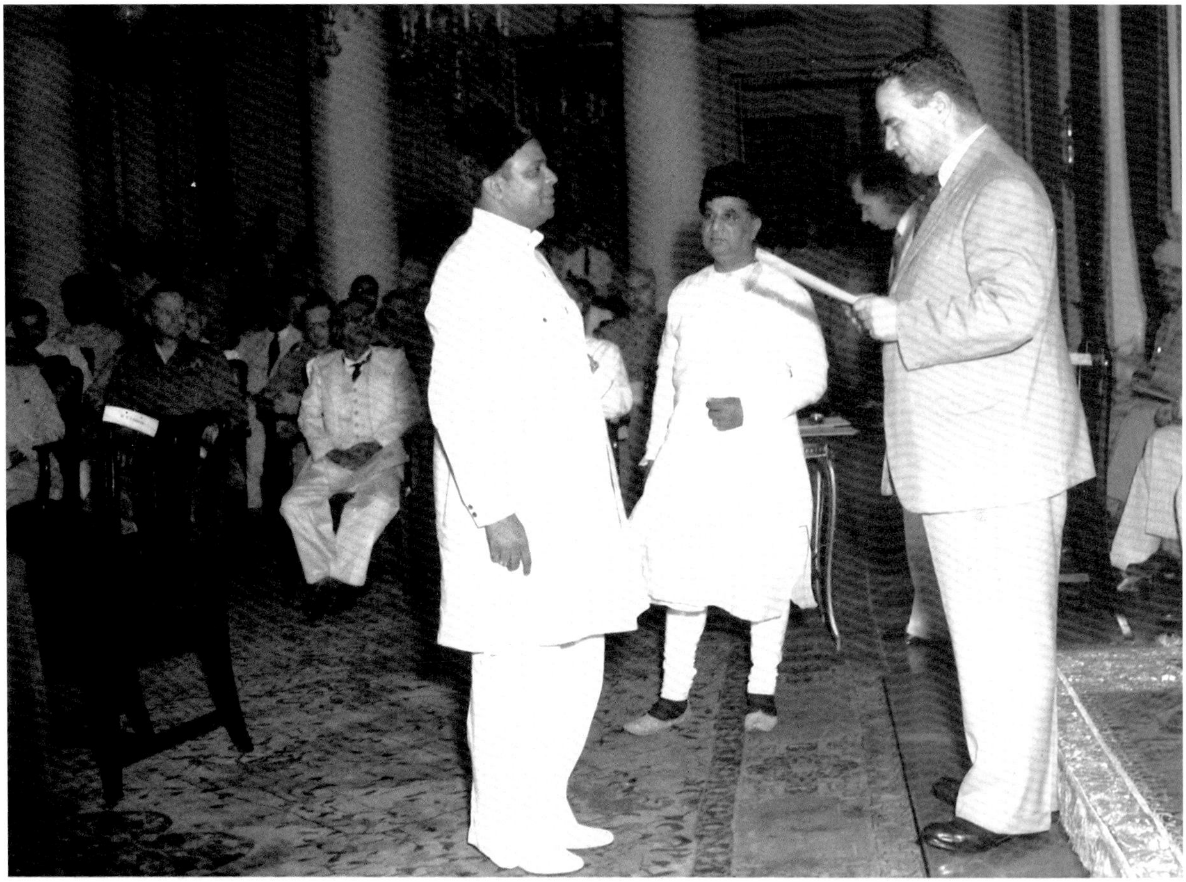

Governor Sir Fredrick Burrows swearing in Muslim League minister, Mohammed Ali, in the presence of Suhrawardy

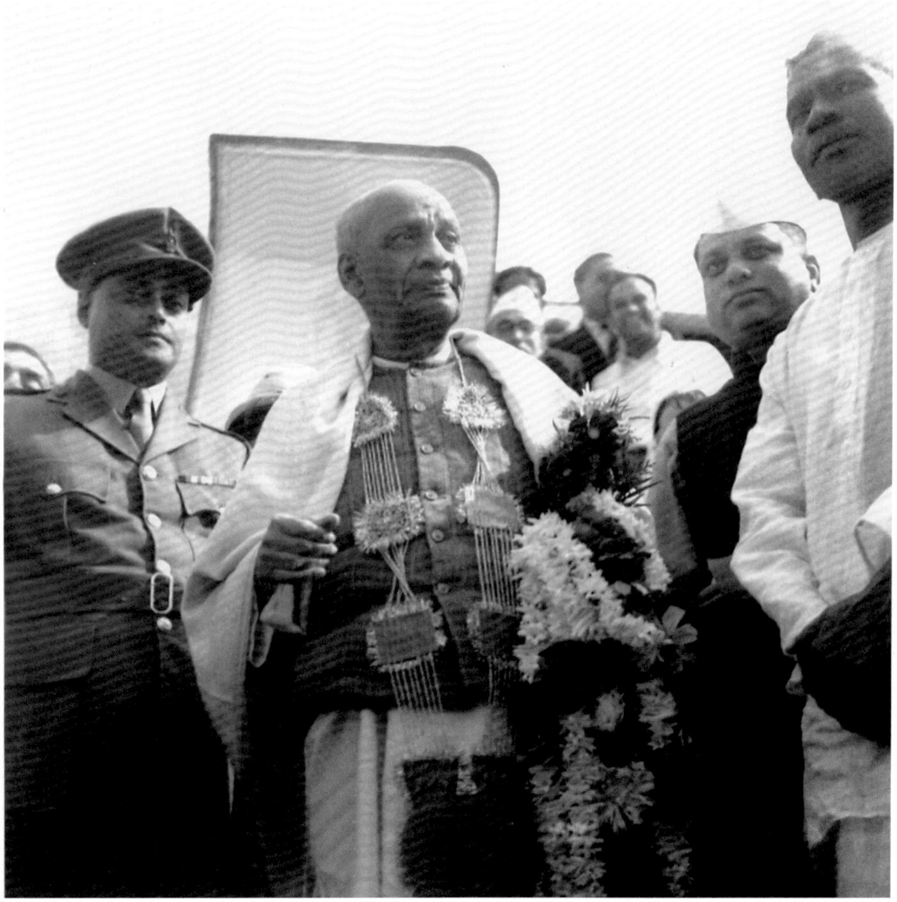

Sardar Patel being received at Calcutta airport

1947

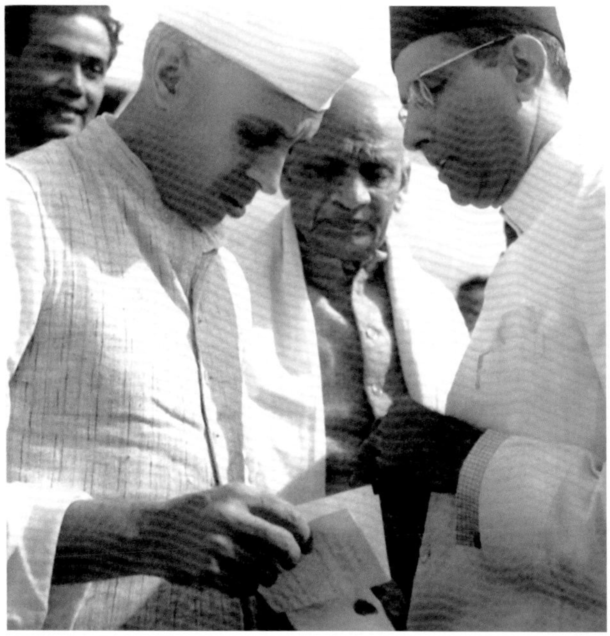

Pt Nehru with Sardar Patel and G.D. Birla

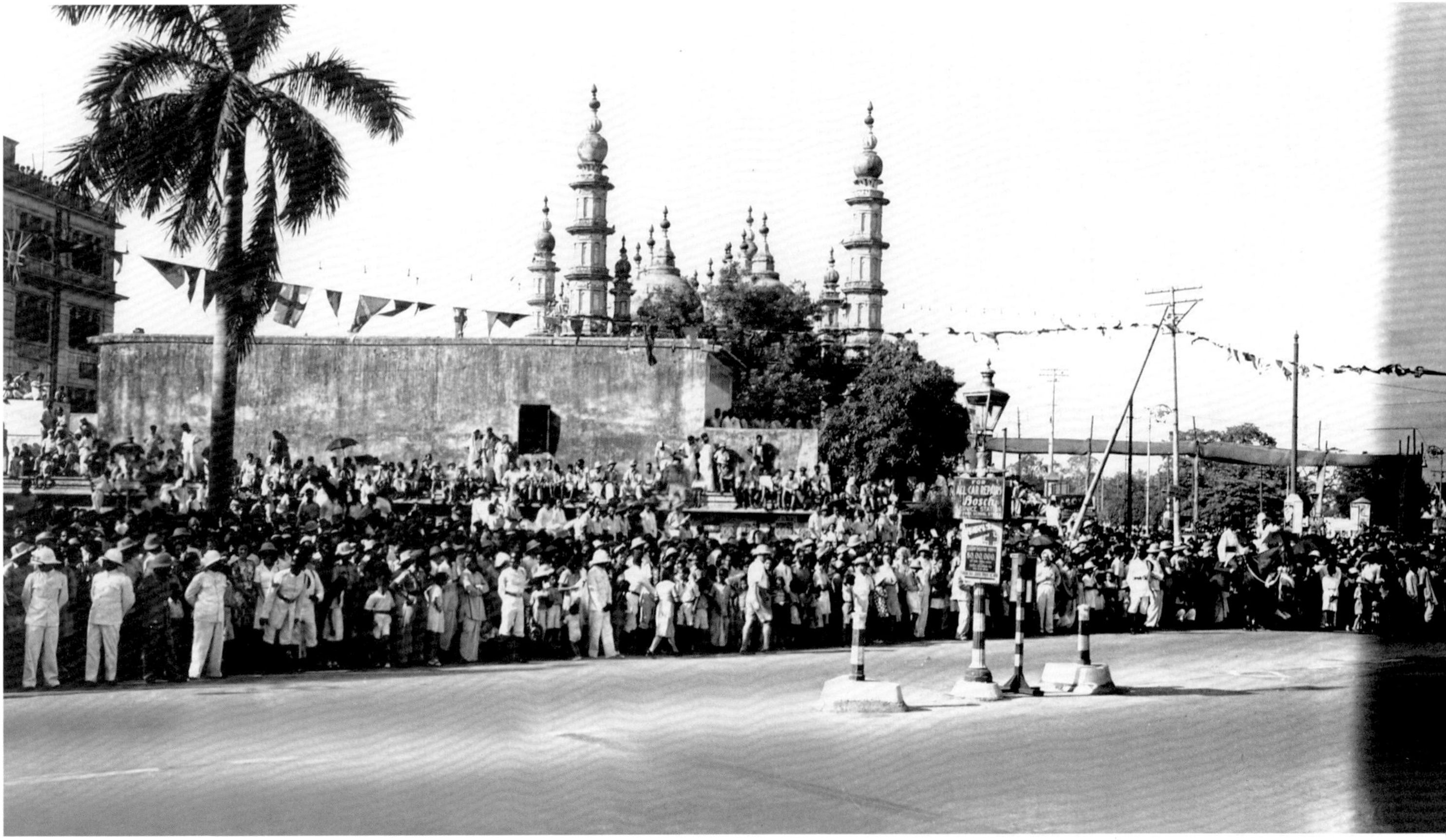

A crowd waiting for Pt Nehru's arrival along Central Avenue. In the background is Tipu Sultan's Mosque

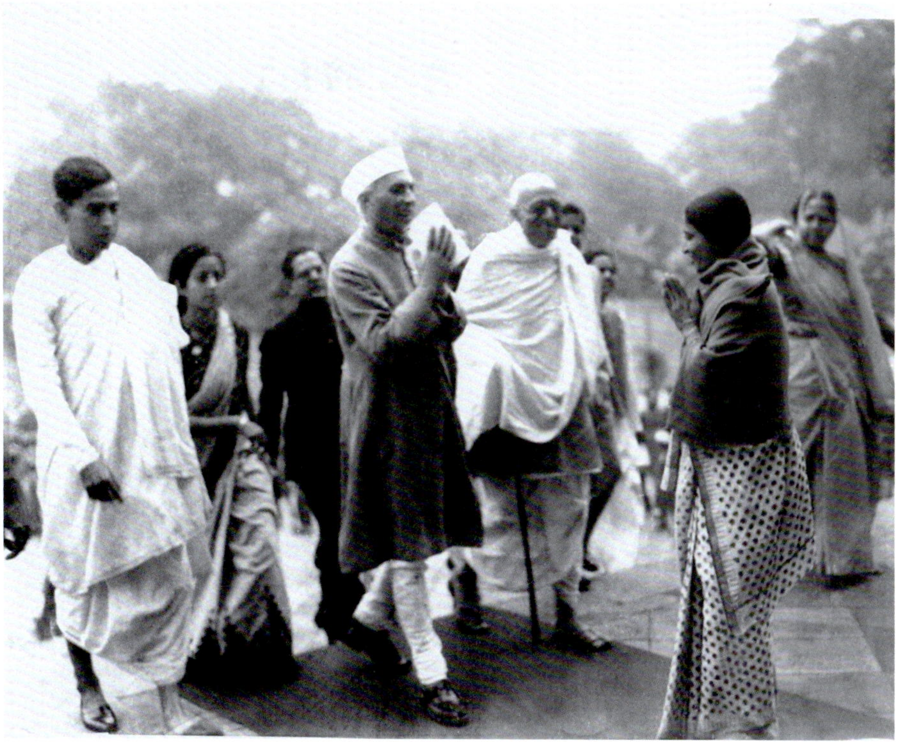

Pt Nehru with Governor Rajagopalachari greeting Namagiri, Shri Rajagopalachari's daughter

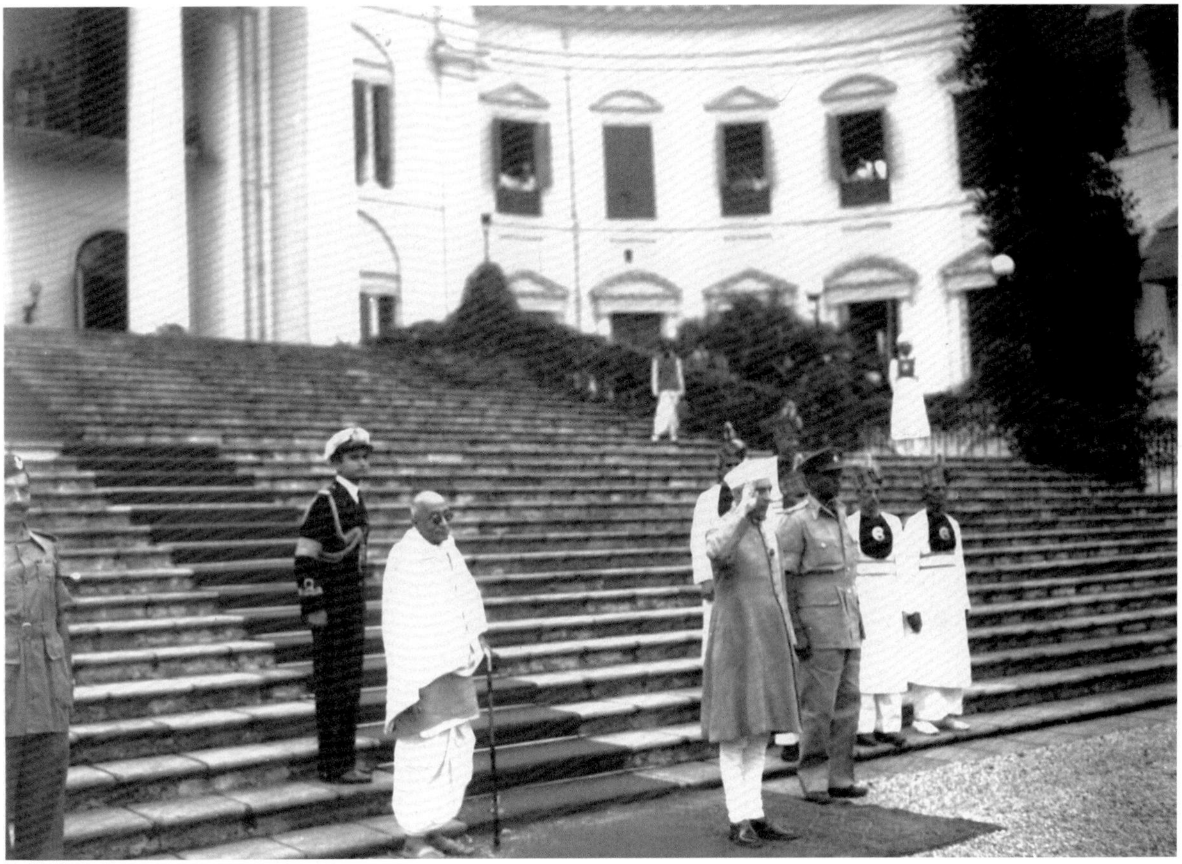

Pt Nehru taking the salute at Raj Bhavan while Governor Rajagopalachari watches

1947

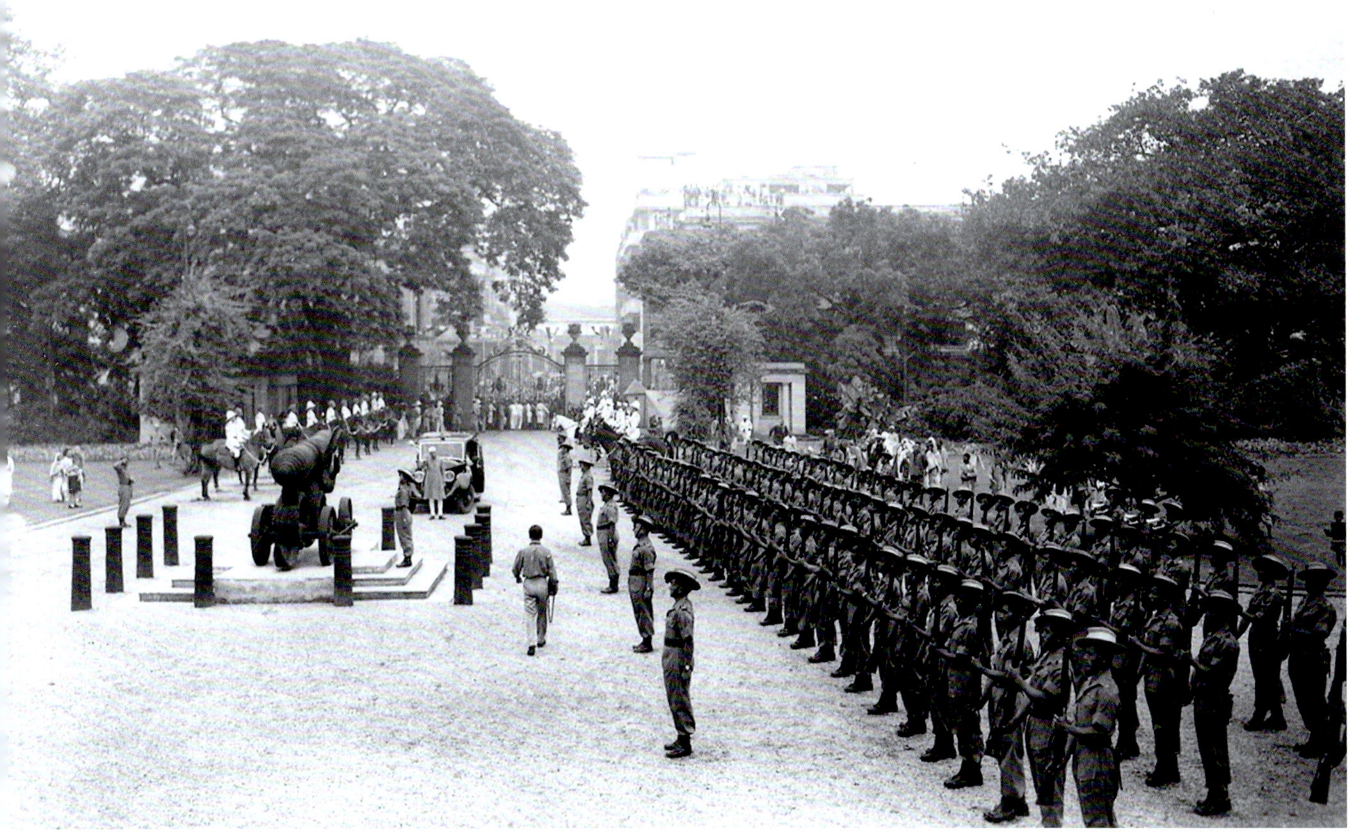

Pt Nehru saluting troops at the north gate of Raj Bhavan

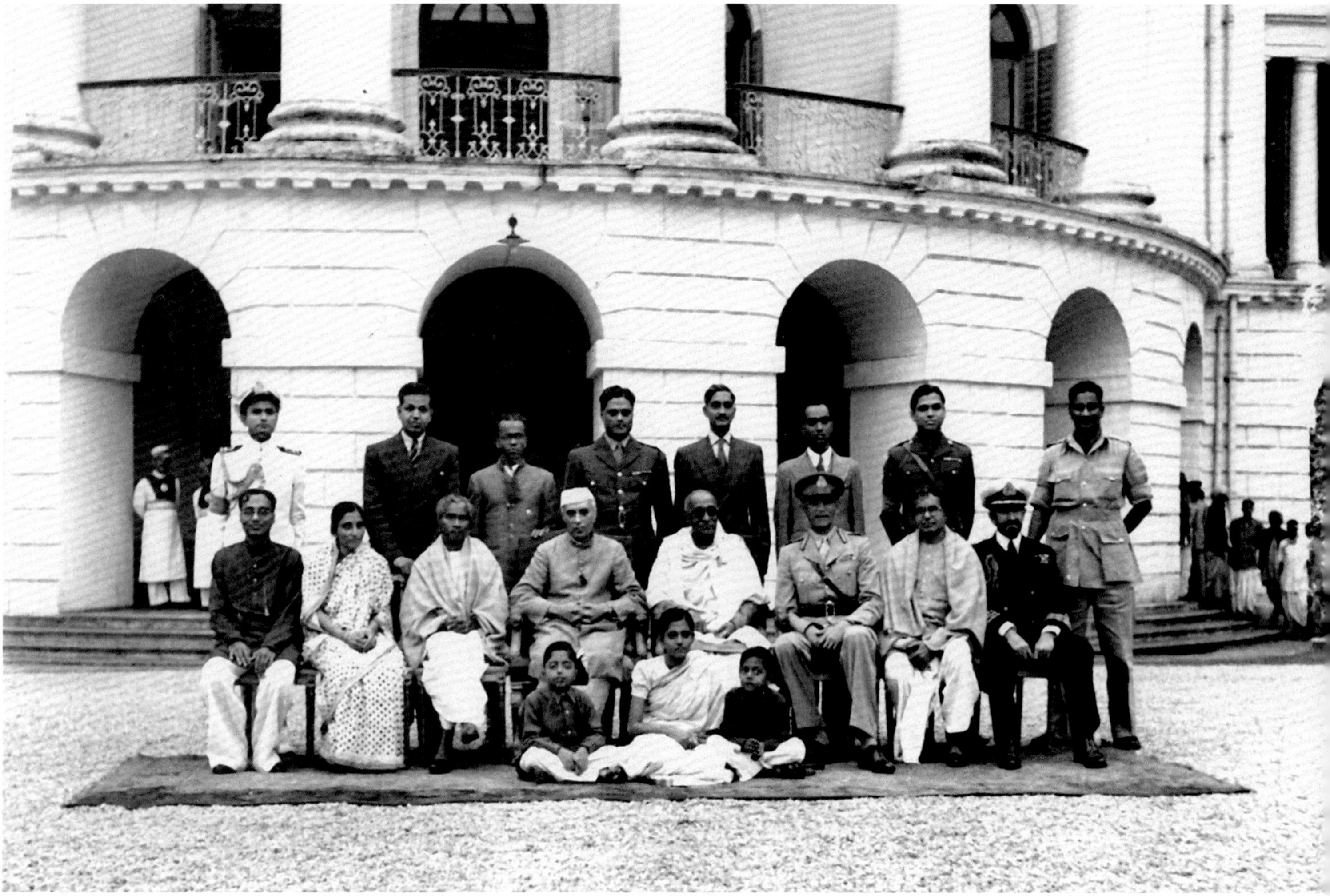

Governor Rajagopalachari at the centre with General Cariappa to his left. To his right are Pt Nehru, P.C. Ghosh, daughter Namagiri, and son C.R. Narasimhan. His grandchildren are seated on the ground

1947

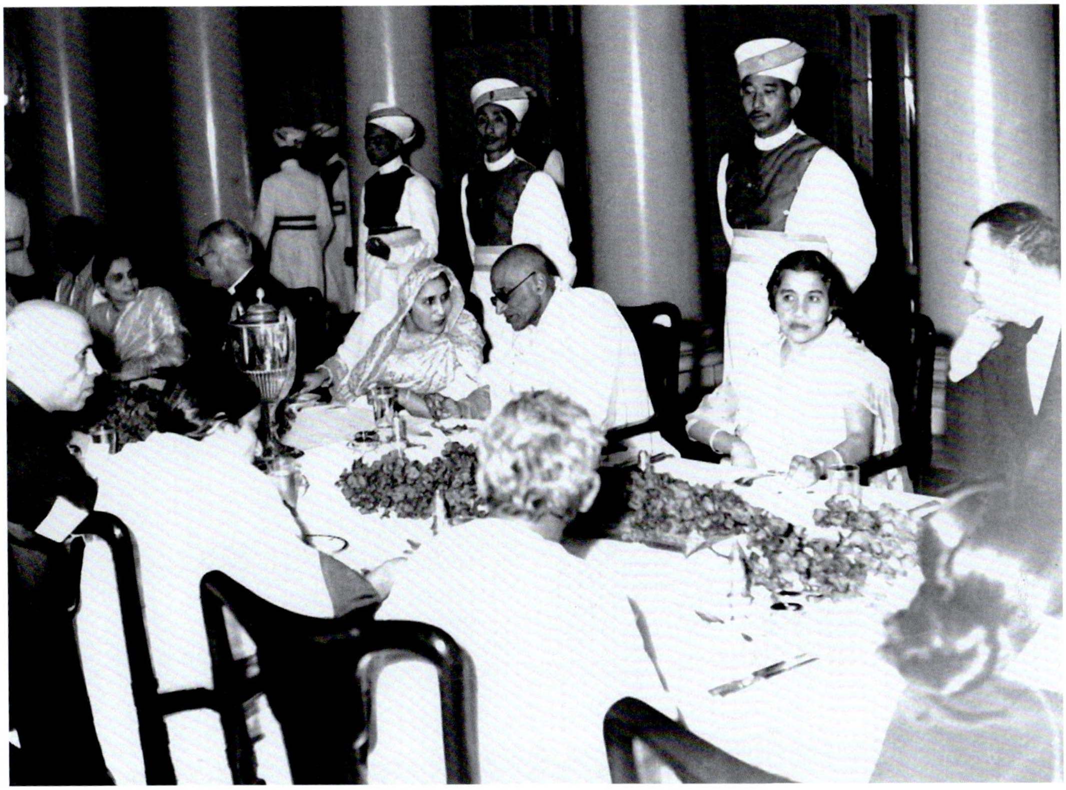

At the table (anti-clockwise) are Pt Nehru, and P.C. Ghosh (second from Nehru). On the opposite side is the Governor, beside Lady Pratima Mitter. He is in conversation with Maharani Radha of Burdwan, whose head is covered with her sari

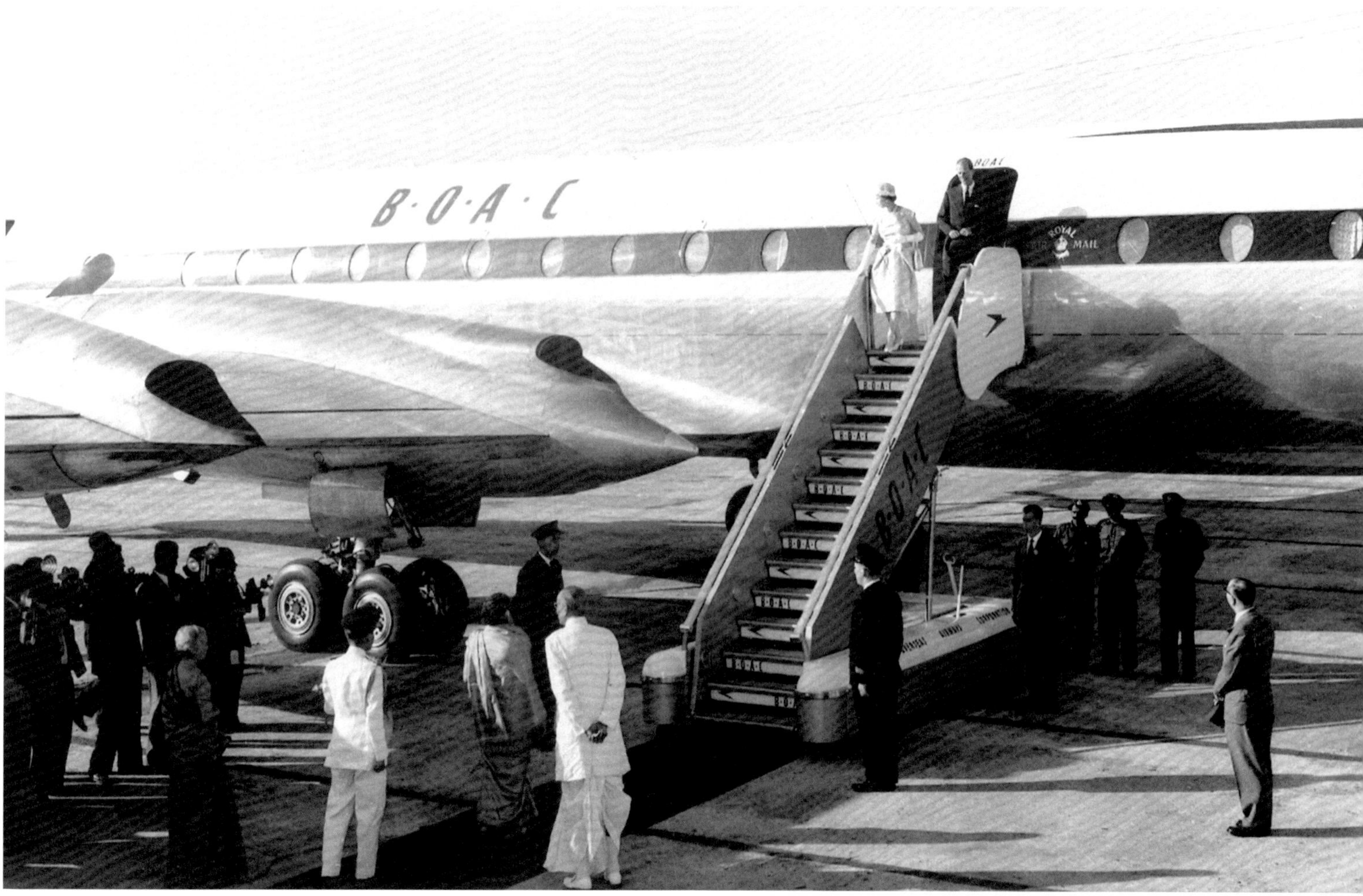

Queen Elizabeth arrives at Calcutta Airport in British aircraft, BOAC. Governor Padmaja Naidu along with Chief Minister Dr B.C. Roy wait to receive her

1961

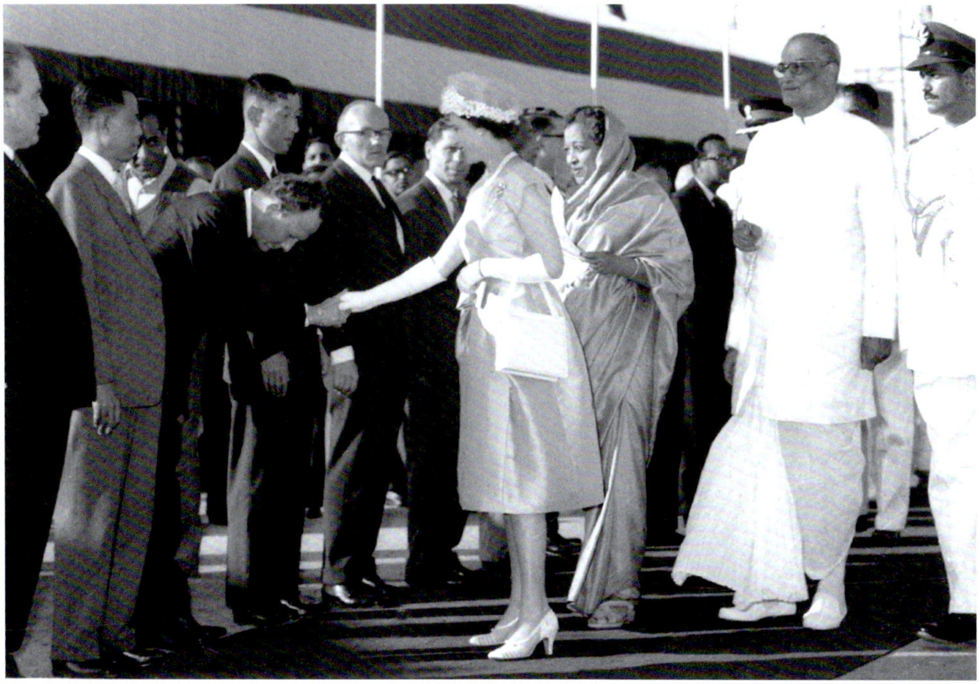

Queen being introduced to the Consular corps in Calcutta by Governor Padmaja Naidu. Dr B.C. Roy, walking alongside

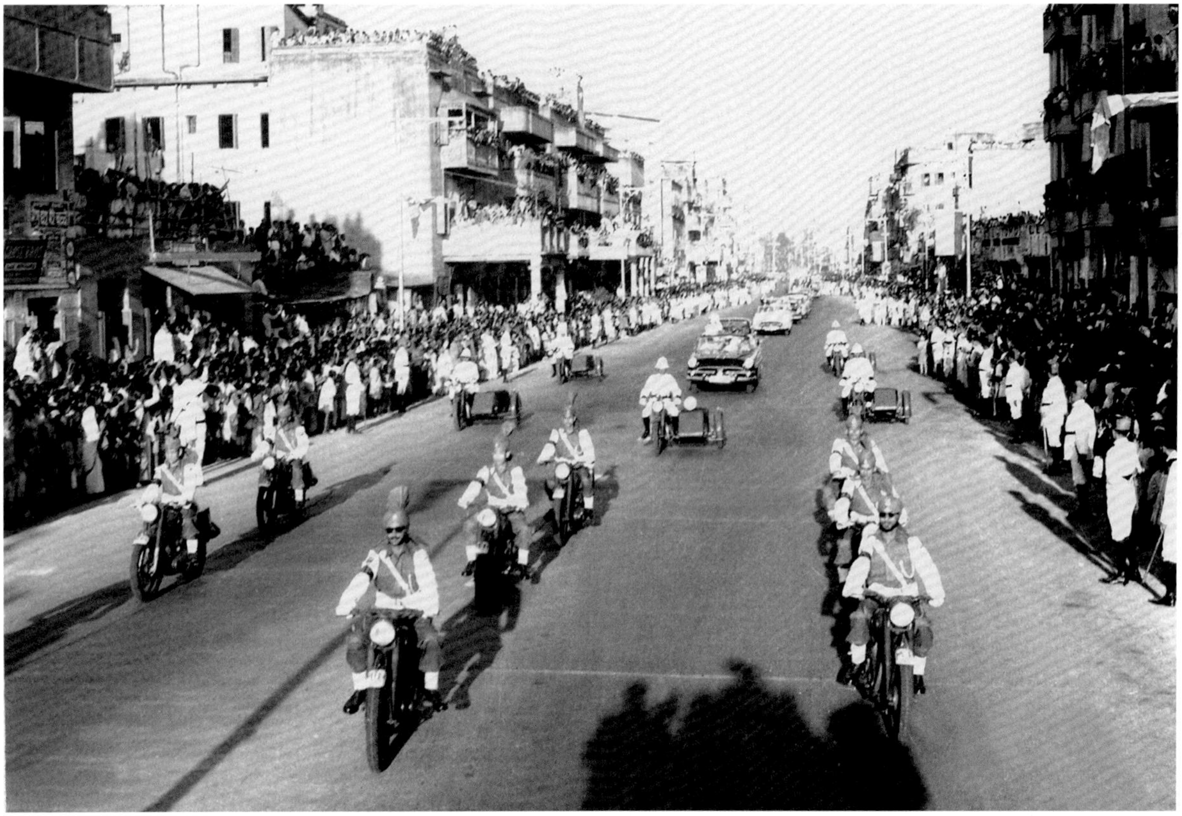

Queen's entourage on the way from the airport

1961

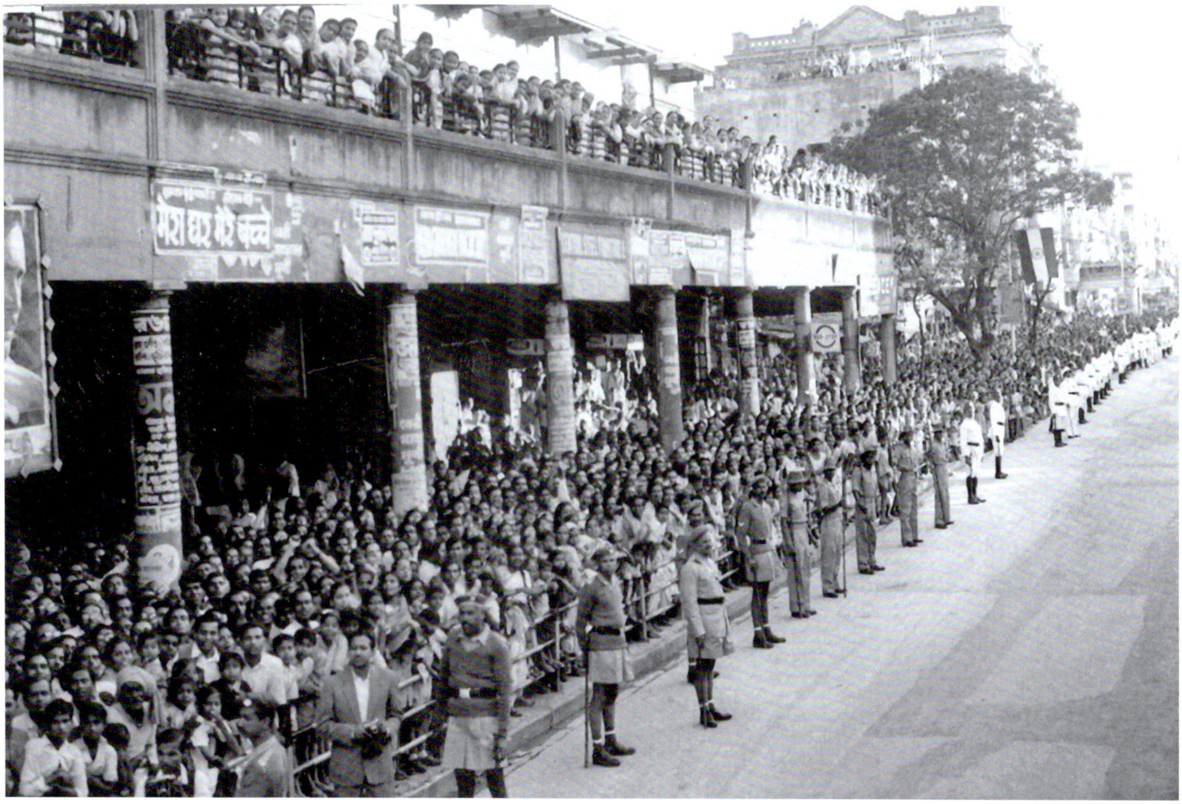

Crowds gathered along Central Avenue, near M.G Road crossing, and on balconies, to catch a glimpse of Queen Elizabeth

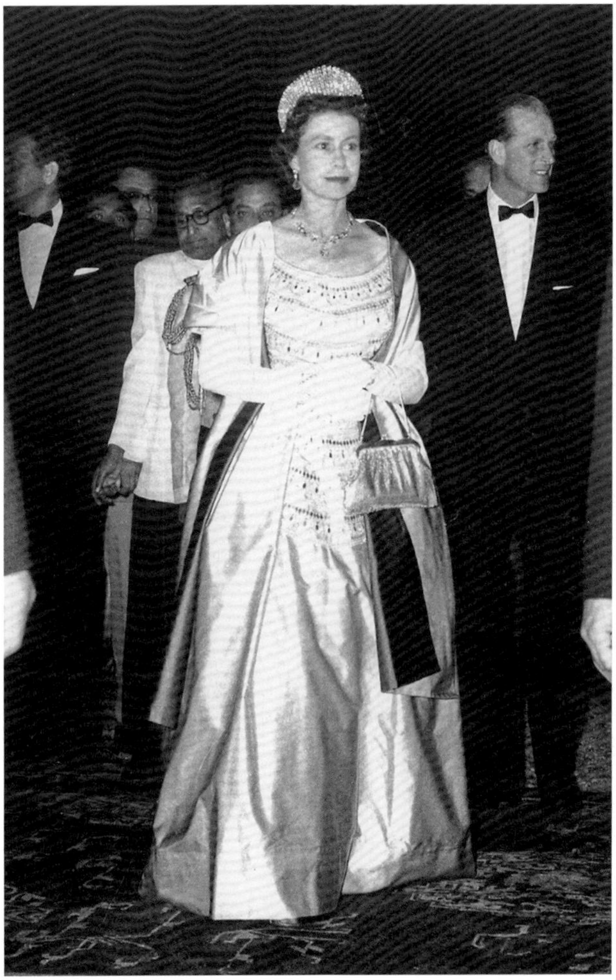

Queen enters Raj Bhavan to attend a banquet organised by Governor Padmaja Naidu

1961

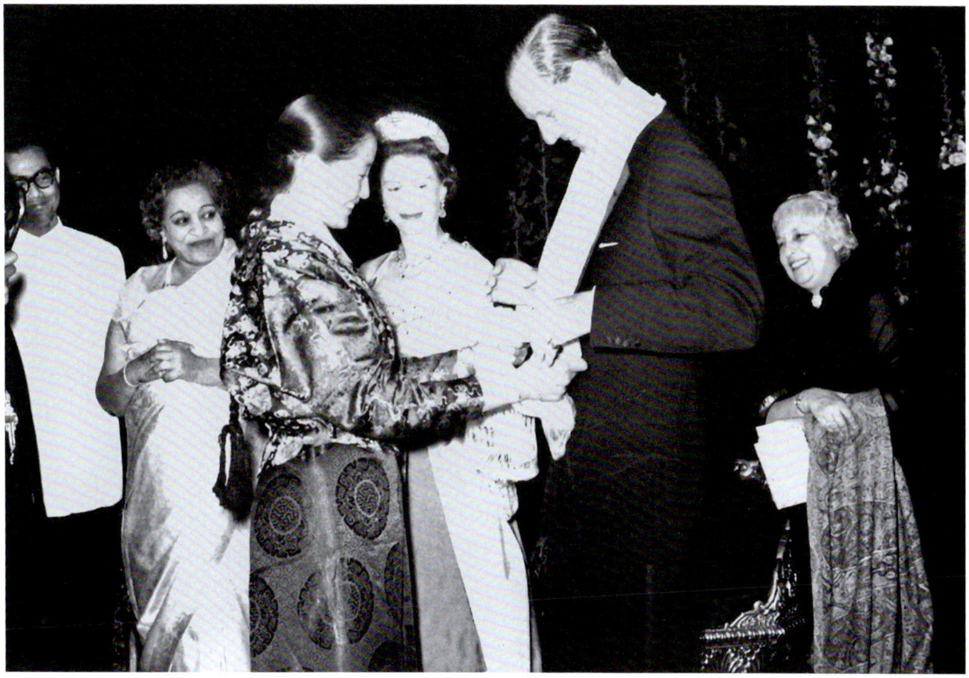

Prince Philip being gifted a scarf by the Princess of Bhutan. Queen Elizabeth watching, along with Governor Padmaja Naidu and Vijaya Lakshmi Pandit

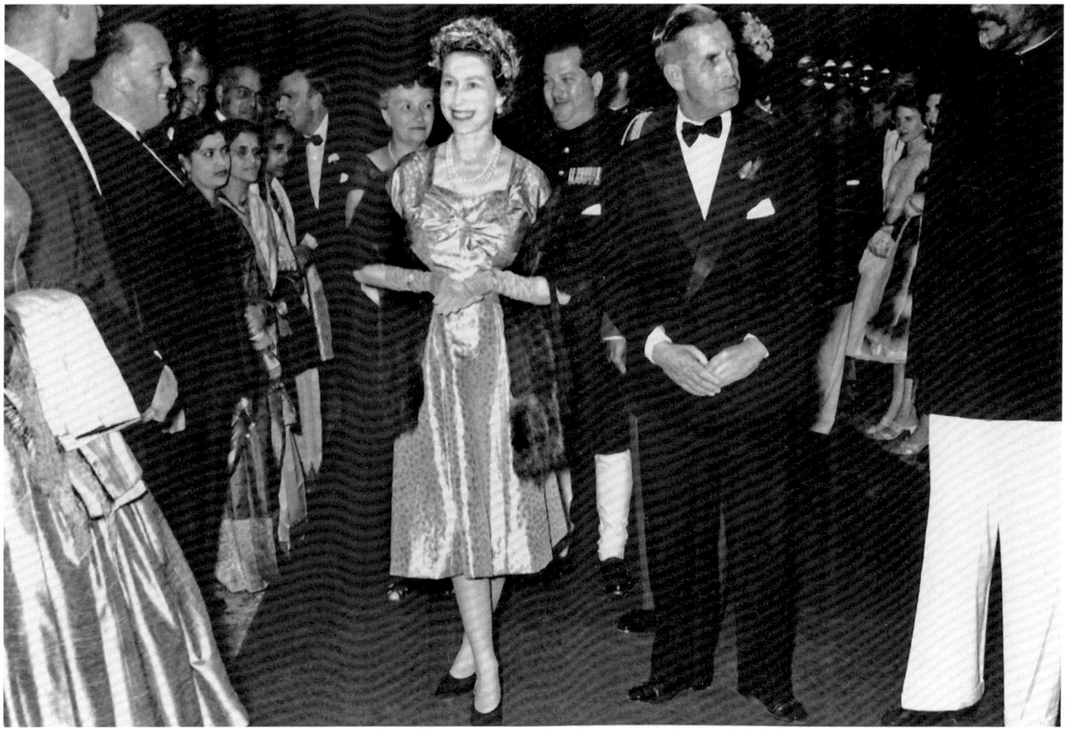

The Queen with the British High Commissioner at the High Commission reception. Ivan Surita behind her

1961

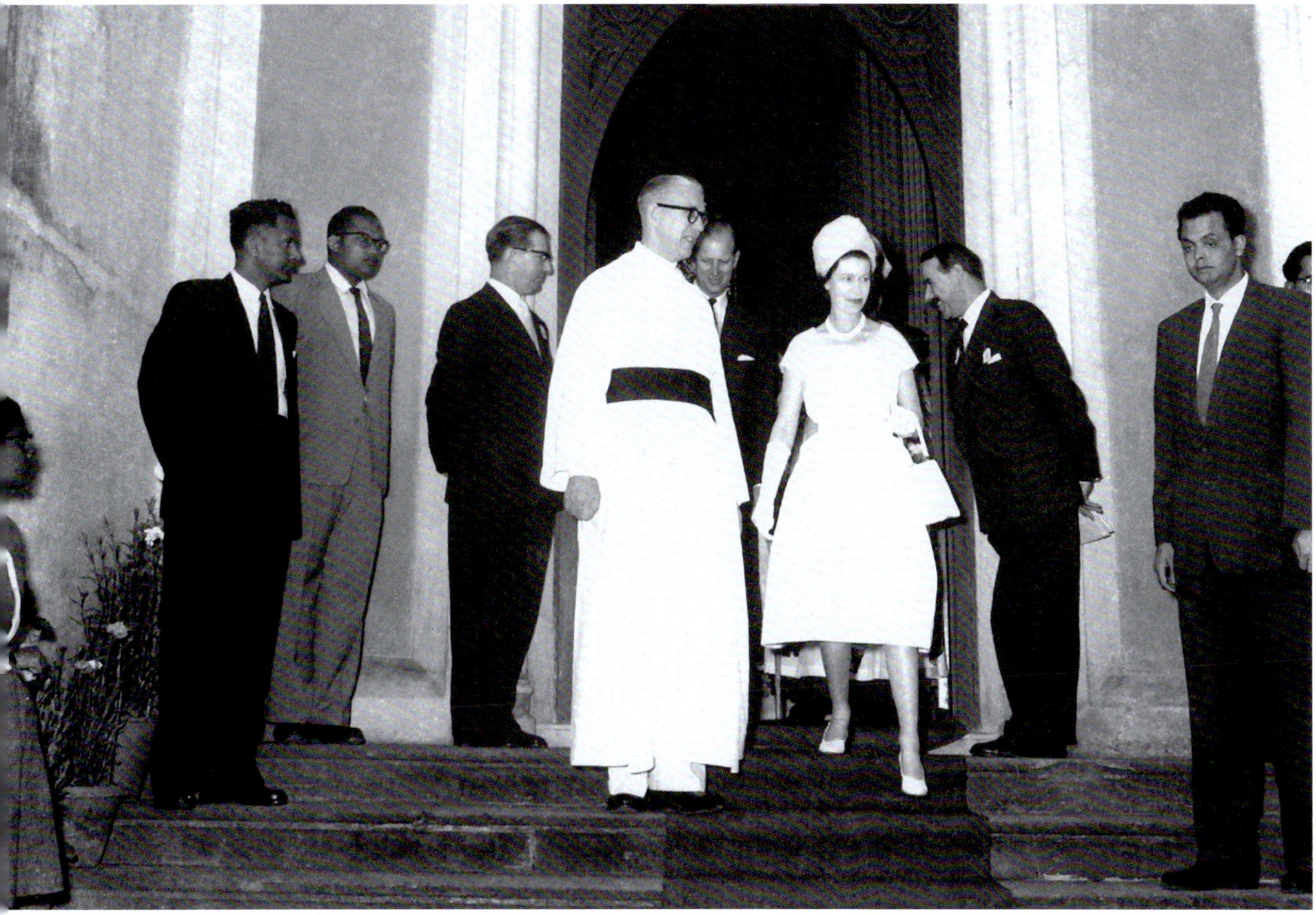

The Vicar with the Queen on her way out of St Paul's Cathedral

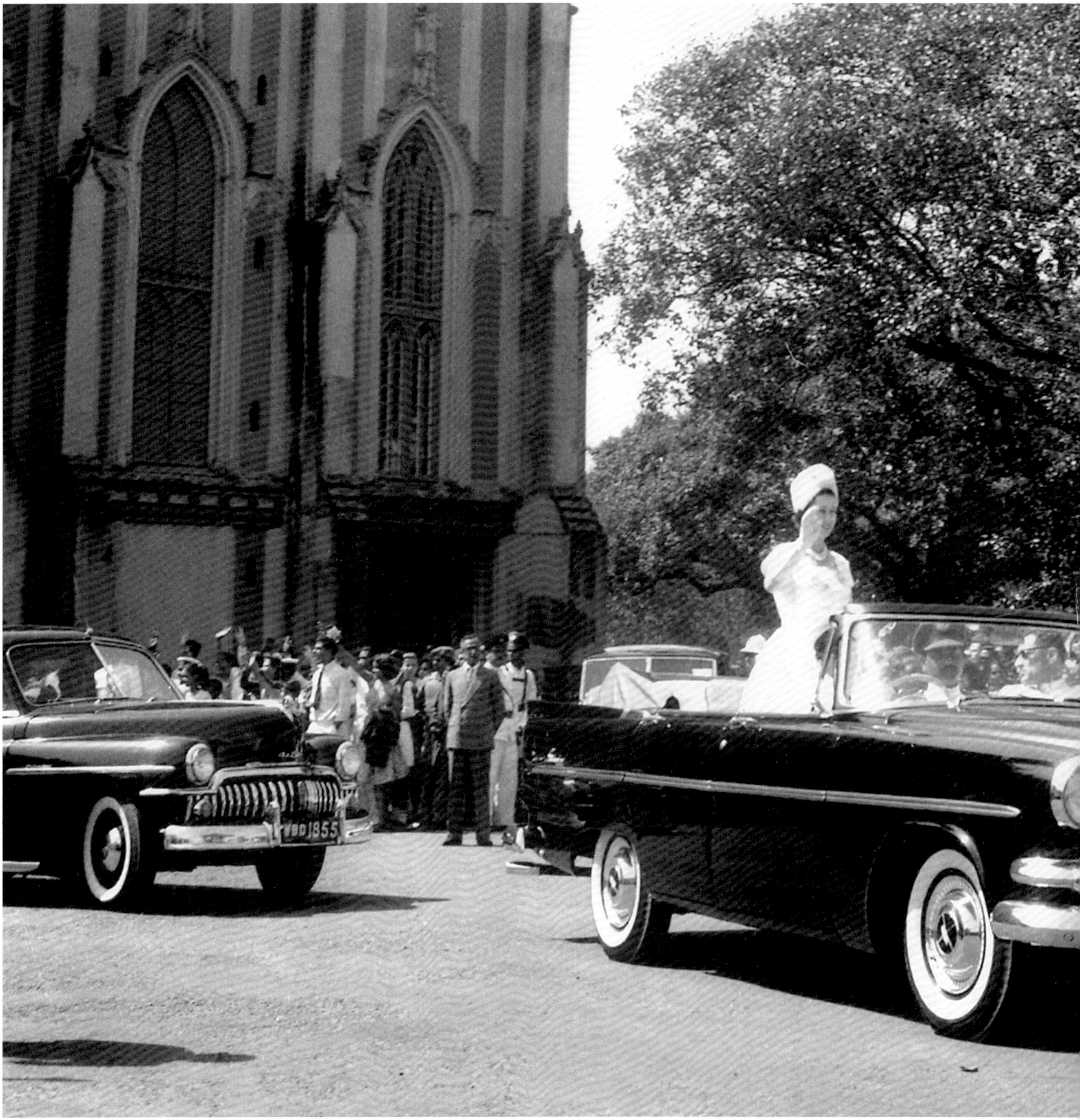
WBD 1855

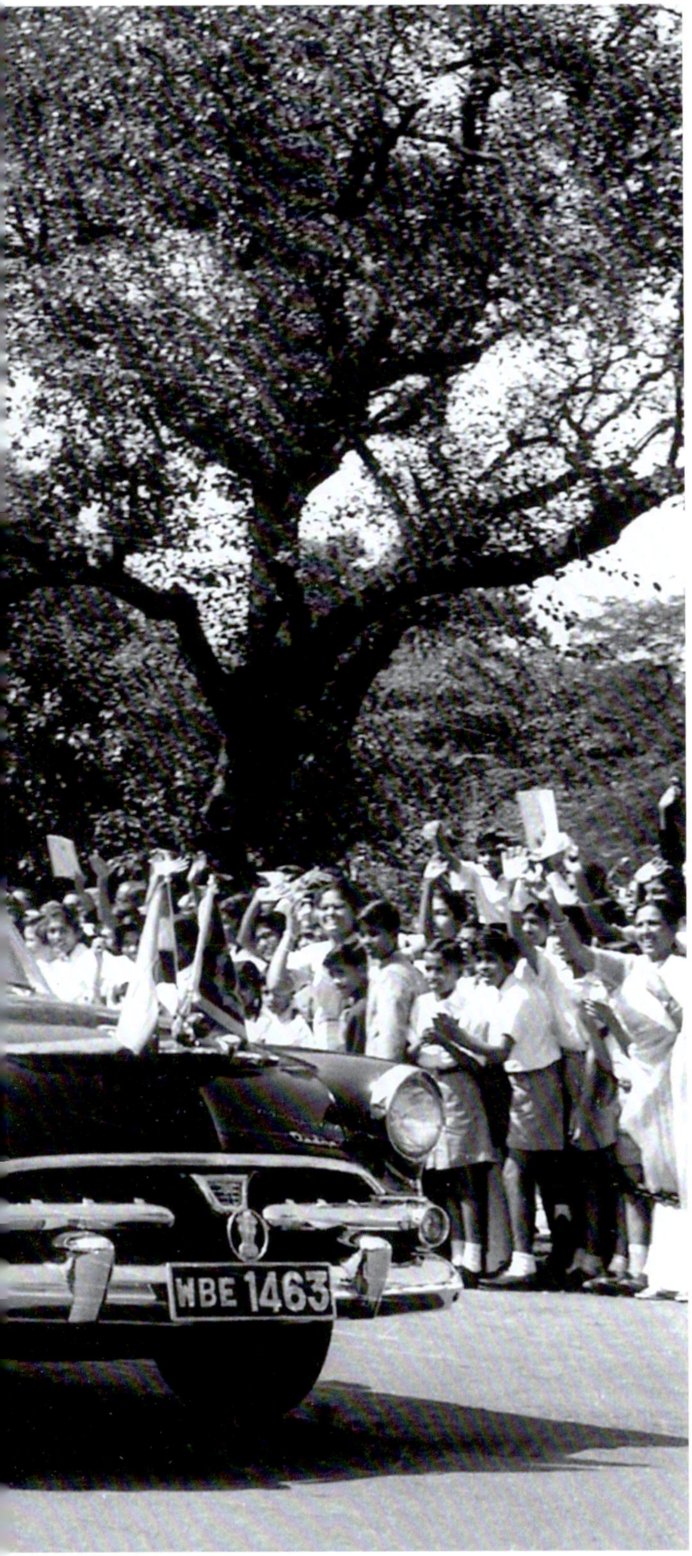

The Queen leaving St Paul's Cathedral in her limousine, waving to the crowd gathered around her

1961

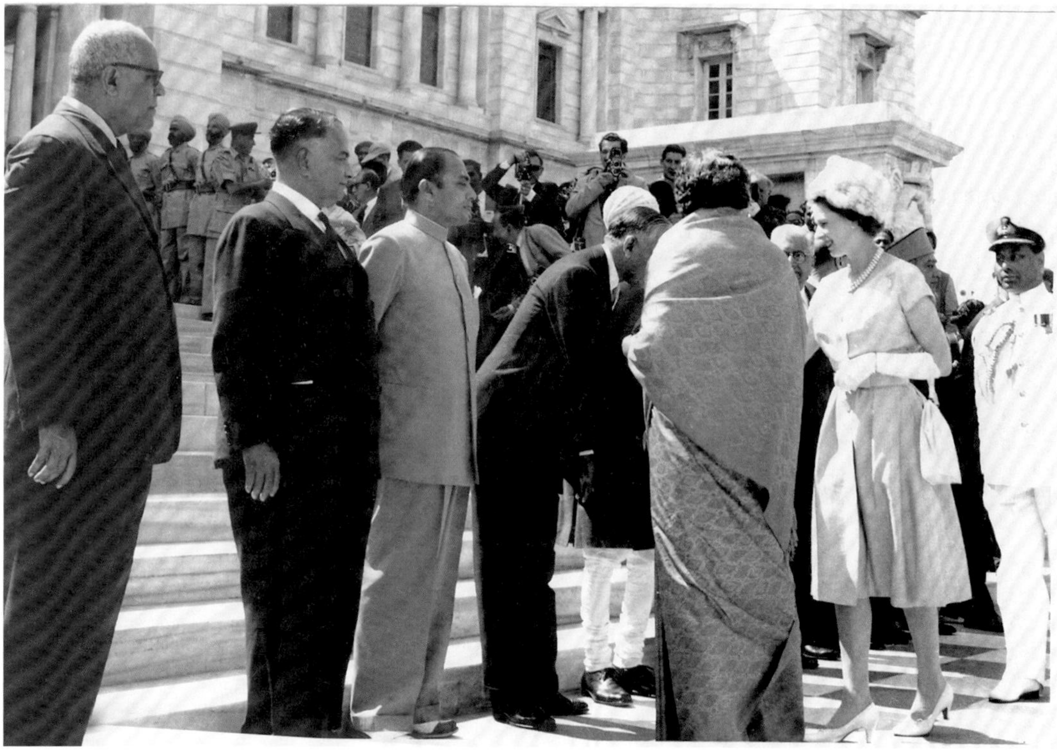

Queen being introduced to the board of trustees of Victoria Memorial by Governor Padmaja Naidu

1961

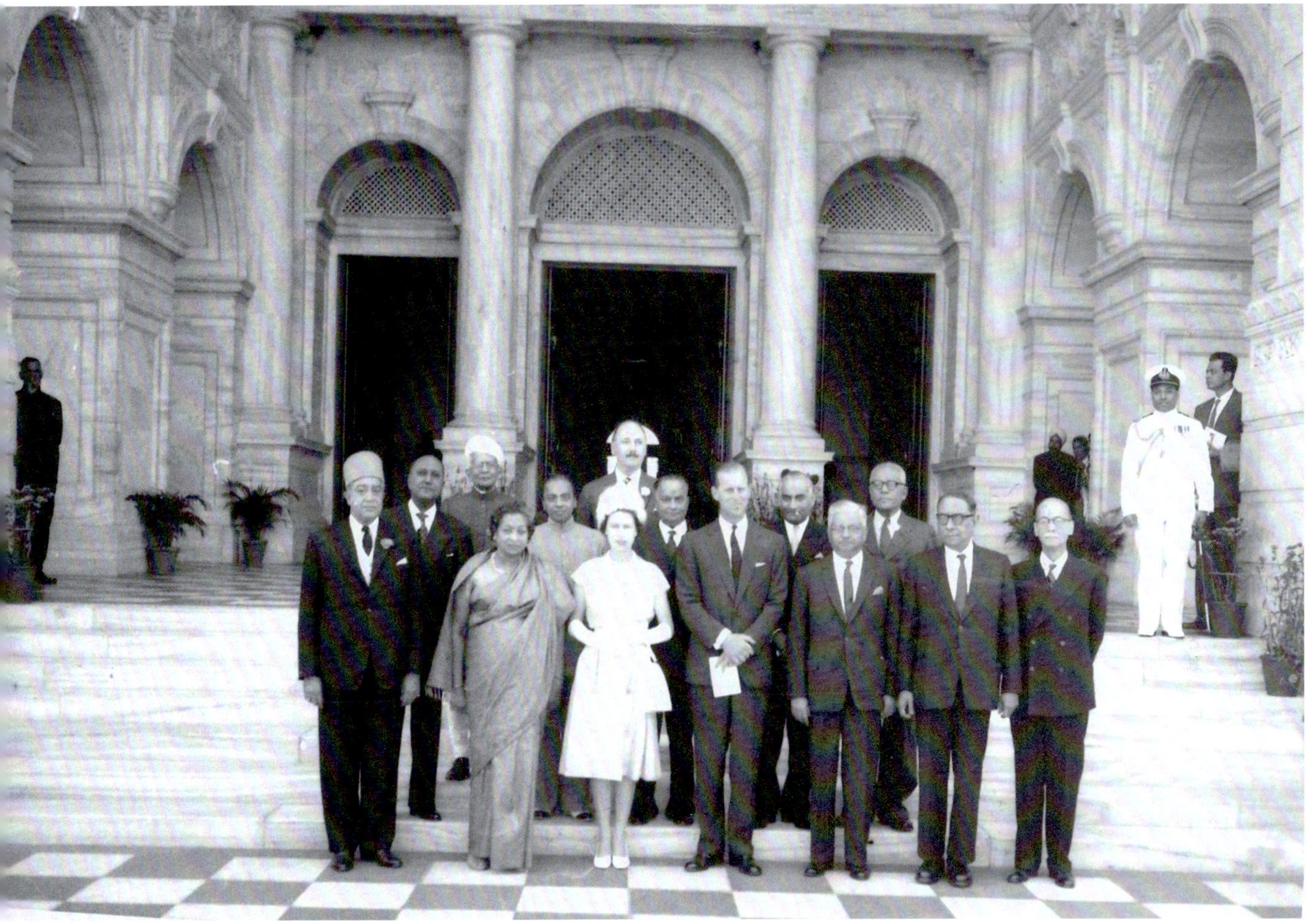

Queen with Governor Naidu and the board of directors of the Victoria Memorial Hall.
FRONT ROW: Maharaja of Burdwan, Padmaja Naidu, Queen, Prince Philip, Sir B.P. Singh Roy.
SECOND ROW: Sir Biren Mookerjee, Maharaja Jivaji Rao Scindia of Gwalior, and Maharaja of Darbhanga, among others. LAST ROW: Sir B.P. Goenka (turbaned)

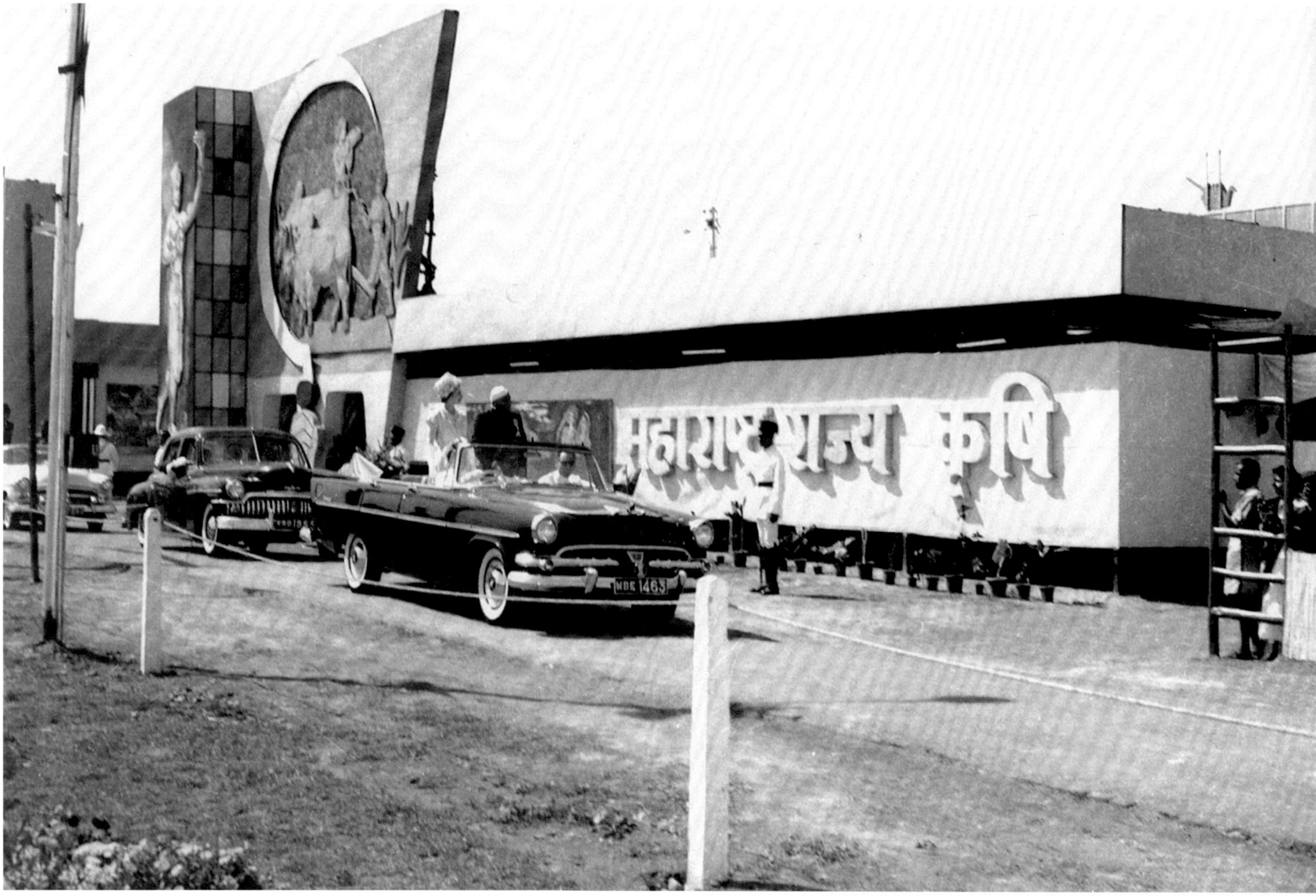

Queen going to the Maharashtra pavilion of the Agriculture Exhibition

1961

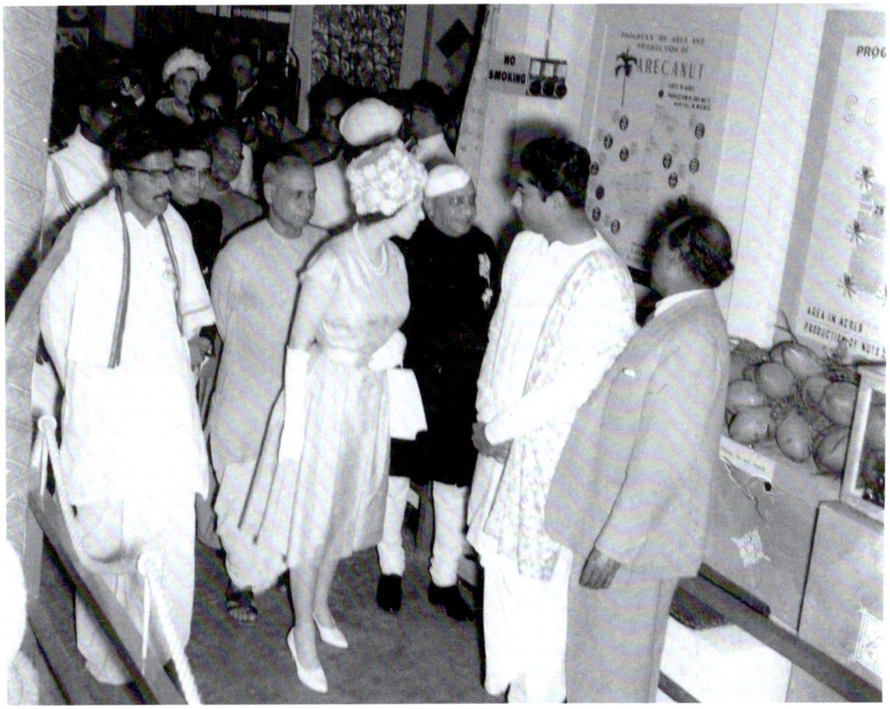

Queen with Ajoy Mukherjee at the agricultural exhibition, speaking to Tarun Kanti Ghosh

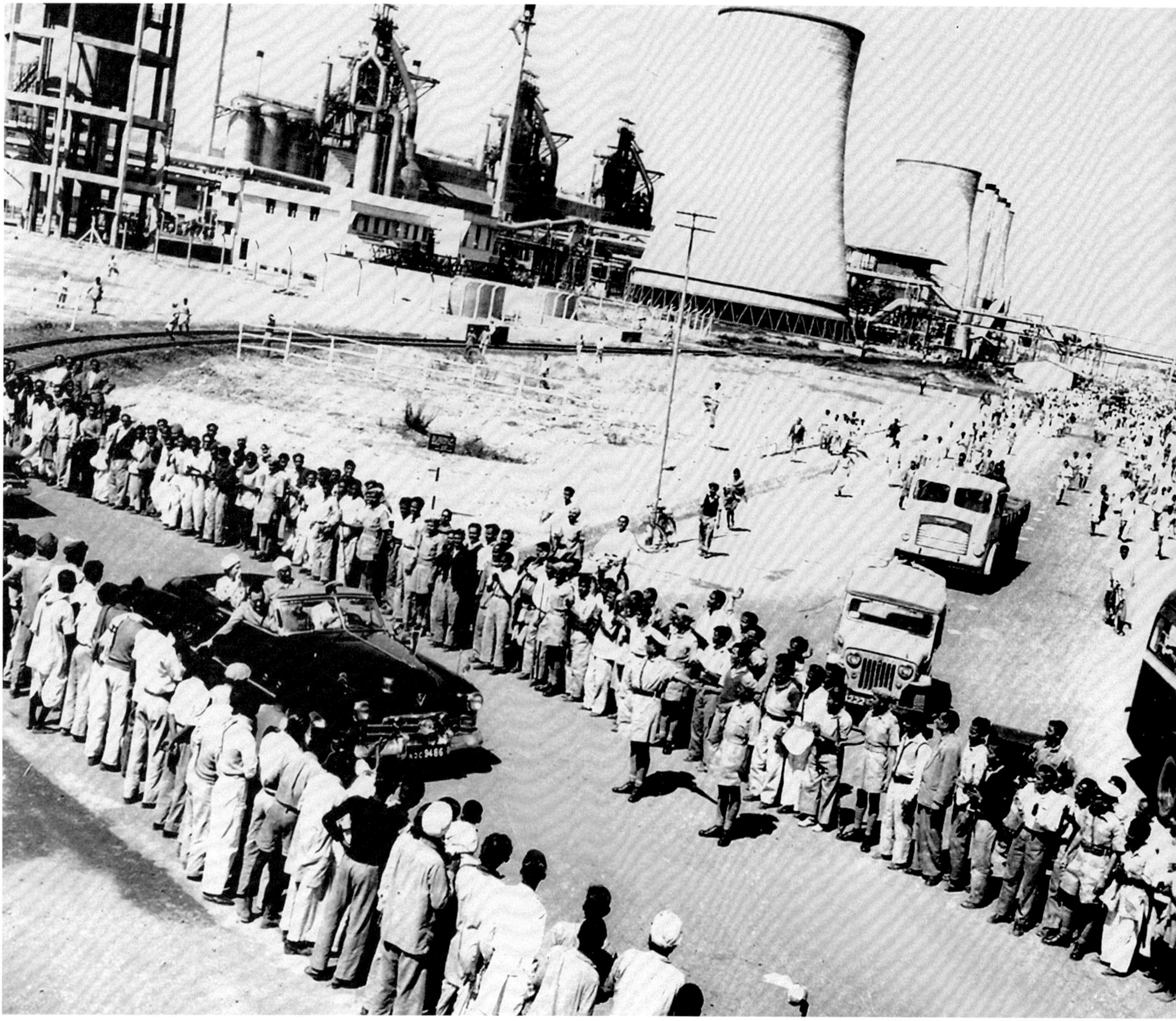

1961

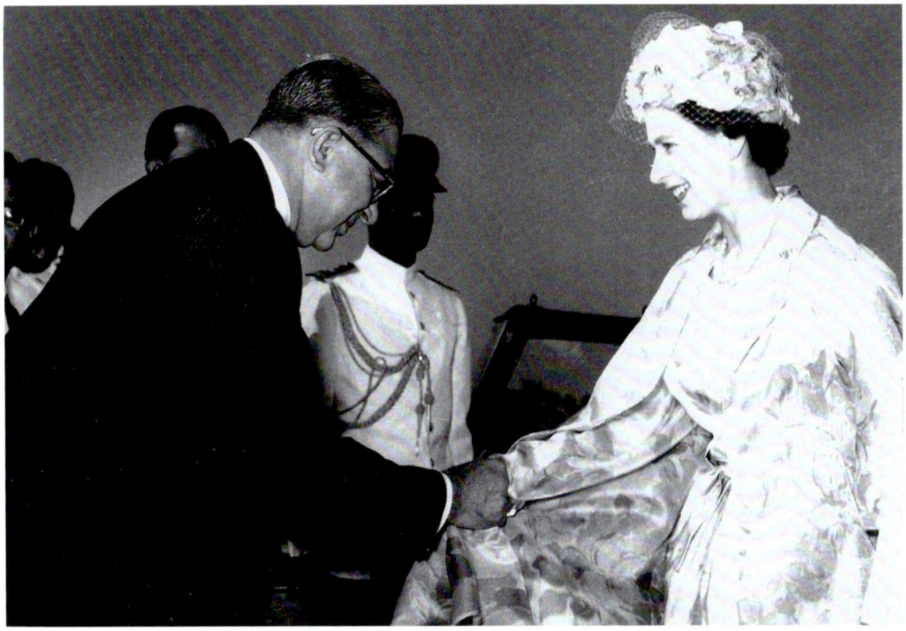

Queen being welcomed at the Royal Calcutta Turf Club by senior steward, Maharaja of Burdwan

LEFT Queen at the First Ingot steel plant in Durgapur

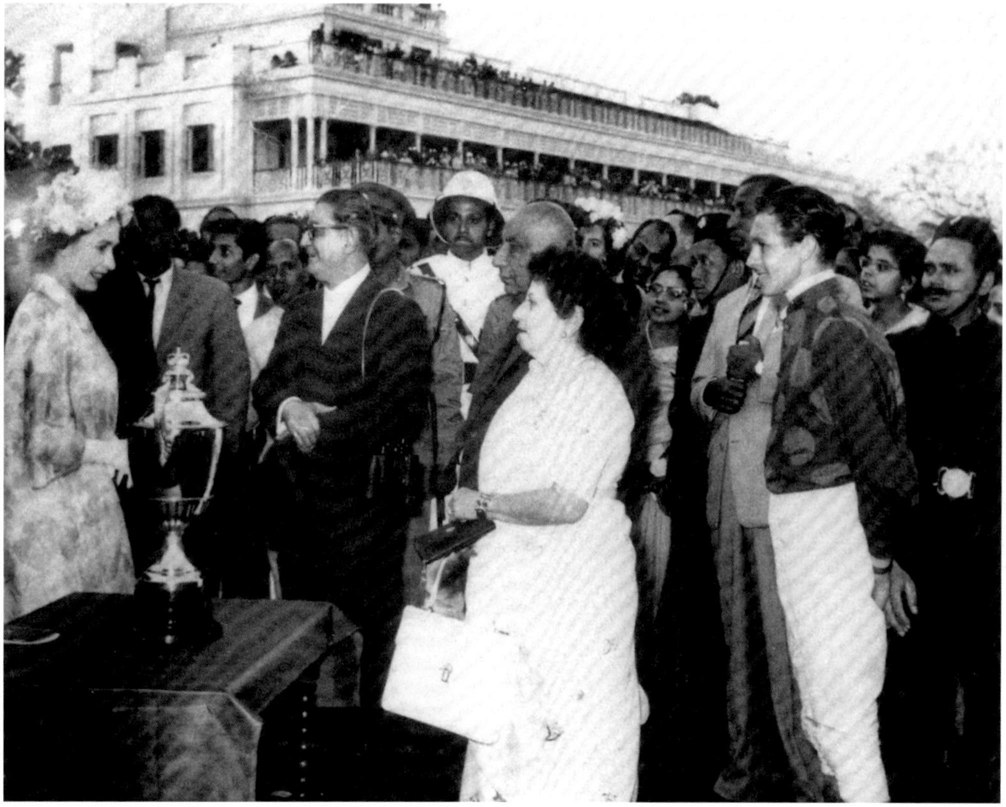

Queen admiring the coveted Queen's Cup on display. Owner Mrs Billimoria, trainer Mac Galstaun, and jockey Wally Swinburn watching

1961

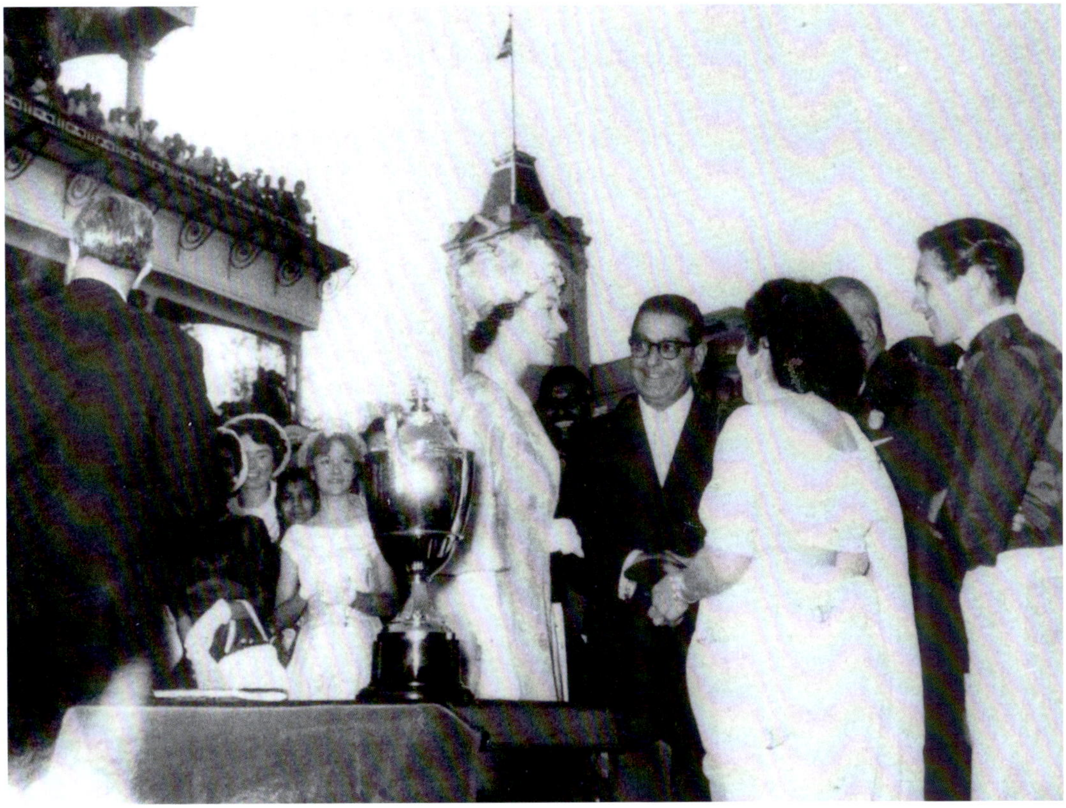

Queen congratulating Pa Bear's trainer, Mac Galstaun, owner, Mrs Billimoria and Mr Billimoria, and jockey, Wally Swinburn

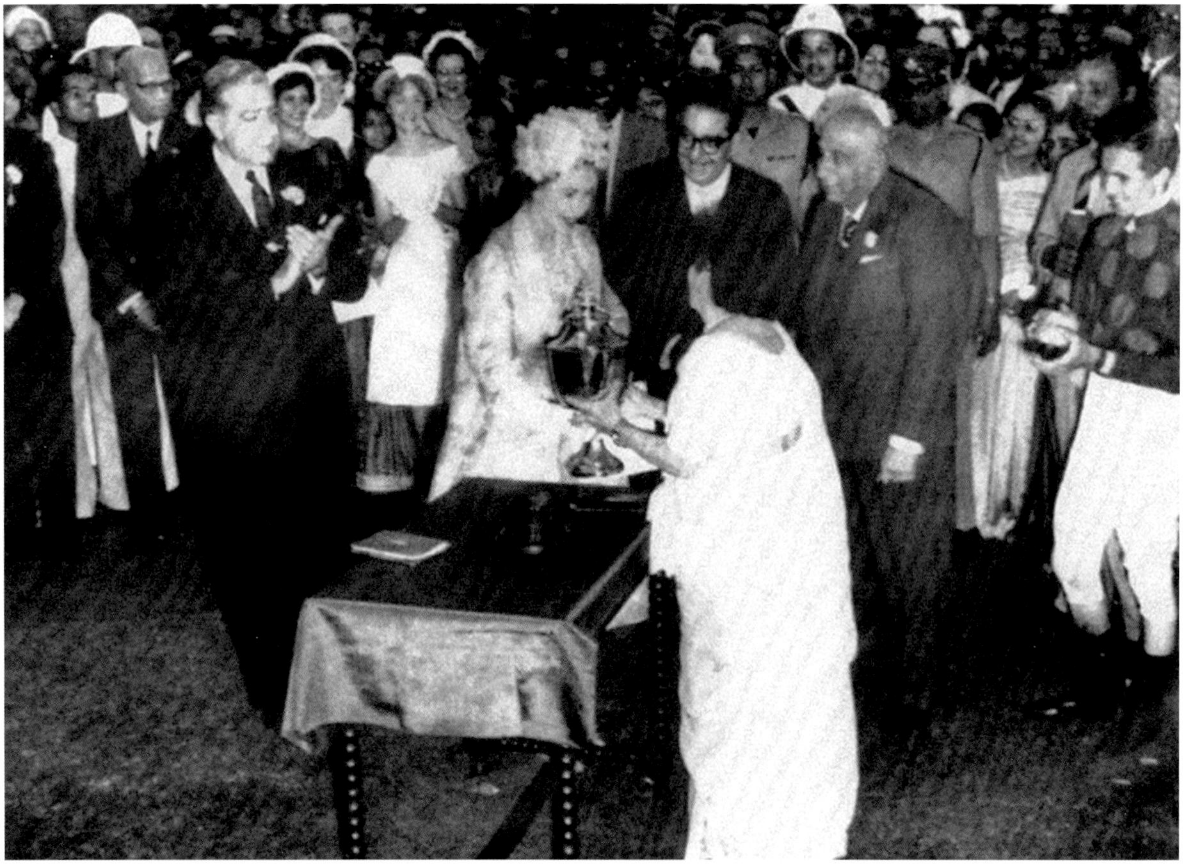

Queen presenting the trophy to Mrs Billimoria. Maharaja of Burdwan clapping with trainer Mac Galstaun, and jockey Swinburn

1961

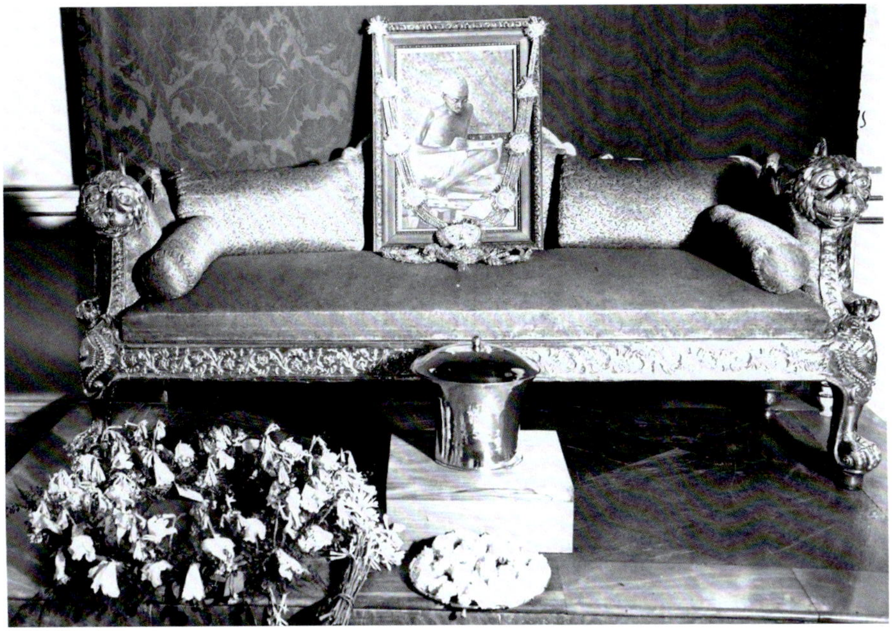

An urn containing the ashes of Mahatma Gandhi in front of his photograph at Raj Bhavan

I would like to thank Governor Shree Gopalkrishna Gandhi for all his encouragement and support to me to do this pictorial book and agreeing to write the Foreword, Anjum Katyal with whose help I met my author Soumitra Das, my sister late Bharati Parekh for her help and unfailing encouragement.

I am thankful to Saroj Mehera and the late Bhaskar Mitter who helped me recognise people and places in the photographs, my author Soumitra Das, Bikash Niyogi and Niyogi Publishers, Payal Parekh and Ruby Radhakrishnan for their help, Pritiranjan Karmakar for scanning the images. Lastly, I would like to thank my family, and especially my daughter Anjani, for always being there for me and for all their encouragement and support.

—LILA PATEL

Acknowledgements

With only scraps of information and the photographs to depend on, writing this book was a tough job. I would not have been able to accomplish it without the help and generosity of my friends, over and above the Internet and Facebook. I am grateful to Anjum Katyal for introducing me to Lila Patel of Bombay Photo Stores. There are many who have been most generous with their time, patience and valuable suggestions. I hope I have expressed my gratitude to all of them. A big thank you to Malavika Karlekar for her tips on reading material, and Bunny Gupta, the late Bhaskar Mitter, Pratap Gupta, Micahel Graf, Abhik Ray, Christopher Taylor, Saroj Mehera, Rupali Ghosh, Peter R. Moore, Anusua Mukherjee, Somnath Ghosh, Chirosree Basu and Gautam Mukherjee for vetting the text, besides other invaluable assistance.

My friends Lorraine Garnet Swinton and Amal Sircar were kind enough to write their personal accounts, which I have used verbatim in this book. I shall remain indebted to them forever. The others who were most indulgent were Katayun Saklat, Pravesh Gupta, Rosie Llwellyn Jones, Swapan Shome, Kaushik Ghosh, Saktidas Roy, Amit Guha, the late Surajlal Mukherjee, Vikram Bachhawat, Aakriti Art Gallery and Saibal Das. Thanks once again to you all.

—SOUMITRA DAS